Truth to Tell

Social History, Popular Culture, and Politics in Germany
Geoff Eley, Series Editor

A complete list of titles in this series is available online at www.press.umich.edu

Truth to Tell

German Women's Autobiographies
and Turn-of-the-Century Culture

Katharina Gerstenberger

Ann Arbor

THE UNIVERSITY OF MICHIGAN PRESS

Copyright © by the University of Michigan 2000
All rights reserved
Published in the United States of America by
The University of Michigan Press
Manufactured in the United States of America
⊛ Printed on acid-free paper

2003   2002   2001   2000   4   3   2   1

No part of this publication may be reproduced,
stored in a retrieval system, or transmitted in any form
or by any means, electronic, mechanical, or otherwise,
without the written permission of the publisher.

A CIP catalog record for this book is available from the British Library.

Library of Congress Cataloging-in-Publication Data

Gerstenberger, Katharina, 1961–
    Truth to tell : German women's autobiographies and turn-of-
the-century culture / Katharina Gerstenberger.
        p.   cm. — (Social history, popular culture, and politics in
Germany)
    ISBN 0-472-11183-3 (alk. paper)
    1. Women—Germany—Biography—History and criticism.
2. Germany—History—1871–1914—Biography.   I. Title.
II. Series.
CT3430 .G44   2001
920.72'0943'09034—dc21   00-010161

Contents

Acknowledgments

The process of writing a book becomes part of its author's biography. This study about women's autobiography has shaped mine in more ways than I can express here. In writing about "my autobiographers" I developed relationships with four very different women across time and culture. Their writings from the last turn of the century meshed with mine as I was working on this book while this century approached its end. I believe that I have come to understand the narratives I construct about my own life better as I attempted to read the stories of their lives. This book has accompanied me for a long time, and I have carried it with me to a number of different places both in the United States and in Europe. Many people have contributed their time and guidance as this project changed shape and scope over the years. Peter Hohendahl's intellectual support and his confidence in my abilities were vital as I began working on it. Sander L. Gilman and Biddy Martin urged me to look at things differently when I thought I had finished a section. Daniel Purdy and John Heins have followed my progress over the years with encouragement and friendship. Margrit Frölich read early drafts and alleviated many of the anxieties most writers face at one point or another.

This work took its decisive turn during my tenure as a research associate at Five College Women's Studies Research Center at Mount Holyoke College in 1996–97. Gail Hornstein and her colleagues were busy at work to allow us researchers-in-residence to live the life of the mind. I thank her and my fellow associates Susan Elizabeth Sweeney, Lucy Knight, Sandra Matthews, and Aorewa McLeod for their insights and ideas. Susan Cocalis, Sara Lennox, Katrin Sieg, Elisabeth Krimmer, and Nele Hempel offered friendship and critique during a lovely New England summer. I have fond memories of our Northampton gatherings.

Back home in Cincinnati, Maura O'Connor, Karla Goldman, and Joanne Meyerowitz helped me narrow the gap that seems to separate historians from literature scholars. Their input enabled me to make this a better book. Lynn Voskuil, Katharina von Ankum, and Karein Goertz never refused to read yet another version of the manuscript. Jerry Glenn encouraged me to continue on and made sure my translations of German quotations were up to stylistic standard. Heidy Margrit Müller's generosity and her expertise in autobiography studies were welcome as I revised the manuscript during a summer spent in Brussels, Belgium. Jeff Loveland coaxed me toward closure during that final summer it took to finish this book, while completing his. Sigrun Haude accompanied me through the final years of production. She never let our friendship get in the way of critical feedback.

The Charles Phelps Taft Memorial Fund and the University of Cincinnati's Research Council have supported this project with several short-term fellowships. I am grateful for that. Geoff Eley and Sidonie Smith offered keen critical insights during the final stages of writing this book. I thank them as well as the anonymous readers at the University of Michigan Press. I would also like to acknowledge the help of my editors, Susan Whitlock and Liz Suhay, at the Press. Rose Glickman patiently helped me to make my prose fit for an American readership. Julia Gerstenberger did library research in Germany when her sister needed obscure sources. Kavindra Malik has been there for me from the inception of this project. This book is for him.

Two chapters of this book have been previously published and have been revised for inclusion here.

Chapter 1 appeared as "Nahida Ruth Lazarus's 'Ich suchte Dich!' A Female Autobiography from the Turn of the Century," *Monatshefte* 86, no. 4 (1994): 525–42. Reprinted by permission of the University of Wisconsin Press.

Chapter 4 appeared as "Her (Per)version: The Confessions of Wanda von Sacher-Masoch," *Women in German Yearbook* 13 (1997): 81–100. Reprinted by permission of the University of Nebraska Press.

True Lives: The Culture of Autobiography in Turn-of-the-Century Germany

This book is about women's autobiographies written at the turn of the century in Germany and Austria. These texts do not immediately come to mind when we explore the point at which the modern age celebrated its achievements and feared their consequences.[1] In the past, some scholars emphasized modernist elite culture to explain the insecurities of an era that defined itself as thoroughly modern while simultaneously searching for its traditions.[2] Others have pointed to the tension in German and Austrian politics between archaic political structures, widespread conservatism, and antisemitism, on the one hand, and the progressive movements on the other.[3] More recently, the crises of the fin de siècle have been explored

---

1. Recent studies on turn-of-the-century culture and modernity are Franz Herre, *Jahrhundertwende 1900: Untergangsstimmung und Fortschrittsglauben* (Stuttgart: dva, 1998); Joachim Radkau, *Das Zeitalter der Nervosität: Deutschland zwischen Bismarck und Hitler* (Munich: Hanser, 1998); and Stephen Eric Bronner and F. Peter Wagner, eds., *Vienna: The World of Yesterday, 1889–1914* (Atlantic Highlands, N.J.: Humanities Press, 1997).

2. These studies focus almost exclusively on turn-of-the-century Vienna. See Carl E. Schorske, *Fin-de-Siècle Vienna: Politics and Culture* (New York: Vintage, 1981); Jürgen Nautz and Richard Vahrenkamp, eds., *Die Wiener Jahrhundertwende: Einflüsse, Umwelt, Wirkungen* (Vienna: Böhlau, 1996); Michael Worbs, *Nervenkunst: Literatur und Psychoanalyse im Wien der Jahrhundertwende* (Frankfurt am Main: Europäische Verlagsanstalt, 1983); Allan Janik and Stephen Toulmin, *Wittgenstein's Vienna* (New York: Simon and Schuster, 1973); and Hilde Spiel, *Vienna's Golden Autumn* (New York: Weidenfeld and Nicolson, 1987).

3. For instance, David Crew, "The Ambiguities of Modernity: Welfare and the German State from Wilhelm to Hitler," in *Society, Culture, and the State in Germany, 1870–1930,* ed. Geoff Eley (Ann Arbor: University of Michigan Press, 1997), 319–44; and John W. Boyer, *Culture and Political Crisis in Vienna: Christian Socialism in Power, 1897–1918* (Chicago: University of Chicago Press, 1995).

through discourses of sexuality and definitions of gender.[4] This book argues that turn-of-the-century readers looked to women's autobiographies for solutions to the quandaries of gender and the vicissitudes of modernity. Readers believed that women's autobiographies offered glimpses into the interiors of femininity and provided authentic answers to the questions raised by "woman." Women's autobiographies both epitomized and explained one of the fundamental problems of the modern age. The cultural meanings of this dual position of women's autobiographies, the deployment of female autobiography in the gender debates and the autobiographical strategies of women writers, are the subject of this book.[5]

In the autobiographies of turn-of-the-century women we encounter voices of modernity that are not necessarily "modern" in intent. For the most part the writers sought to present themselves as traditional women who, for a variety of reasons, felt compelled to respond to the challenges of the changing times. Many of them lament the perceived loss of tradition and the revered roles it presumably afforded women, revealing an uneasy relationship to the demands of the organized women's movement. Given the hostility of the majority culture to the feminist enterprise, this should not surprise us.[6] Yet for many autobiographers the tensions between tradition and change form pieces of a puzzle they strive to sort out in their narratives. Thus, by analyzing women's autobiographies this book takes another look at the meanings of "fin de siècle." Female autobiographers enrich our understanding of the gendered discourses of nation, race, and sexuality that occupied their contemporaries. As reluctant "modernists," they afford us glimpses into the conflicted self-understanding of turn-of-the-century culture.

Autobiography is always more than a private act of self-representation. Any autobiographical text responds to a generic tradition. The writer typically has an ideal reader in mind and, in most cases, seeks to make a statement that transcends the individual life. Perhaps more than any other literary genre, autobiography fuses individual and collective modes of self-

---

4. See Rita Felski, *The Gender of Modernity* (Cambridge: Harvard University Press, 1995); Elaine Showalter, *Sexual Anarchy: Gender and Culture at the Fin de Siècle* (New York: Viking, 1990); Bram Dijkstra, *Idols of Perversity: Fantasies of Feminine Evil in Fin-de-Siècle Culture* (New York: Oxford University Press, 1986); and Nike Wagner, *Geist und Geschlecht: Karl Kraus und die Erotik der Wiener Moderne* (Frankfurt am Main: Suhrkamp, 1982).

5. My study focuses on modernity and tradition as overarching concerns rather than on Germany and German-speaking Austria as distinct cultures.

6. See also Ute Planert, *Antifeminismus im Kaiserreich: Diskurs, soziale Formation und politische Mentalität* (Göttingen: Vandenhoeck & Ruprecht, 1998).

representation.[7] Traditionally, autobiographies have been read either as a particular kind of literary text or have been used selectively to support historical analyses.[8] The literary approach runs the risk of neglecting the historical context that enabled certain narratives in the first place; the documentary approach might overlook the intricacies of the text as literary construct.

This book foregrounds close readings of autobiographical texts and historicizes these analyses by embedding them in the texts' contemporary reception to assess the kind of cultural work these narratives intended. "The literary," as feminist historian Joan W. Scott has termed the linguistic qualities of autobiographical expressions of experience, produces subjectivities in excess of the sociohistorical facts that delimit the individual.[9] It allows the autobiographer to cast her experience in ways that at times exceed her explicit intentions and undercut her readers' expectations. Close readings tease out the "excess" contained in these texts. The contemporary attempts to use these narratives to cope with modernity reveal anxieties as well as strategies to appease the fears caused by changing roles and identities. Reading autobiographies by women, I also read turn-of-the-century readers reading.

This book moves beyond "femininity" as a focus of feminist analysis without losing sight of its importance. The four autobiographers under consideration shared gender and race but were of different class, religious, and national background. Their texts, published between 1898 and 1909, were not chosen to "cover" certain categories of identification but to understand how these categories were defined, deployed, linked, and redefined around 1900. Protestant-born Nahida Lazarus explains in her autobiography why she converted to Judaism; the German colonizer Mar-

7. Barbara Green makes a similar argument in *Spectacular Confessions: Autobiography, Performative Activism, and the Sites of Suffrage, 1905–1938* (New York: St. Martin's Press, 1997). She maintains that the autobiographies of suffragists helped shape feminist culture. I suggest that the influence of women's autobiographies reached beyond feminism or women's concerns.

8. Literary scholars such as Ralph-Rainer Wuthenow in his *Das erinnerte Ich: Europäische Literatur und Selbstdarstellung im 18. Jahrhundert* (Munich: Beck, 1974), and Gunter Niggl in *Geschichte der deutschen Autobiographie im 18. Jahrhundert: Theoretische Grundlegung und literarische Entfaltung* (Stuttgart: Metzler, 1977), carefully distinguish between autobiography and novel and seek to define the generic boundaries of autobiography. Jochen Loreck, *Wie man früher Sozialdemokrat wurde: Das Kommunikationsverhalten in der deutschen Arbeiterbewegung und die Konzeption der sozialistischen Parteipublizistik durch August Bebel* (Bonn: Verlag Neue Gesellschaft, 1977) uses working-class autobiographies as historical documents.

9. Joan W. Scott, "Experience," in *Feminists Theorize the Political,* ed. Judith Butler and Joan W. Scott (New York: Routledge, 1992), 34.

garethe von Eckenbrecher writes about her experiences as a settler's wife in Germany's Southwest African protectorate. The Austrian Adelheid Popp tells the story of her working-class childhood and youth in Vienna, and her compatriot Wanda von Sacher-Masoch relates the story of her relationship with Leopold von Sacher-Masoch, the father of literary masochism. All four autobiographers regarded the writing and publishing of their life stories as a daring and yet necessary act. They promised their readers honest insights into their unusual lives, hoping to explain to themselves and others the subjectivities they had won as women in a world increasingly dominated by divisions of class and race. Their texts demonstrate not just how gender and class shaped them, but also how they came to understand these categories. For the working-class autobiographer Adelheid Popp, to give an example, the discovery of class provided her with the key to her sufferings as a woman. In Nahida Lazarus's autobiography race is the central yet unspoken referent as she constructs herself as a woman, a German, and a Jew. Women's autobiographies are no more authentic than other texts by or about women. Yet they provide insights into "processes of identity production," in Scott's words, at a time when notions of femininity were increasingly bound up with definitions of nation and race.[10]

Two of the autobiographers, Nahida Lazarus and Margarethe von Eckenbrecher, were born in Germany, but lived elsewhere for long periods of time. The other two, Adelheid Popp and Wanda von Sacher-Masoch, were born in Austria. Popp remained in Austria, and Wanda von Sacher-Masoch took up residence in France and Switzerland. Writing from different geographic and national locations, they all considered German high literature in the tradition of Goethe and Schiller to be their cultural home. The contemporary reception placed the Austrian books, both of which were published in Germany, in the context of modern German culture.

At the turn of the century Germany witnessed a "memoir boom."[11]

---

10. Ibid., 37.

11. I borrow the term from a special issue of the *Women's Review of Books,* "The Memoir Boom," July 1996. A comparable phenomenon can be observed in the United States in the 1990s. With more than two hundred memoirs published in 1995 alone, cultural critic Zoë Heller characterized the 1990s as the "decade of the memoir" (*New York Times Book Review,* March 15, 1998, 10). James Atlas declared the "triumph of memoir" (*New York Times Magazine,* May 12, 1996, 25), while Michiko Kakutani described the phenomenon somewhat pejoratively as the "current memoir craze" (*New York Times,* October 21, 1997, B6). Others have referred to the "publishing explosion in memoirs" (*New York Times,* June 18, 1997, A26). The majority of autobiographers in the United States today are women. Defenders of the trend insist that these texts reflect a multitude of female voices and experiences. The most frequently voiced criticism against the memoir boom contends that autobiographical narratives by both men and women are often narcissistic, self-pitying, and poorly written.

Publishers promoted autobiographical literature, journals reviewed it, and the public—with a literacy rate of almost 90 percent—avidly read it. Until the 1890s history had been considered the leading discipline in the humanities. Its practitioners promised an understanding of the present through the study of the past.[12] Nietzsche's famous critique of history as dead, or, worse, deadening, knowledge only emphasizes its significance. The importance of history as the foremost *Geisteswissenschaft* began to wane in the late 1890s, its position challenged by new academic enterprises such as economics, sociology, and psychology. At about the same time, an increasing number of autobiographies became available to German readers.[13] Historiography enabled the academic elite to understand processes of change. Memoir literature, the consensus ran, helped a general audience to cope with the onslaught of change. Autobiographies, whether they espoused tradition or bore witness to change, offered firsthand and therefore authentic insights into the mechanisms of history and historical change. The upsurge in autobiographical literature was an individual as well as collective response to the profound shifts in political, social, and national identities.

Not surprisingly, some critics hailed and encouraged the trend, while others condemned it, hoping to stem a veritable flood, in their opinion, of the wrong kind of memoir literature. Even though the memoir boom included a large number of translations, reviewers for the most part agreed that the increase in "books of memory" was a phenomenon of modern German culture, and they endeavored to define the kind of cultural work this thriving genre should be permitted to do. Autobiographers, reviewers agreed, invited readers to consider the fundamental questions of the day. The history of German unification, the plight of the lower classes, and Germany's colonial quest, for instance, could be grasped most authentically through the autobiographies of those who had shared in these experiences. In their commentaries critics pondered whose life stories were qualified to shape the new nation's understanding of itself. The debates about autobiography and its rightful purpose thus extended beyond questions of genre. At stake were the identity politics of a modern nation.

Around 1900 autobiography embraced a diversity of textual prac-

---

12. See Thomas Nipperdey, *Deutsche Geschichte, 1866–1918,* vol. 1, *Arbeitswelt und Bürgergeist* (Munich: Beck, 1994), 635. One need only think of gargantuan projects such as the *Monumenta Germaniae Historica,* to this day one of the most important archives of German medieval sources, or the prestige enjoyed by nineteenth-century historians such as Theodor Mommsen and Leopold von Ranke.

13. This included a significant number of translations into German. Memoirs of aristocrats from major European courts enjoyed great popularity, as did the autobiographies of actresses and other female performers.

tices, including works of high culture and popular literature, writings by men and women, and narratives by members of all social classes. Because autobiographical modes of literary expression had become available to more people than ever before as writers and as readers, the memoir boom had a democratizing effect on literary production and consumption. Many critics found this development alarming. By 1900 class and gender had lost some of their traditional power to control access to literary production. The memoir boom now challenged the notion that "talent" was a necessary precondition for writing. The sense of change that pervaded fin de siècle culture empowered greater numbers of people to bear witness to the history that took place during their lifetime. And since contemporaries recognized that historical change affected people across class and gender, a life no longer needed to be outstanding to merit writing about it. The upsurge in autobiographical production itself had become a symptom of sociocultural shifts and an expression of the modern age.

Much of turn-of-the-century autobiography, including but not limited to the majority of texts by women, did not share in the stylistic and linguistic experiments of what Barbara Green terms a "'minority' modernist aesthetic."[14] A look beyond the conventional canon of high literature directs the researcher toward what is alternately—with different political agendas in mind—called trivial literature, mass literature, or popular literature.[15] Popular literature, moreover, is not a monolithic category but includes different types of texts, ranging from the high-volume output of the popular press to pulp fiction.[16] In *After the Great Divide,* a collection of essays exploring the relationship between high and mass culture, Andreas Huyssen argues that mass culture connoted feminization and a loss of manliness in artistic production. Only with the emergence of feminism did "formerly devalued forms and genres of cultural expression," among which Huyssen includes "autobiographic texts," gain new recogni-

---

14. Green, *Spectacular Confessions,* 23.

15. Peter Nusser, *Trivialliteratur* (Stuttgart: Metzler, 1991), 3, opts for the term *trivial literature* because it reflects aesthetic categories as well as the accessible nature of such texts. Andreas Huyssen uses the term *mass culture* to distinguish it from modernist high art in *After the Great Divide: Modernism, Mass Culture, Postmodernism* (Bloomington: Indiana University Press, 1986). Huyssen explores the juxtaposition of early-twentieth-century elite culture and mass culture in aesthetic theory. Kirsten Belgum in *Popularizing the Nation: Audience, Representation, and the Production of Identity in "Die Gartenlaube," 1853–1900* (Lincoln: Nebraska University Press, 1998), speaks of popular culture in her analysis of the content, function, and marketing of the nineteenth-century magazine *Die Gartenlaube.*

16. A recent study on popular culture is Helmut Schmiedt, *Ringo in Weimar: Begegnungen zwischen Hochkultur und Popularkultur* (Würzburg: Köngishausen & Neumann, 1996). Schmiedt argues that high culture and popular culture should be examined in context rather than as separate entities.

tion.[17] Turn-of-the-century critics repeatedly commented on women's penchant for autobiography, suggesting that the fear of autobiography was also a response to its feminized proximity to mass culture. Autobiography was not only literature for the masses but also—potentially—literature by the masses. On the other hand, the general accessibility of autobiography was considered its foremost asset because memoirs possessed an immediacy lacking in other texts. Autobiography was allotted a special position within popular culture, and critics enlisted these narratives for various and at times contradictory purposes. The autobiographies discussed here belong to popular culture by virtue of their comparatively simple, sometimes clichéd, language and their realist style but differ in intent and reception from pulp fiction.[18] Their authors enjoyed a degree of public recognition even before they published their autobiographies and could count on an audience interested in their true life stories rather than aesthetics.

A number of scholars have accounted for the unique appeal of autobiography by theorizing the relationship between writer and reader, the institution of criticism, and the market mechanisms through which autobiographies are circulated. Philippe Lejeune, one of the first scholars to address the special relationship between the autobiographer and her readers, proposes the concept of the "autobiographical pact." According to Lejeune, the author's name on the front page implies the writer's promise to tell his or her life truthfully. The autobiographical pact, Lejeune believes, accounts for the fundamental difference between autobiography and fiction.[19] Other scholars have expanded upon Lejeune's work, distinguishing between different groups of readers. There has "never yet been an autobiography written for a readership of theorists," American critic John Sturrock maintains, insisting on a privileged relationship between autobiographers and lay readers.[20] Unlike the theorist, the lay reader is willing to

---

17. Huyssen, *After the Great Divide,* 59.

18. They are also not autobiographies of lay authors with little formal education who do not otherwise claim any public significance. On "popular autobiography" as a tool in everyday history *(Alltagsgeschichte)* see Bernd Jürgen Warneken, *Populare Autobiographik: Empirische Studien zu einer Quellengattung der Alltagsgeschichtsforschung* (Tübingen: Tübinger Vereinigung für Volkskunde, 1985); and Monika Bernold, "Representations of the Beginning: Shaping Gender Identity in Written Life Stories of Women and Men," in *Austrian Women in the Nineteenth and Twentieth Centuries: Cross-Disciplinary Perspectives,* ed. David F. Good, Margarete Gardner, and Mary Jo Maynes (Providence: Berghahn, 1996), 197–212.

19. Philippe Lejeune, *On Autobiography,* ed. Paul John Eakin, trans. Katherine Leary (Minneapolis: University of Minnesota Press, 1989).

20. John Sturrock, "Theory versus Autobiography," in *The Culture of Autobiography: Constructions of Self-Representation,* ed. Robert Folkenflik (Stanford, Calif.: Stanford University Press, 1993), 24.

share in the autobiographer's truth and to grant authenticity to the self that emerges from the text. Australian-born historian and autobiographer Jill Ker Conway makes a similar argument in the opening sentence of her volume on autobiography, *When Memory Speaks,* asking: "Why is autobiography the most popular form of fiction for modern readers?"[21] Conway, proposing that autobiography is a "form of fiction," nonetheless responds to her own question that the "satisfaction comes from being allowed *inside* the experience of another person who really lived and who tells about experiences which did in fact occur."[22] Turn-of-the-century Germans experienced the intimate pleasures of autobiography as they devoured the life stories of the rich and powerful or read the confessional memoirs of women and men whose lives fell outside of the parameters defined by bourgeois society. Readers were shocked by the poverty and deprivation chronicled in the life stories of members of the lower classes, and they identified with the fate of those who succeeded in their endeavors. Most importantly, autobiographies offered their readers exclusive truths no other kind of writing could proffer.

Autobiographical truth, whether pledged by the writer or assumed by the reader, is central to the cultural function of autobiography. Traditionally, literary critics and cultural commentators felt called upon to decide whose truth to admit into the canon, autobiographers devised strategies to make their version of the truth heard, and readers sought, perhaps, to determine the importance of these truths for their own lives.[23] Recent theory immensely complicates the issue of truth. The search for autobiographical truth has been replaced by the analysis of the "construction of self," "technologies of self," and the "performance of identity." The genuineness attributed to autobiography accounts for the continuing appeal of the genre, challenging the contemporary critic to analyze the function of truth within the culture of autobiography.

Turn-of-the-century Germans could choose among almost two hundred monthly or bimonthly magazines dedicated to politics and culture, from conservative to liberal, Catholic to Protestant, Prussian to South German. Many of these publications took a considerable interest in autobiography: they reviewed memoir literature under special headlines and regularly

---

21. Jill Ker Conway, *When Memory Speaks: Reflections on Autobiography* (New York: Knopf, 1998), 3.

22. Ibid., 6.

23. On the question of women and autobiographical truth see Sidonie Smith, "Construing Truths in Lying Mouths: Truthtelling in Women's Autobiography," *Studies in the Literary Imagination* 23, no. 2 (1990): 159; and Leigh Gilmore, *Autobiographics: A Feminist Theory of Women's Self-Representation* (Ithaca: Cornell University Press, 1994).

published autobiographical narratives. Marie von Ebner-Eschenbach's *Meine Kinderjahre* (My years of childhood),[24] for instance, was serialized in the *Deutsche Rundschau* (German review) before it appeared in book form, and *Das literarische Echo* (Literary echo) featured a series "Autobiographical Sketches."[25] Beginning in 1901 the *Neue Deutsche Rundschau* (New German review) reviewed "Letters, Diaries, Memoirs" as a separate category. The Berlin-based *Literary Echo* periodically surveyed autobiographies under such collective titles as "Works of Memoirs," "Memoirs and Correspondences," or "Books of Remembrance"; and the *German Review,* Julius Rodenberg's cultural magazine, regularly included critical assessments under headers such as "On Recent Memoir Literature."

Autobiographical literature became so abundant that editors recognized it as a category that deserved its own headlines within the magazines' book review sections. In their reviews and comments on this rapidly proliferating body of writing, cultural critics introduced criteria for evaluating new memoir publications. Some reviewers welcomed the increase in memoir literature and called for more. For these critics autobiography served political and social rather than literary purposes. "All social policy has begun with drastic descriptions of workers' misery," a reviewer remarked on working-class memoirs.[26] He endorsed autobiography as a tool in the struggle against poverty and as an important source for learning about lives presumably very different from the reader's own. Others professed to be inspired by outstanding lives and urged their readers to heed the lessons of failed ones. Reviewers also enlisted autobiography to propagate German national identity. In the decades after unification, cultural magazines promoted the memoirs of Germans of different classes who had participated in the founding of the nation-state as significant documents of recent German history. The upsurge in autobiography, in the minds of the intellectual elite, demanded a response. One such response was to place memoir literature in the service of a variety of social and political agendas.

The majority of critics, however, tried to delimit the trend toward autobiography because they feared its resemblance to popular culture. They wished to curb the genre's popular appeal by distinguishing between "good" and "bad" memoirs, basing their judgment on both literary quality and the importance of the writer's life and warning readers away from gossipy or vulgar memoirs. They hoped to rein in the proliferation of memoir literature by demanding that these narratives possess didactic

---

24. Marie von Ebner-Eschenbach, *Meine Kinderjahre* (Berlin: Paetel, 1906).

25. Thomas Mann, Ilse Frapan-Akunian, and Gabriele Reuter, among others, published autobiographical essays in this series.

26. Heinrich Herkner, "Seelenleben und Lebenslauf in der Arbeiterklasse," *Preußische Jahrbücher* 140 (1910): 393.

qualities to provide insights into history, society, politics, and the unfolding of an outstanding life. Whether supportive or averse, critics assumed a special relationship between autobiography and national culture. In trying to curb popular autobiography, they defended the exclusivity of German high culture.

The debates on the pages of the cultural magazines had a counterpart among academics. In 1900 the Königlich Preussische Akademie der Wissenschaften (Royal Prussian Academy of Sciences) solicited a "history of autobiography in the strictest sense (with exclusion of all memoir literature)" for its annual prize question, encouraging potential contributors to analyze the "representative works of the most important European nations."[27] The academy's formulation made clear that literary quality was the criterion to distinguish between popular works of remembrance and the literary autobiography whose appreciation required the expertise of the scholar. Like their colleagues from the cultural press, the members of the academy proposed a tangible relationship between the autobiographer's nation and his *Werk,* and the judges expected the submissions to illuminate this correlation. The winner of the competition was the philosopher Georg Misch with his *History of Autobiography.*[28] Autobiographies by women, predictably, played a marginal role in Misch's study. Since Misch set out to define the genre, he had to create an ideal autobiographer, who by definition was male, endowed with unique individuality and a claim to historical representativeness. "Though essentially representations of individual personalities, autobiographies are bound always to be representative of their period . . . the contemporary intellectual outlook revealed in the style of an eminent person who has himself played a part in the forming of the spirit of his time," as Misch expanded on the academy's formulation.[29] For feminist scholars of autobiography, the work of Misch and his followers has served as a negative point of departure because he constructed an autobiographical tradition without female autobiographers.[30] The academy's interest in "representative works" and Misch's

27. *Sitzungsberichte der Königlich Preussischen Akademie der Wissenschaften zu Berlin* (Berlin: Verlag der Königlichen Akademie der Wissenschaften, 1900), 55.

28. The academy received only two submissions by the 1904 deadline. Misch's competitor was Kurt Jahn, a literary scholar and coeditor of the *Jahresberichte für neuere deutsche Literatur.*

29. Georg Misch, *A History of Autobiography in Antiquity,* trans. E. W. Dickes (Cambridge: Harvard University Press, 1951), 12–13.

30. Sidonie Smith has provided one of the most pertinent feminist critiques of Misch's work in *A Poetics of Women's Autobiography: Marginality and the Fictions of Self-Representation* (Bloomington: Indiana University Press, 1987), 7–9. Misch's intellectual legacy manifests itself in the fact that the distinction between autobiography and memoir, as well as the difference between autobiography and novel, continued to occupy German literary scholars into the 1980s. See Wuthenow, *Das erinnerte Ich;* and Niggl, *Geschichte der deutschen Autobiographie.*

subsequent definition of "representative" autobiographical subjects forges an alliance of European high culture against the countless practitioners of the autobiographical genre, among them German-speaking women from different classes and from different religious and national backgrounds, who told the stories of lives that contributed to the spirit of their time in ways Georg Misch chose not to account for.

Autobiography became a veritable industry as publishers and editors furthered the public interest in personal narratives.[31] In 1899 the Robert Lutz publishing house in Stuttgart inaugurated a series titled Memoirenbibliothek (Memoir library) that by 1927 had swelled to more than ninety volumes. Appropriately, the series opened with the autobiography of the Prussian general Hermann von Boyen. It featured autobiographies, diaries, and letters by outstanding personalities of European history, including the *Erinnerungen der Kaiserin Katharina II* (Memoirs of Empress Catherine II).[32] The series also included the memoirs of remarkable ordinary people such as deaf and blind American Helen Keller, who had overcome her disabilities through sign language. The attractive volumes were of uniform size and coloring with an emblem stamped into the cover, impressing upon the buyer the serial nature of these books. Other publishers launched similar undertakings with titles such as the Bibliothek wertvoller Memoiren: Lebensdokumente hervorragender Menschen aller Zeiten und Völker (Library of valuable memoirs: Life documents of extraordinary people of all times and nations), which featured memoirs of historical personalities like the thirteenth-century explorer Marco Polo and the leader of the Italian unification, Guiseppe Garibaldi. Often adorned with an image of the author, these books were "for the educated layman rather than the trained historian," as the editor of this series described the popular appeal of his enterprise in his preface to one of the first volumes.[33] These series suggested to their readers that History could be understood through the collected life stories of people who in different ways had made

---

31. See Linda H. Peterson, "Institutionalizing Women's Autobiography: Nineteenth-Century Editors and the Shaping of an Autobiographical Tradition," in Folkenflik, *The Culture of Autobiography,* 80–103, for a discussion of English-language "memoir libraries" from the early to the middle nineteenth century.

32. *Erinnerungen der Kaiserin Katharina II* (Hamburg: Gutenberg, 1907).

33. Ernst Schultze, "Vorwort des Herausgebers zu der Bibliothek wertvoller Memoiren," in *Die Eroberung von Mexiko: Drei eigenhändige Berichte von Ferdinand Cortez an Kaiser Karl V,* ed. Ernst Schultze (Hamburg: Gutenberg, 1907), 16. Other publishing houses launched similar undertakings. Beginning in 1898 the Berlin-based publisher Schuster und Loeffler, for instance, joined the trend with a series of artists' autobiographies titled Contemporary Self-Biographies (Zeitgenössische Selbstbiographien). Other memoir libraries are Fried & Co.'s fifteen-volume Memoiren-Bibliothek: Berühmte Menschen und ihre Geschichte (1892*),* and Hüpeden und Merzyn's Memoiren-Sammlung (1905ff.).

history. The publicity blurb for Ernst Schultze's Library of Valuable Memoirs declared:

> No time period has sensed the general value of good memoirs more clearly than ours. . . . It is thus especially peculiar that nowhere in the world has the attempt been made to unite the most significant *Memoirs of all Times and Peoples* in one series. The present collection therefore wants to bring together the most valuable memoirs of world literature.[34]

The advertisement suggests a privileged relationship between the autobiographical genre and turn-of-the-century culture, urging potential readers to be at the vanguard of their times. Inclusion in the series assured readers of the quality of the individual volumes and allowed them to display in their private libraries their appreciation for "good memoirs." The publisher's encyclopedic approach conveyed to readers that the value of memoirs lay in their sum as much as in the individual narrative.

While the advertisement did not, of course, define the criteria a good memoir had to meet, it certainly implied that memoirs as such carried intrinsic value. Less scholarly than history books but more truthful than fiction, autobiography bridged the gap between the scholar and the lay reader who wanted to learn about history. The historian Hermann Oncken (1869–1945), writing in the *Deutsche Monatsschrift* (German monthly), maintained that "our knowledge of history gains vital depth from all those sources that are associated with the achievement and development of the individual: diaries, collections of letters, memoirs, autobiographies."[35] The private documents of outstanding individuals revealed to lay readers as well as to scholars how history was made. Women's autobiographies, though far outnumbered by men's, were explicitly included in the offerings of the memoir libraries.[36]

---

34. Schultze, *Die Eroberung von Mexiko,* n.p. Memoir collections go back to the eighteenth century. Johann Gottfried Herder's *Selbstbekenntnisse* and Friedrich Schiller's *Sammlung historischer Memoires* are the most prominent. These multivolume editions were indebted to the project of universal history as a philosophy of life. In the introduction to his *Sammlung,* Schiller appealed to a general audience by assigning the memoirs of European political and military leaders a status between the serious historical treatise and the entertaining historical novel.

35. Hermann Oncken, "Aus der neueren Memoirenliteratur," *Deutsche Monatsschrift* 7 (1905): 616.

36. Ernst Schultze lists among contributors of autobiographies "statesmen and generals, leaders and seducers of the people, conquerors and explorers, intellectuals and artists, extraordinary women, simple citizens and soldiers—in short, all those whose lives contained elements that are of interest for a larger public" ("Vorwort des Herausgebers," 13). Among the autobiographies by women are the memoirs of sensational personalities such as the Russian empress Catherine II; Lola Montez, lover of Ludwig I of Bavaria; and the marquise de Pompadour, lover of Louis XV.

The publishing industry promoted autobiography to a general reading public as reading material that was easily comprehensible yet distinguished from popular fiction by its truthful content and its ability to instruct the reader. "Memoir libraries" like Lutz's and those who followed his model are precursors of what Joan Shelley Rubin has described as middlebrow culture in her study of institutions such as the Book-of-the-Month Club in post–World War I America or the weekly publication of literary supplements by major newspapers.[37] These projects variously tried to steer educated nonexperts toward "good" literature while simultaneously attempting to create a class of discerning readers. The proponents of middlebrow culture sought to ensure that Americans adhered to certain cultural standards and in turn assured their audience that the right kind of reading secured membership among the "cultured" class.

Turn-of-the-century memoir libraries and series were most of all commercial undertakings. Yet they promoted their merchandise with a similar set of arguments meant to satisfy readers that they were reading good books and were joining an educated reading public beyond the ranks of the expert few. Unlike the offerings of the American book-of-the-month club or those of their German precursors, the book societies *(Buchgemeinschaften)*, memoirs at the time were not marketed for their literary qualities.[38] Rather, they were considered accessible historical sources, including but not limited to German history, and authorized perspectives on social concerns. The projected outcome was a better-educated reader who could judge more competently the vicissitudes of his times.

While undertakings like the Memoirenbibliothek specialized mainly in the exceptional lives of great people, other publishers gave a voice to the hitherto mute. Under the title Leben und Wissen (Life and knowledge) Paul Göhre, Protestant minister and later Social Democratic member of parliament, edited the first series of workers' memoirs. Karl Fischer's *Denkwürdigkeiten und Erinnerungen eines Arbeiters* (Reminiscences and memories of a worker) opened the series.[39] In the introduction to the second volume of the series, Moritz Bromme's *Lebensgeschichte eines modernen Fabrikarbeiters* (Life story of a modern factory worker), Göhre explained the meaning of the series' title; to further the "general knowledge of the real life of the contemporary proletariat."[40] The "lives" were

---

37. Joan Shelley Rubin, *The Making of Middle Brow Culture* (Chapel Hill: University of North Carolina Press, 1992); also Janice A. Radway, *A Feeling for Books: The Book-of-the-Month Club, Literary Taste, and Middle-Class Desire* (Chapel Hill: University of North Carolina Press, 1997).

38. The first *Buchgemeinschaft* was founded in 1919 (Rubin, *Middle Brow Culture,* 95).

39. Karl Fischer, *Denkwürdigkeiten und Erinnerungen eines Arbeiters* (Leipzig: Diederich, 1903).

40. Paul Göhre, in Moritz William Theodor Bromme, *Lebensgeschichte eines modernen Fabrikarbeiters* (Frankfurt am Main: Athenäum, 1971), v.

proletarian, yet the "knowledge" they were expected to impart was meant for the education of the middle class. Six years later, on the initiative of August Bebel, the Ernst Reinhardt publishing house in Munich established a series Lebensschicksale in Selbstschilderungen Ungenannter (Anonymous lives in self-descriptions) that published the anonymous first edition of Adelheid Popp's *Jugendgeschichte einer Arbeiterin* in 1909. In the same year, the Social Democrat Adolf Levenstein edited a series of letters and memoirs by workers to provide middle-class readers authentic insights into an alien world.[41] When the *Literary Echo* recommended Karl Fischer's *Reminiscences* as an "excellent yardstick for all those beautiful theories that nonworkers have written about workers," it attributed to autobiography a higher level of truth than academic tracts and elevated the genre as a much-needed antidote to "theory."[42]

Other publishers concentrated on particular subjects. Ernst Mittler in Berlin, for instance, specialized in military memoirs and colonial autobiographies. The publisher's program included Margarethe von Eckenbrecher's colonial autobiographies and the memoirs of Theodor Leutwein (1849–1921), the governor of German Southwest Africa from 1898 to 1905.[43] The Fontane Verlag, also in Berlin, "specialized" in the autobiographies of lower-class women. Its program included Margarete Böhme's *Tagebuch einer Verlorenen* (Diary of a lost one),[44] one of the commercially most successful books of 1905, and Marie Sansgêne's *Jugenderinnerungen eines armen Dienstmädchens* (Childhood memories of a poor servant girl).[45] In 1913 the series Memoiren jüdischer Männer und Frauen (Memoirs of Jewish men and women), published by the Jüdischer Verlag, opened with a High German translation of *Denkwürdigkeiten der Glückel von Hameln* (Reminiscences of Glückel von Hameln), a seventeenth-century autobiography by a German-Jewish woman. The introduc-

---

41. *Aus der Tiefe. Arbeiterbriefe. Beiträge zur Seelenanalyse moderner Arbeiter; Proletariers Jugendjahre. Lebenstragödie eines Tagelöhners;* and *Arbeiter-Philosophen und-Dichter* (all titles Berlin: Frowein, 1909).

42. Wilhelm Hegeler, "Erinnerungen eines Arbeiters," *Das Litterarische Echo* 6 (1903–4): 30.

43. Ernst Mittler's program included titles such as Ludwig Schmitz, *Aus dem Feldzuge 1870/71: Tagebuchblätter* (1907); *Aus meinem Leben: Aufzeichnungen des Prinzen Kraft zu Hohenlohe-Inselfingen* (1905); *Heinrich Abeken: Ein schlichtes Leben aus bewegter Zeit, aus Briefen zusammengestellt* (1898); Theodor Leutwein, *Elf Jahre Gouverneur in Deutsch-Südwestafrika* (1907); Kurd Schwabe, *Mit Schwert und Pflug in Deutsch-Südwestafrika. Vier Kriegs-und Wanderjahre* (1899).

44. Margarete Böhme, ed., *Tagebuch einer Verlorenen: Von einer Toten* (Berlin: Fontane, 1905). Translated into English as *The Diary of a Lost One* (New York: The Hudson Press, 1908).

45. Marie Sansgêne, *Jugenderinnerungen eines armen Dienstmädchens* (Berlin: Fontane, 1905).

tion addressed a general female readership rather than a Jewish audience: "This portrait of an independent woman who energetically shaped her own life, from a time when no one yet thought about the struggle for women's rights, offers women in particular abundant material for reflection and comparison."[46]

Speculation about why autobiographies enjoy popularity at any given time is an inquiry into the culture that produced them. In the introduction to *Getting a Life* Smith and Watson comment, "Autobiographical narratives, their citation, and their recitation have historically been one means through which the imagined community that was and is America constitutes itself on a daily basis as American."[47] The struggle over autobiography in turn-of-the-century Germany reflects the struggle over German self-definitions. A good number of critics looked to autobiography to define and confirm what it meant to be German. Thirty years after the nation's unification under Bismarck reviewers allotted a special status to the life stories of active participants in the unification process, and they stressed the importance of such memoirs for those who came after. The journalist Gustav Manz, for instance, could count on broad agreement when he claimed in the pages of the *Literary Echo* in 1901 that the memoirs of "outstanding men and women from the most varied of intellectual climates" documented and completed the struggle toward German unification.

> One can hardly imagine cultural-historical reading material better suited to build character in the national sense: there lies a compelling eloquence in the simple narration of such individual German fates during the epoch of the desired yet repeatedly impeded unification.[48]

Julius Rodenberg's *German Review* also hailed autobiography as an important tool in the creation of national identity. Under headers such as "New Memoir Literature" the journal reviewed almost exclusively the memoirs of members of the Prussian military and the Prussian intellectual elite, praising their contributions to German unification: "The memoirs, letters, life descriptions, and comparable related records by those men who created the new Germany have by no means all come to light," a reviewer observed in 1905, calling for more autobiographies.[49] Cultural critics who

---

46. Alfred Feilchenfeld, ed., *Denkwürdigkeiten der Glückel von Hameln* (Berlin: Jüdischer Verlag, 1913), 9, 10.

47. Sidonie Smith and Julia Watson, eds., *De/Colonizing the Subject: The Politics of Gender in Women's Autobiography* (Minneapolis: University of Minnesota Press, 1992), 4.

48. Gustav Manz, "Memoirenwerke," *Das Litterarische Echo* 4 (1901–2): 310.

49. *Deutsche Rundschau* 125 (1905): 153.

wished to promote German national identity through the autobiographies of people who had helped forge the nation also enlisted the memoirs of common people for their purposes. Often these autobiographies specifically addressed the lay reader rather than the historian and sought to instill in a nonspecialist audience a sense of German history from below. A reviewer for the *Preußische Jahrbücher* (Prussian yearbooks) recommended three memoirs by volunteers who had fought in the Franco-Prussian War: "Innumerable literary creations of this kind may yet appear; all of them will stimulate the nation's most lively interest."[50] As soldiers, the autobiographers had contributed to the formation of the nation. The nation now rewarded them by incorporating their stories into its self-understanding.

Many reviewers considered the politics of unification inseparable from cultural politics: "The only area . . . in which German literary production remained quantitatively behind that of other civilized peoples was until a few years ago the field of *memoir* literature." They found the reason as well as the remedy for Germany's comparative lack of memoir literature in politics: "The years 1866 and 1870–71 also signified turning points in that area," the *German Review* asserted in 1906.[51] Two years before, the historian Hermann Oncken had put forth a similar argument in the *German Monthly:*

> For a long time the Germans lagged behind the memoir literature of France and England. This has long since changed. As we are melting together again into one people we can look back on shared glorious memories; thus the lively interest in all personal matters that have contributed to our new development with such powerful significance.[52]

The printed autobiography, according to Oncken, embedded individual memoirs in the collective memory of the German people and thus helped constitute Germans as a nation.

Reviewers singled out certain moments in German history that lent themselves especially well to memoir writing and the politics of nation building. Autobiographies that recalled the Napoleonic occupation from 1806–12, the so-called French period, the revolution of 1848–49, and the Franco-Prussian War of 1870–71 were considered vital to the formation of the German nation. In *Imagined Communities* Benedict Anderson insists on the importance of print capitalism for the formation of the "nation's

---

50. Emil Daniels, "Notizen und Besprechungen," *Preußische Jahrbücher* 132 (1908): 155.

51. *Deutsche Rundschau* 128 (1906): 311.

52. Oncken, "Aus der neueren Memoirenliteratur," 616.

biography."[53] German critics around 1900 were very much aware of print capitalism's centrality for the creation of Germany as a national community. The autobiographies and memoirs of those who had witnessed the defeats and victories of German nineteenth-century history transformed historical events into the biography of the German nation. Memoir literature thus was thought to continue and to complete the work of German unification. The production of national memoirs presupposed the existence of a nation, but without such narratives the nation was bound to remain incomplete.

By 1900 Germany defined itself as a *Kulturnation* with a nation-state and no longer adhered to the early-nineteenth-century notion of the German nation bound together by high culture in the absence of political unity. This shift is pertinently—if peculiarly—encapsulated in the fact that for reviewers as well as for writers of national memoirs Bismarck's *Gedanken und Erinnerungen* (Reflections and reminiscences) had become as important as Goethe's seminal literary autobiography *Dichtung und Wahrheit.* The *German Monthly,* for instance, credited Bismarck not only with having achieved German unification but also for having written the "milestone" *(Markstein)* memoir of the period.[54] Memoir literature reminded readers that to be German meant to belong to a nation "born late" out of struggle and to be obliged to prove the nation's equality with its European neighbors, most importantly England and France. In perusing the life stories of those who had contributed to national unity, readers relived and shared in the formation of the German nation.

Women participated in the memoir boom of the late nineteenth and early twentieth centuries as writers, critics, and readers. Yet until recently their contributions were not accorded scholarly recognition.[55] Thus, beginning in the 1980s, feminist scholars approached women's autobiographies from the premise of "exclusion." Autobiographical narratives by women, they argued, had traditionally been barred from the canon of autobiography, and they set themselves the task, often against institutional pressures, of

---

53. Benedict Anderson, *Imagined Communities: Reflections on the Origin and Spread of Nationalism,* rev. ed. (London: Verso, 1991), 205.

54. Oncken, "Aus der neueren Memoirenliteratur," 616.

55. Before 1990 there are no German studies on German autobiography that include women in any significant way. Important works such as Niggl's *Geschichte der deutschen Autobiographie* and Ralf-Rainer Wuthenow's *Das erinnerte Ich,* or even later studies such as Manfred Schneider's *Die erkaltete Herzensschrift: Der autobiographische Text im 20. Jahrhundert* (Munich: Hanser, 1986), do not discuss autobiographies by women. This pattern changes in the mid-1990s with contributions such as Magdalene Heuser's edited volume *Autobiographien von Frauen: Beiträge zu ihrer Geschichte* (Tübingen: Niemeyer, 1996), and Michaela Holdenried's anthology *Geschriebenes Leben: Autobiographik von Frauen* (Berlin: Schmidt, 1995).

retrieving women's autobiographies from oblivion and making them available to other feminist readers and scholars.[56] Scholars asked why women traditionally had not been considered suitable autobiographers and argued that Western culture since the eighteenth century defined the subject as male. Women, they suggested, developed a variety of strategies to achieve autobiographical agency despite their cultural status as unsuitable subjects.[57] These arguments, valid in their own right and pathbreaking when they were first proposed, have been challenged by critics such as Linda H. Peterson, who has invited scholars of autobiography to revisit the "fact of exclusion."[58] Peterson has urged critics to reinvestigate the formation of literary traditions, suggesting that scholars ask how women's autobiographies are situated within a given literary culture, in which she includes marketing strategies and editorial policies. Peterson has also cautioned us not to assume that gender is the central concern in women's personal narratives, urging us to look critically at the function and role of gender. We should not take for granted that we know how women used literary traditions and how they might have changed them.

German.

In the two decades between 1890 and 1910 more women than ever before wrote autobiographies; publishers solicited women's autobiographies; previously unpublished memoirs were made available, and foreign-language autobiographies were translated into German. Eda Sagarra's 1986 bibliography lists about 120 autobiographies by women during that period, and more have been discovered since.[59] The documented proliferation of autobiographical literature by women around the turn of the century illustrates that the argument of exclusion does not adequately describe the status of women's autobiography. At a time when the "woman question" loomed large, female autobiographies occupied a special position in the already complicated cultural politics of the autobiographical genre, whose shifting definitions, purposes, and growing numbers of practitioners were perceived to have an impact on the nation's

---

56. In the United States the interest in women's autobiographies begins about fifteen years earlier than in Germany. Mary Mason's collection of excerpts *Journeys: Autobiographical Writings by Women* (Boston: G.K. Hall, 1979) and Estelle Jelinek's *Women's Autobiography* (Bloomington and London: Indiana University Press, 1980) have broken new ground. Katherine Goodman's *Dis/Closures: Women's Autobiography in Germany between 1790 and 1914* (New York: Lang, 1986) is the first study dedicated to German women's autobiographies.

57. Sidonie Smith has argued this point very elegantly and eloquently in her *Poetics of Women's Autobiography*. See also Felicity A. Nussbaum, *The Autobiographical Subject: Gender and Ideology in Eighteenth-Century England* (Baltimore: Johns Hopkins University Press, 1989).

58. Peterson, "Institutionalizing Women's Autobiography," 81.

59. Eda Sagarra, "Quellenbibliographie autobiographischer Schriften von Frauen im deutschen Kulturraum, 1730–1918," *Internationales Archiv für Sozialgeschichte* 11 (1986): 175–231. Sagarra's bibliography lists only a few of the twenty or so autobiographies by female colonizers.

culture. Women's autobiographies raise the question of gender, whether foregrounded by the writer or assumed by the reader. Contemporaries regarded these texts as privileged insights into the interiors of femininity that thus were authoritative on one of the central issues of modernity.

Women's literature *(Frauenliteratur)*, which could mean literature by women as well as books about women, enjoyed considerable popularity in the late nineteenth century. Readers could consult encyclopedias for the bio-bibliographies of women authors, peruse anthologies of women's poetry, and choose among several volumes with titles such as *Geschichte der Frauen und ihre Stellung in der menschlichen Gesellschaft bei allen Völkern und zu allen Zeiten* (History of women and their position in human society in all peoples and during all times).[60] The interest in women's lives and histories was spurred by progressive as well as conservative motivations. The emergence and the pressures of the women's movements explain some of the attention lavished on women's lives. Commercial interests are another important factor. Most importantly, the majority of these works confirmed rather than questioned traditional gender expectations. They celebrated women's difference from men and highlighted their subjects' ability to preserve femininity under extraordinary circumstances.

There were no "libraries" dedicated exclusively to women's autobiographies. Publishers marketed women's personal writings in anthologies such as *Frauenbriefe aller Zeiten* (Women's letters from all times), the ten-volume collection of biographies *Frauenleben* (Women's lives), and selections of autobiographical essays such as *Als unsre großen Dichterinnen noch kleine Mädchen waren* (When our great women writers were little girls).[61] The *German Review* confirmed the fashionableness of autobiogra-

---

60. *Geschichte der Frauen und ihre Stellung in der menschlichen Gesellschaft bei allen Völkern und zu allen Zeiten* (Leipzig: Dyk, 1853). Poetry collections included volumes such as Karl Schrattenthal's *Die deutsche Frauenlyrik unserer Tage* (Stuttgart: Greiner und Pfeiffer, 1888), and Hermann Kletke, *Deutschlands Dichterinnen* (Berlin: Hermann Hollstein, n.d.). Similar undertakings were Heinrich Gross, *Deutsche Dichterinnen und Schrifstellerinnen in Wort und Bild* (Berlin: Thiel, 1885); and, significantly earlier, Karl Wilhelm August von Schindel, *Die deutschen Schriftstellerinnen des neunzehnten Jahrhunderts*, 3 vols. (Leipzig: Brockhaus, 1823–25). Sophie Pataky's *Lexikon deutscher Frauen der Feder: Eine Zusammenstellung der seit dem Jahre 1840 erschienenen Werke weiblicher Autoren, nebst Biographieen der lebenden und einem Verzeichnis der Pseudonyme*, 2 vols. (Berlin: Schuster und Loeffler, 1898), is one of the first literary encyclopedias exclusively dedicated to women writers.

61. Bernhard Ihringer, ed., *Frauenbriefe aller Zeiten* (Stuttgart: Krabbe, 1910); Hanns von Zobeltitz, ed., *Frauenleben* (Bielefeld: Velhagen und Klasing, 1907–8). *Als unsre großen Dichterinnen noch kleine Mädchen waren* (Leipzig: Moeser, 1912), which is a follow-up of *Als unsere großen Dichter noch kleine Jungen waren* (Leipzig: Moeser, 1911), contains autobiographical narratives by Ida Boy-Ed, Hedwig Dohm, Enrica von Handel-Mazzetti, Charlotte Niese, Clara Viebig, Hermine Villinger, and Luise Westkirch. Incidentally, a recurring motif in these narratives is the topic of female handiwork and the authors' suffering through endless hours of unsuccessful knitting instruction.

phies by women when it recommended to its readers "images of German women . . . in the form of memories and memoirs that is so popular nowadays" among its selection of Christmas books for the year 1908.[62]

Turn-of-the-century women created a diverse body of autobiographical texts. The writers came from different class and ethnic backgrounds and were involved in a range of careers. Some were professional writers, others published only their autobiography; some were highly visible public figures; many belonged to the first generation of professional women who earned a living as schoolteachers and nurses.[63] Aristocratic women published memoirs about life at German and other European courts at the same time that women of the working class began to write their life stories.[64] German translations of foreign-language autobiographies such as Helen Keller's fascinated German readers.[65] The autobiographies of public figures such as Malwida von Meysenbug's multivolume *Memoiren einer Idealistin* (1882), Lily Braun's *Memoiren einer Sozialistin* (1909–11), and Bertha von Suttner's *Memoiren* (1909) were widely read and were reviewed in most of the major literary magazines. Marie von Ebner-Eschenbach's *Meine Kinderjahre* is one of the few autobiographies by a woman that was accepted into the canon of high literature.

Other well-known writers told their life stories in the form of autobiographical novels; Gabriele Reuter's *Aus guter Familie: Leidensgeschichte eines Mädchens* (1895) and Franziska von Reventlow's *Ellen Olestjerne* (1903) are examples of fictionalized life writing. We may surmise that the authors of such texts could express only in fictionalized form their severe criticism of the social limitations placed on women.[66] In addition to the memoirs of contemporary women, unpublished or out-of-print texts were published, such as the memoirs of the eighteenth-century aristocrat Elisa von der Recke (1900) and the *Lebensschicksale* (1908) of her contemporary Angelika Rosa. The letters and diaries of Susanna Catharina von Klettenberg, Goethe's model for his "beautiful soul," were published

62. *Deutsche Rundschau* 137 (1908): 471.

63. For instance, the teacher Helene Adelmann's *Aus meiner Kinderzeit* (Berlin: Appelius, 1892); and the nurse Emmeline Zagori's *Aus dem Leben eines Weihnachtskindes* (Leipzig: Ungleich, 1908).

64. For instance, *Sophie Schwerin. Ein Lebensbild aus ihren eigenen hinterlassenen Papieren zusammengestellt von ihrer jüngeren Schwester Amalie von Romberg,* ed. Paul Schreckenbach (Leipzig: Eckart, 1911); and Ferdinande Freiin von Brackel, *Mein Leben* (Cologne: Bachem, 1905).

65. Helen Keller, *Die Geschichte meines Lebens,* trans. Paul Seliger (Stuttgart: Lutz, 1905). The interest in Helen Keller persists. Her autobiography was republished in Germany in 1997 under the title *Mein Weg aus dem Dunkel: Blind und gehörlos,* trans. Werner DeHaas (Munich: Knaur, 1997).

66. See Karin Tebben, *Literarische Intimität: Subjektkonstitution und Erzählstruktur in autobiographischen Romanen von Frauen* (Tübingen: Francke, 1997).

under the appropriate title *Die schöne Seele* (1911); the diaries of Fanny Lewald (1900; *Gefühltes und Gedachtes*) were edited by literary historian Ludwig Geiger. The sociocultural differences among women autobiographers and the stylistic variety of texts they produced prohibit generalizations about their autobiographical strategies. Neither reviewers nor publishers, however, failed to emphasize the writer's gender in discussing or promoting women's autobiographies.

In "The Relative and the Absolute in the Problem of the Sexes" (1911), the sociologist Georg Simmel observes that women cannot separate their identity from their gender and therefore always remain representatives of their sex.[67] Men, by contrast, can "forget" their gender and act as individuals. In his insightful contemporary critique of male universalism's effect on women, Simmel writes that

> it seems as if the woman never loses the feeling—which may be more or less clear or obscure—that she is a woman. This forms the subterranean ground of her life that never entirely disappears. All the contents of her life transpire on its basis.[68]

The pervasive interest in the gendered essence of a woman's life was the single most important factor in the reception of female autobiography. Consequently, reviewers focused on how the autobiographers represented themselves as women and what insights their texts provided into the female "soul." They often judged women's narratives according to the writer's adherence to or defiance of traditional femininity. Malwida von Meysenbug's *Memoirs of an Idealist,* for instance, was praised in the *Prussian Yearbooks* for its womanly qualities ("A century in the mirror of a woman's soul—that is the meaning of these three volumes of memoirs") and not as a means to "learn philosophy."[69] Another reviewer, discussing the same book, applauded von Meysenbug for never forgetting that the key to her "female fortune" lay in motherly love.[70] A reviewer of Bertha von Suttner's *Memoirs* downplayed the writer's political career, remarking that her book consisted of two sections, the "interesting novel of her rich life" and the "somewhat dry account of the peace movement."[71] He com-

67. Georg Simmel, "The Relative and the Absolute in the Problem of the Sexes," in *On Women, Sexuality, and Love* (New Haven: Yale University Press, 1984), 102–32.

68. Ibid., 103.

69. Max Lorenz, "Memoiren einer Idealistin von Malwida von Meysenbug," *Preußische Jahrbücher* 98 (1899): 561.

70. *Deutsche Rundschau* 101 (1899): 197.

71. Alfred von Mensi, "Die Memoiren Bertha von Suttners," *Hochland* 6, no. 2 (1909): 219.

mended this activist's memoirs for her supposed rejection of bluestockings.[72] The Reform Catholic journal *Hochland* (Highland) praised the "significance" of Lily Braun's memoirs for "Catholic womankind," noting the "selfless commitment of her personality," yet raised doubts that socialism would provide her with a lasting "element of life."[73] Marie von Ebner-Eschenbach's autobiography, finally, was especially recommended to female readers because it presumably chronicled the author's development into an "ideal type of woman."[74] The quality of a female autobiography was measured by the writer's position on the "woman question" and the positive model the narrative could provide to female readers.

Women's autobiographies were primarily marketed and reviewed in the service of conservative agendas aimed at validating gender difference. "Women and men experience [the world] differently," asserted writer and critic Lulu von Strauß und Torney (1873–1956) in a collective review article of male and female autobiographies in the *Literary Echo:* "Their philosophy of life, and therefore also their portrayal of their experience, has a different orientation . . . a man will always put foremost emphasis on his professional life, how he was able to shape his environment; whereas a woman will relate how her environment shaped her." And she added for emphasis: "That always has been and will continue to be the case, as long and as truly nature will not let even the most fervent human striving to meddle with her straightforward course."[75] Von Strauss und Torney, a conservative who also wrote regularly for *Hochland,* enlisted life writing as evidence in the gender debates.[76] More often than not, the reviewers' emphasis on the autobiographer's gender and on traditional femininity as the criterion of evaluation resulted in sanitized interpretations of the autobiographies of women who had made a name for themselves as philosophers, writers, and political leaders. Von Strauss und Torney's emphatic insistence on natural gender difference also betrays an anxiety that these differences might not be enforceable.

Some critics suggested an even closer connection between women's autobiographical production and the questions posed by modernity. In an 1896 article titled "Women's Confessions," the journalist Felix Poppen-

---

72. Ibid., 222.

73. Franz Herwig, "Neue Romane," *Hochland* 7, no. 2 (1910): 97.

74. Ernst von Wolzogen, "Marie Ebners Kinderjahre," *Das Literarische Echo* 9 (1906): 1441.

75. Lulu von Strauß und Torney, "Memoirenwerke," *Das Literarische Echo* 14 (1911–12): 1272.

76. Other female reviewers include Margarete Danneel, Marie Fuhrmann, Marie Goslich, and Gertrud Prellwitz, all of whom published in *Preußische Jahrbücher.* Their interpretations of gender and gender roles in women's autobiographies do not differ from those of their male colleagues.

berg contended that the desire to reveal the truth about the "problem of woman in modern society" enticed women to become writers in the first place. The "impossibility of denying the nature of her gender," he surmised, moved female writers to testify to the "feminine emotionality of woman" [Weibempfinden der Frau].[77] A tangible connection between women's gender identity and their literary production was central to a reading public for whom the difference between the sexes presented one of the big questions of their time. Gender provided the key to interpreting women's texts. Their autobiographies, male and female critics concurred, served an important cultural purpose because they confirmed traditional femininity.

Autobiography enjoyed such popularity in turn-of-the-century German culture because it satisfied a desire for authenticity and truth in the face of waning certainties. "In periods of cultural insecurity," Elaine Showalter writes about European fin de siècle culture, "when there are fears of regression and degeneration, the longing for strict border controls around definition of gender, as well as race, class, and nationality, becomes especially intense."[78] Women's autobiographies were enlisted to confirm such borders. At the same time, memoir literature was seen as dangerously close to popular culture, encouraging unsuitable subjects to circulate their stories in the public sphere. Women's confessional memoirs with their revelations about female sexuality, such as Wanda von Sacher-Masoch's *Lebensbeichte,* ranked among the most disturbing autobiographies of the time. The memoir boom was both symptom and cure for modern anxieties.

Turn-of-the-century readers valued women's autobiographies beyond the individual story they told because these narratives promised to answer the many questions raised by "woman." For women, the gender debates opened up narrative spaces despite the conservative tendencies of these discussions. Moreover, I suspect that questions of gender motivated readers and reviewers more than the writers themselves. In any case, female autobiographers could assume that the stories of their lives would find readers. In the following chapters I show that individual women used this favorable climate to stake out identities both within and beyond the gender debates by linking their gender to issues of class, race, and national identity. Nahida Lazarus's conversion narrative explores the problem of

cryptic [handwritten annotation]

---

77. Felix Poppenberg, "Frauen-Bekenntnisse," *Die Gegenwart* 49 (1896): 165. Poppenberg discusses among others Gabriele Reuter's *Aus guter Familie* and Lou Andreas-Salome's short novel *Ruth.*

78. Showalter, *Sexual Anarchy,* 4.

Jewish and German identity between religion and race. Both Adelheid Popp and Wanda von Sacher-Masoch were born into the lower class; for Popp class provided the key to explain her suffering as a female child; Sacher-Masoch transgressed boundaries of sexuality and gender, class and race in her quest for conventional femininity. Colonialist Margarethe von Eckenbrecher offered to her German readers the racial fantasy of the "white woman." All four writers negotiated between the traditions they themselves espoused and the desire for "modern" identities. This book traces the fault lines of modernity and tradition that run through their texts.

[handwritten notes:]

used interchangeably

problems of definition —   but cf. 10 IN 30 in
autobiography   (which happens IN 5)
    memoir
problematize of memoir - cf. FN 11, p.4.
why such a reception? connected to
assertion / fact that most autob. in US
now ff ??

NO PNG book - -
historical account (5.6 etc.) seem very
simplistic reporting
    use of "authenticity" totally un-
problematized ??

no indication of problematic relationship
betw. autob + ff   (~ 6)

    15. mistake —
repetitive re Ger. identity + autob. etc. etc. on
                                      also sec. on
                                           women
very German - based - cf. very confession on
    p. 17

but nicely written even so

RACE — connected to Judaism? (here + later)

CHAPTER 1

Becoming An/Other:
The Conversions of
Nahida Ruth Lazarus

In 1895, at the age of forty-six, fiction writer, journalist, and intellectual Nahida Remy, a baptized Protestant who never underwent confirmation, converted to Judaism. Three years later, under her new name, Nahida Ruth Lazarus, she told the story of her conversion in her autobiography, *Ich suchte Dich!* (I sought you!).[1] Converts to Judaism, two-thirds of them women, were a numerically insignificant minority in turn-of-the-century Germany and Austria.[2] As an autobiographer among these converts Nahida Lazarus is unique. Lazarus's resolve to become a Jew had its roots in her personal history. Her complicated relationship with her divorced

---

1. Nahida Lazarus, *Ich suchte Dich! Biographische Erzählung von Nahida Ruth Lazarus (Nahida Remy)* (Berlin: Cronbach, 1898). Subsequent references are given in the text. All translations are mine. The title of the handwritten manuscript, in the Leo Baeck Institute New York, AR 3754, reads: "*Ich suchte dich. Eine Erzählung aus dem Leben von Nahida Ruth Lazarus* (Nahida Remy)." The parenthetical mention of her previous name allows the reader to recognize Lazarus as the author of numerous literary and scholarly works.

2. Between 1870 and 1900 several hundred Christians in Germany and two thousand in Austria had taken this step. For statistics, conditions, and debates about Christian conversion to Judaism see Katharina Gerstenberger, "January 31, 1850: Conversion to Judaism Is Protected under the Constitution of the North German Confederation," in *Yale Companion to Jewish Writing and Thought in German Culture, 1096–1996*, ed. Sander Gilman and Jack Zipes (New Haven: Yale University Press, 1997), 186–92. Austrian law prohibited marriage between Christians and Jews, thus the comparatively higher numbers. Among female converts were the writer Paula Buber-Winkler (1877–1958), wife of the Jewish philosopher Martin Buber, and Paula Beer-Hofmann (1879–1939), wife of the Austrian-Jewish writer Richard Beer-Hofmann. Paula Winkler wrote a brief newspaper article about her conversion, "Betrachtungen einer Philozionistin," *Die Welt* 36 (1901): 4–6. On Paula Buber and Paula Beer-Hofmann see Barbara Hahn, *Unter falschem Namen: Von der schwierigen Autorschaft der Frauen* (Frankfurt am Main: Suhrkamp, 1991), 92–108.

parents plays a role, as does her quest for the spiritual fulfillment she did
not find in Christianity, and, importantly, her deep admiration for her
teacher and second husband, the Jewish philosopher Moritz Lazarus
(1824–1903). But her conversion and the autobiography she wrote about it
are also a response to modernization and what she perceived to be a loss of
tradition. More specifically, Lazarus believed that Judaism afforded
women the revered position denied them by patriarchal Christian society.
The autobiographer's religious search is also the search of a woman who
had to find her way in a world in which women's life choices continued to
be restricted, while many of them could no longer rely on the securities
presumably provided by their traditional status. Lazarus's response to
women's changing roles is both idiosyncratic and paradoxical. She took
more freedoms for granted than many of her female contemporaries yet
longed for traditional gender roles. That she found her answer to the problems posed by a rapidly modernizing society in Judaism makes her case
significant beyond its singularity. Lazarus's step against the tide of the
time offers a new perspective on the confluences of gender and race and
how these markers of difference figured in the conflict between tradition
and modernity.

Nahida Lazarus's spiritual quest took place in the context of antisemitism, on the one hand, and widespread secularization, on the other.
As religious distinctions were losing their importance, nineteenth-century
science began to conceive of Jewish difference as racial difference.[3] To
become a Jew in turn-of-the-century Germany thus meant to identify with
a group that the Christian-German majority perceived as racial others.
Lazarus was well aware of antisemitism and publicly condemned it. Yet
she was even more concerned about the growing secularization among
German Jews. For the convert Nahida Lazarus Jews had to be different
from Christians, but they could not be racially different from Germans.
She therefore understood the distinction between Christians and Jews to
be rooted in religious culture, most notably in the treatment of women.
The Jews she met and admired in late-nineteenth-century Berlin were middle-class Germans with whom she shared a deep commitment to both Jewish tradition and German high culture. *Ich suchte Dich!* is fundamentally
about insider and outsider positions and the concomitant attribution of
sameness and difference. In that, Lazarus is a product of her time. Racial
difference between German and Jews, however, which preoccupied so
many of her contemporaries, remains an unspoken referent in her autobiography. Instead, her focus is on women's difference from men and Jewish

---

3. See Sander Gilman, *Freud, Race, and Gender* (Princeton, N.J.: Princeton University
Press, 1993), 3ff.

Fig. 1. Nahida Ruth and Moritz Lazarus. (Courtesy of the Jewish National and University Library, Jerusalem.)

difference from Christians. The Jewish woman, who combines both, is a central figure in Lazarus's thinking because it was her duty, the autobiographer agreed with many Jewish men, to uphold the difference between Jewish and non-Jewish culture.[4]

Nahida Lazarus found her spiritual home in the Reform Jewish community of turn-of-the-century Berlin. She thus joined a group that sought to adapt the Jewish religion to the demands of a modern society without altogether renouncing its traditions and its sense of difference.[5] Reform

---

4. I agree with Barbara Hahn's suggestion, in "Die Jüdin Pallas Athene. Ortsbestimmungen im 19. und 20. Jahrhundert," in *Von einer Welt in die andere: Jüdinnen im 19. und 20 Jahrhundert,* ed. Jutta Dick and Barbara Hahn (Vienna: Brandstätter, 1993), that Lazarus found in Judaism a "tradition that was foreign to her as a bulwark against the thrust of modernization at the end of the nineteenth century" (16). For the realities of Jewish women in Wilhelmine Germany see Marion Kaplan, *The Making of the Jewish Middle Class: Women, Family, and Identity in Imperial Germany* (New York: Oxford University Press, 1991).

5. See Michael A. Meyer, *Response to Modernity: A History of the Reform Movement in Judaism* (New York: Oxford University Press, 1988).

Judaism, in addition, was most open to converts. The balance between tradition and modernity that the Reformers sought to achieve might have reminded Lazarus of her own predicaments as a woman whose unconventional life was more "modern" than she perhaps wanted it to be. The Reform Jewish community welcomed her as someone who had chosen to become one of them. Its members enthusiastically received her autobiography because it illustrated the attraction and validity of Jewish tradition beyond the ranks of born Jews.[6] Lazarus's conversion and her defense of Judaism were appreciated as a courageous statement against antisemitism. Her choice was also enlisted as a counterargument against secularization among Jews and her autobiography especially recommended to Jewish women, whose identification with Judaism Lazarus sought to reinforce with her own example. Lazarus never commented on antisemitism as an issue of race. But as a convert to Judaism in turn-of-the-century Germany she became a symbol in the two-pronged debates about Jewish difference.

An unusual degree of geographical and intellectual mobility, relative financial independence, and a remarkable courage not to conform characterize the life and work of Nahida Lazarus. When she published her autobiography in 1898, she could look back on a varied career as an actress, painter, and, most importantly, widely recognized fiction writer and dramatist.

Nahida Ruth Lazarus was born Nahida Anna Maria Sturmhoefel in Berlin on February 3, 1849, to the writer and feminist Nahida Sturmhoefel[7] and the art historian Max Schasler (1819–1903). Her parents married after she was born and separated a few years later. Young Nahida was raised by her mother. She spent her childhood and early adulthood in Berlin and in the small village of Flatow in West Prussia, in southern France, and in different parts of Italy, repeatedly crossing national bound-

---

6. Gustav Karpeles, "Ein autobiographisches Glaubensbekenntnis," *Allgemeine Zeitung des Judenthums* (hereafter *AZJ*), October 15, 1897, 499–501; Ludwig Jacobowski, "Nahida Ruth Lazarus," *Die Gesellschaft* 15, no. 1 (1899): 235; for a critical review see S. Lublinski, "Eine Bekehrte," *Die Zeit,* July 16, 1898, 38–39.

7. Nahida Sturmhoefel (1822–1889), daughter of a Prussian major, was the author of several philosophical and lyrical works, including a treatise *Neulatein als Weltsprache* (Berlin: Apolant, 1884), and articles on women's work in the socialist newspaper *Der Arbeiterfreund.* According to Pataky, *Lexikon deutscher Frauen,* 348, Sturmhoefel published a feminist newspaper in Dresden in 1848. This information could not be confirmed. For further biographical and bibliographical information see Franz Brümmer, ed., *Lexikon der deutschen Dichter und Prosaisten des neunzehnten Jahrhunderts,* 5th ed, vol. 3 (Leipzig: Reclam, 1901), 12; and Elisabeth Friedrichs, *Die deutschsprachigen Schriftstellerinnen des 18. und 19. Jahrhunderts. Ein Lexikon* (Stuttgart: Metzler, 1981), 304.

aries and acquiring fluency in several languages and cultures. In the mid-1860s she returned to Germany. After short-lived engagements as an actress in Breslau (Wrocław) in 1866 and Bad Warmbrunn (Cieplice Śląskie Zdrój) in 1867,[8] she enrolled at the newly founded academy for women painters in Berlin, where she pursued her art studies until she married the journalist and art critic Max Remy (1839–1881) in 1873. After her first husband's death in 1881, Nahida Remy lived by herself in Berlin, supporting herself with book reviews and art commentary for the *Vossische Zeitung*.[9] In the early 1880s, Nahida, now in her midthirties, met Moritz Lazarus, the philosopher of Reform Judaism and together with Heyman Steinthal (1823–1899) the founder of the nineteenth-century science of *Völkerpsychologie* (ethnopsychology).[10] Over the course of the next one and one-half decades, Moritz Lazarus became her teacher of Jewish religion, culture, and philosophy. Nahida Remy, in turn, assumed an active role as his biographer and editor, a task she began as early as 1884 and continued to fulfill until after his death.[11]

Immediately following her conversion to Judaism in Freiburg in 1895, she married Moritz Lazarus.[12] In 1897 the couple moved to the Alpine city of Merano, then part of the Habsburg monarchy, where Moritz Lazarus died in 1903. After his death, Lazarus published several of her late husband's works, including three autobiographical accounts that owe their existence largely to her initiative and persistence. With the exception of two booklets dedicated to her Tyrolean environment, Lazarus did not publish any works of her own during the last three decades of her life. A "victim of the inflation," according to one obituary, she died in Merano in January 1928.[13]

Political geography suggests itself as a point of entry into the story of Nahida Lazarus's life because her understanding of difference was shaped

---

8. See Karl A. Leimbach, ed., *Die deutschen Dichter der Neuzeit und Gegenwart. Biographien, Charakteristiken und Auswahl ihrer Dichtungen* (Leipzig: Kesselringsche Hofbuchhandlung, 1899), 429.

9. See *Moritz Lazarus' Lebenserinnerungen*, ed. Nahida Lazarus and Alfred Leicht (Berlin: Georg Reimer, 1906), 126; see also Adolf Hinrichsen, *Das literarische Deutschland*, 2d ed. (Berlin: Verlag des "literarischen Deutschlands," 1891), 1093.

10. On Moritz Lazarus see Ingrid Belke, ed., *Moritz Lazarus und Heymann Steinthal: Die Begründer der Völkerpsychologie in ihren Briefen* (Tübingen: Mohr, 1971).

11. Moritz Lazarus, *Aus meiner Jugend*, ed. Nahida Lazarus (Frankfurt am Main: J. Kauffmann, 1913), 68. Members of Moritz Lazarus's family apparently objected against the close relationship between the widowed Nahida Remy and the married Moritz Lazarus.

12. His first wife, Sarah Lebenheim, had died in 1894.

13. Gerhard Lüdtke, ed., *Nekrolog zu Kürschners Literatur-Kalender, 1901–1935* (Berlin: de Gruyter, 1936), 407.

by her many places of residence. Since the mid–nineteenth century European politics were increasingly dominated by the erection of national boundaries intended to ensure cultural, linguistic, and racial homogeneity within their confines.[14] Lazarus lived major parts of her life in geographical locations where nationalisms repeatedly redrew the political map. Italian and German unification are the most prominent examples. Throughout the century, Polish patriots fought for the unification of the divided Polish nation. After her first years in a small village in West Prussia, one of Prussia's "Polish provinces," she spent her childhood and early adolescence in the Italian cities of Pisa, Palermo, and Naples. Before unification, Pisa was under Austrian rule, while Palermo and Naples belonged to the Kingdom of the Two Sicilies ruled by the Spanish house of Bourbon. In 1861 all three cities became part of the newly founded Kingdom of Italy. In West Prussia, Lower Silesia, and Tyrol Lazarus witnessed the competition of German-Protestant minority culture with Polish and Italian Catholicism. Both West Prussia and Silesia, moreover, were home to large and diverse Jewish communities, ranging from the shtetl-community Lazarus knew in her native Flatow to the Jewish bourgeoisie of Breslau, who might have seen her perform on stage. Between 1871 and 1900, Berlin, capital of the newly united Germany and Lazarus's residence for the last three decades of the nineteenth century, saw an increase in population from eight hundred thousand to 2.7 million inhabitants, radically changing the city's demographic composition. The hierarchies of insider and outsider positions she experienced and observed in these diverse national and cultural settings are reflected in her writings: The position of the German in non-German contexts, the oppression of the religious outsider, and the silencing of the female voice in a male-dominated world are primary concerns in Lazarus's fiction, in her scholarly writings, and in her autobiography.

Nahida Lazarus was a prolific writer throughout extended periods of her adult life. Her creative output can be divided into three distinct phases.[15] Between 1870 and 1890 she wrote seven popular dramas, two novels, and a collection of stories, all of which enjoyed popular and criti-

---

14. For a discussion of nation formation in nineteenth- and twentieth-century Europe see Miroslav Hroch, "From National Movement to the Fully-Formed Nation: The Nation-Building Process in Europe," in *Becoming National: A Reader,* ed. Geoff Eley and Ronald Grigor Suny (Oxford: Oxford University Press, 1996), 60–77.

15. See Bettina Kratz-Ritter, "Konversion als Antwort auf den Berliner Antisemitismusstreit? Nahida Ruth Lazarus und ihr Weg zum Judentum," *Zeitschrift für Religions- und Geistesgeschichte* 46 (1994): 16–17.

cal success, according to contemporary sources.[16] During the second phase of her professional life, from 1890 to 1898, Lazarus dedicated herself to "Jewish cultural studies." In 1891 she published her first and most widely acclaimed book on Jewish religion and culture, entitled *Das jüdische Weib.*[17] Subsequently translated into English, Hebrew, and Hungarian, the book earned her a certain fame as a Christian "scholar of Judaism." Other studies on Judaism followed, including a small pamphlet entitled *Das Gebet in Bibel und Talmud* (Prayer in Bible and Talmud) and *Culturstudien über das Judenthum* (Cultural studies about Judaism).[18] She also contributed stories and poems to the Reform Jewish *Allgemeine Zeitung des Judenthums* (General newspaper of Judaism).[19] The publication of her autobiography in 1898 concludes this second phase of her creative career.

Nahida Lazarus spent the final stage of her professional life preserving and enhancing Moritz Lazarus's reputation as an ethnopsychologist and philosopher of Judaism. She oversaw the publication of his scholarly works and edited a collection of his aphorisms. After his death in 1903 she wrote and published a number of newspaper articles dedicated to his memory, and, most importantly, she compiled, edited, and published his voluminous autobiographical works.[20] Nahida Lazarus's considerable

---

16. Her first theater play, a one-act comedy titled *Rechnung ohne Wirth,* was produced by the Vienna Burgtheater in 1872. In the following years her dramas were performed by several Berlin theaters: *Constanze* premiered at Residenz-Theater on April 26, 1879; *Schicksalswege* (1879) premiered at the Belle-Alliance Theater on May 9, 1879 and at the Ostendtheater. Her other dramas include *Die Grafen Eckhardstein* (1880), *Domeniko* (1884), *Nationale Gegensätze* (1884), and *Liebeszauber* (1887). Her novel *Wo die Orangen blühen* (1872), her story collection *Sizilianische Novellen* (Berlin: Richard Eckstein, 1886), and her two-volume novel *Geheime Gewalten* (Dresden: Pierson, 1890), genre pieces set in the Catholic world of the Italian south, earned Remy praise for her lively renditions of a world unfamiliar to her German readership. The publication of *Geheime Gewalten* marks the end of the first stage of her professional life.

17. Nahida Remy, *Das jüdische Weib* (Leipzig: Malende, 1891), trans. Louise Mannheimer as *The Jewish Woman* (Cincinnati: Brehbiel, 1895).

18. Nahida Remy, *Das Gebet in Bibel und Talmud* (Berlin: Apolant, 1892); *Culturstudien über das Judenthum* (Berlin: Carl Duncker, 1893).

19. Nahida Remy, "Auch eine Geistergeschichte!" *AZJ,* June 30, 1893, 311–12; "Eine Spazierfahrt," *AZJ,* November 2, 1894, 527–28, November 16, 1894, 550–52; "Frühlingsfabel," *AZJ,* March 24, 1899, 144. During this period of her life Nahida Lazarus lectured on Jewish topics in different European countries, including the Netherlands and Austria.

20. *Aus meiner Jugend* (1913) is the chronologically earliest of these accounts, relating his memories of childhood and adolescence in the Prussian village of Filehne, and his years as a student in Braunschweig and Berlin. *Ein deutscher Professor in der Schweiz* (Berlin: Dümmler, 1910) chronicles his years in Bern. *Moritz Lazarus' Lebenserinnerungen* (1906) is a collection of letters and documents. It was the first volume to be published, covering the

reputation as a dramatist and novelist has not persisted into this century. Her position as female convert, by contrast, has ensured her some modest fame. Studies on Judaism such as Jacob Raisin's voluminous *Gentile Reactions to Jewish Ideals* honor her as a convert and author of books on the Jewish woman.[21] A brief obituary in *Blätter des jüdischen Frauenbundes* (Pages of the Jewish Women's Organization) encapsulates the reception of the person and the work of Nahida Lazarus: "The deceased was an offspring of a Christian family of Aryan descent. In her later years a profound sense of conviction moved her to convert to Judaism. She made a name for herself as the author of several valuable works, in particular the book on *The Jewish Woman.*"[22] "Conversion to Judaism" and her publications on the "Jewish woman" are Lazarus's personal and intellectual legacy.[23] Life and writing, however, do not form a seamless continuum. Lazarus's struggle with the lure of tradition and the promises of modernity becomes visible in the fissures between the two.

Ich suchte Dich! spans the early 1850s to 1895, from the autobiographer's childhood to her conversion to Judaism in 1895 and her subsequent marriage to Moritz Lazarus. Like all autobiographers, Nahida Lazarus presents a selective account of her life. In *Ich suchte Dich!* she narrates the story of her religious coming-to-consciousness and glosses over her acting career or her considerable accomplishments as a fiction writer. Indeed, most of the autobiography speaks of childhood and adolescence. Only the last two chapters portray the autobiographer as an adult, relating the story of her first marriage and, finally, her resolve to convert. Lazarus's omission of her artistic accomplishments can be interpreted as her desire to portray herself as a woman who remained within the social boundaries of acceptable female conduct. More accurately, perhaps, her narrative choices suggest that she conceived of her conversion at the age of forty-five as the interpretative key to her life.[24] In *Ich suchte Dich!* Lazarus traces the

---

height of his career in the 1870s and 1880s. In addition, Nahida Lazarus published articles on her husband; for instance, "Wie Steinthal und Lazarus Brüder wurden," *Jahrbuch für jüdische Geschichte und Literatur* (1900): 149–66.

21. Jacob S. Raisin, *Gentile Reactions to Jewish Ideals: With Special Reference to Proselytes,* ed. Herman Hailperin (New York: Philosophical Library, 1953).

22. *Blätter des jüdischen Frauenbundes,* February 2, 1928, 6.

23. See Barbara Hahn's entry on Lazarus in Jutta Dick and Marina Sassenberg, eds., *Jüdische Frauen im 19. und 20. Jahrhundert: Lexikon zu Leben und Werk* (Reinbek bei Hamburg: Rowohlt, 1993), 238–39.

24. Kratz-Ritter's argument that she would not have converted had she not met Moritz Larazus ("Konversion," 16) does not give sufficient consideration to Lazarus's spiritual struggles and her resolve to remain without religious affiliation until well into her forties, both of which suggest strong motivations of her own that precede her relationship with Moritz Lazarus.

spiritual and psychological foundation of her conversion to her childhood and adolescence. The act of conversion retrospectively allowed her to endow with meaning the suffering of the first two decades of her life.

Since Augustine's fourth-century *Confessions,* religious conversion has figured prominently among the classic themes of autobiography. The conversion experience represents the central turning point in the autobiographer's story, marking the renunciation of a life of sin and the beginning of a life of redemption. The language of these narratives is often formulaic because their purpose is not so much to reveal the autobiographer's individuality as to invite the reader to emulate the converted subject's path to salvation. Unlike the majority of Christian conversion narratives, Nahida Lazarus did not intend *Ich suchte Dich!* to be a guidebook for religious conversion, nor is her conversion experience based on a radical change of mind and heart.[25] She describes her life before her conversion as spiritual isolation rather than sin and the act of conversion as the outward manifestation of a long-hidden identity. Her resolve to become a Jew results from her rejection of Christian religious dogma and what she understood to be the lowly position of women, in particular of mothers, in the New Testament. Arguing passionately against the Christian religion, Lazarus works out her role as a woman, as an artist, and as a daughter in late-nineteenth-century Germany.

Lazarus's spiritual journey shows affinities with what Virginia Lieson Brereton in her study of women's conversion narratives has termed "twentieth-century out-of-church narratives."[26] Brereton reads lesbian coming-out stories as contemporary versions of the conversion autobiography, comparing the writer's act of proclaiming her sexual preference to the act of conversion. Coming-out stories describe the dilemmas posed by an identity that cannot be put into words in the narrator's preconversion environment. Often, the autobiographer herself has no language for the incompatibility between her inner self and the role she projects to the outside world. The autobiographical pronouncement of this identity places the subject in contrast to the heterosexual, or, in Lazarus's case, Christian majority. The declaration is experienced as a liberating, if risky, event because a long-suppressed truth is revealed and a new community found.

Thus, Lazarus's experience of isolation and the pressures to conform to a Christian patriarchal environment parallels that of twentieth-century

---

25. See Virginia Lieson Brereton, *From Sin to Salvation: Stories of Women's Conversions, 1800 to the Present* (Bloomington: Indiana University Press, 1991). In her excellent study on American Protestant conversion narratives Brereton shows that the vast majority of conversion narratives do not involve a change of religion but rather a fundamental shift from a nonreligious life to a life of religious observance within Protestantism.

26. Brereton, *From Sin to Salvation,* 102.

lesbian autobiographers. She, too, bases her self-understanding on the existence of an essence that cannot yet be put into words. The pronouncement of her Jewish identity gives a name to her difference. Her Jewishness, moreover, serves to explain her deviations from the conventional female gender role. In *Ich suchte Dich!* Lazarus traces the path she had to take for this identity to become speakable.

In the 220-page narrative, the autobiographical subject initially appears under the author's first name, Nahida, or "the young German"; as the narrator matures, she refers to herself as "the young woman" or "the young scholar."[27] Lazarus offers herself in different identities, to herself and the reader. The first-person pronoun appears in the title, in direct speech, and after the act of conversion toward the very end of the narrative. Only as Jew was the autobiographer Nahida Ruth Lazarus able to say "I." The story breaks off at that point. Her newly found identity required no narrative.

The use of the third person places narrative distance between the autobiographer and her younger alter ego as she develops from child to convert. This structure permitted Lazarus to create her younger self as a "fictional" character and to take some of the liberties available to an omniscient narrator. She was thus less vulnerable to questions of credibility as she reconstructed childhood events from an adult perspective. The third-person perspective grants the adult autobiographer and the subject of her narrative a certain independence of one another; Lazarus included only those events she considered relevant to the story of her conversion.

The opening scene of *Ich suchte Dich!* introduces the young autobiographer and her mother as foreigners in the Mediterranean environment of Pisa. "A tall German woman, still young, with her child by her hand, was walking along the Lungarno in the quiet university town of Pisa." The mother's height and the daughter's blond hair identify them as German and, the narrator fantasizes, captivated the admiring attention of passersby. "The seven-year-old girl attracted general attention with the splendor of her light blond locks billowing around her little head. Almost without exception the passers-by turned their heads, and several stopped to gaze after the strikingly beautiful child; yet neither mother nor daughter paid any attention" (1). Germanness is a category of visible difference that elicits the admiration of the non-German spectators.

The bond between the self-absorbed mother-daughter pair immediately reveals itself to be precarious. Entitled "Separation," the introduc-

---

27. Lazarus gave public lectures on her life story. In these speeches she used the same formulations as in her autobiography but referred to herself in the first-person singular. See "Zweiter Lazarusabend. Vortrag der Frau Nahida Ruth Lazarus," *Oesterreichische Wochenschrift* 17 (1897): 361–63.

tory chapter signals an end rather than a beginning, recording the first in a series of ruptures in a relationship that should be inseparable. A chronic respiratory disease rendered Nahida Sturmhoefel, the autobiographer's mother, incapable of caring for her child and forced her to place her young daughter with an English countess in Pisa. Neither her mother's poor health nor financial pressures, however, fully explain the separation of mother and child. Seven-year-old Nahida's naive request that her mother preserve the mother-child union by marrying the French writer Eugène Sue suggests that the absence of a male provider was responsible for the disintegration of the nuclear family. Max Schasler, Nahida's father, remains unnamed and virtually unmentioned in the autobiography. The autobiography thus begins with an experience of double abandonment. The absence of both parents and the loneliness of her childhood are fundamental to Lazarus's autobiographical search for a society in which women can be mothers because men fulfill their obligations as fathers.

Jewish culture, in particular Jewish women, represent an alternative world of intact family relationships. The first Jewish character to appear in *Ich suchte Dich!* is a lower-class butcher woman from Lazarus's West Prussian hometown of Flatow. Her introduction into the narrative is abrupt and out of chronological sequence. While waiting for her mother's return from her negotiations with the countess in whose house she is to spend the next years of her life, Nahida recalls memories that date back to her early years in West Prussia. Lazarus interweaves anguished and comforting childhood experiences and thus situates the seven-year-old subject of narration between the warmth of Jewish culture and the coldness of the Christian household she is about to enter. Distressed by the impending separation from her mother, the child remembers a Jewish butcher woman who was routinely mocked because her name, Veilchen (Violet), was at odds with the old woman's appearance. "Indeed, she did not look like a violet," Nahida confirms, "but there was something so good and so patient about her."[28] The butcher woman's wrinkled face did not confirm the expectation of blossoming youth; her descriptive name identified her as a Jew and stigmatized her as an outsider.[29] The unspecified feeling that "this

---

28. Lazarus offers no explanation of why her family purchased meat from a Jewish butcher.

29. On Jewish names see Dietz Bering, *The Stigma of Names: Antisemitism in German Daily Life, 1812–1933*, trans. Neville Plaice (Ann Arbor: University of Michigan Press, 1992). The Veilchen episode brings to mind the young Bettina Brentano's encounter with a Jewish woman named Veilchen. In "Clemens Brentanos Frühlingskranz" she recalls in a letter to her brother Clemens how she helped her needlework teacher, a young Jewish woman named Veilchen, sweep the street in front of her house. Her aunt responded to this incident by pronouncing her niece Bettina "lost for a better life" (16). Bettina emphasizes her admiration for Veilchen's motherly and housewifely qualities, adding that from then on she had lost

called for atonement" motivated the child to offer the old woman her handshake, and Veilchen's response rewards the child's good intentions: "Her withered, thin face always turned red with joy when the child offered her its small hand" (11). The encounter with a religious outsider and the autobiographical subject's experiences of isolation occupy a central position in Lazarus's narrative. Young Nahida's gesture toward Veilchen distinguishes her from the rest of her family and establishes a foundational link between the child and the Jewish woman. The alliance between the German as foreigner and the Jewish butcher woman, both of whom the narrative introduces as vulnerable outsiders, forms the emotional basis for Lazarus's version of a specifically female German-Jewish symbiosis.[30]

Nahida spends the next years of her life in luxurious isolation within the massive walls of the countess's house, where she receives the nineteenth-century education of upper-class girls: foreign-language instruction and piano lessons, mathematics and religious training. Nahida, much to the dismay of her benefactress, cannot overcome her longing for her mother. With her pleasing physical appearance and her artistic talents, "the little German with her blond locks, always dressed in white," attracts the attention of the distinguished guests in the countess's house (24). Their superficiality and insincerity, however, earn them nothing but the child's disdain. An exception is the French painter Rosa Bonheur, whose frank speech and "somewhat fantastic" dress intrigue young Nahida.[31] Under Bonheur's influence, she resolves to become a painter. The inclusion of her encounter with the successful and nonconforming artist Bonheur suggests that she was receptive to female role models that differed from her talented but sickly mother. Lazarus indeed joined the newly founded academy for women painters in Berlin in the late 1860s and included a substantial discussion of this phase of her life in her autobiography.

---

all respect for her aunt's rules of proper social conduct. Bettina von Arnim, *Ein Lesebuch* (Stuttgart: Reclam, 1987), 15ff. There is no evidence that Lazarus was familiar with this incidence in Bettina von Arnim's life.

30. In *The Jewish Woman* Lazarus attributes key importance to the butcher woman. "I shall never forget the small, slim wife of a butcher, who used to come with her basket heavily laden to my aunt in Flatow. The cheerfulness with which she bore our sometimes rather rough jokes won my childish affections, and had, perhaps, awakened my sympathies for Jewish ways and manners" (247).

31. Rosa Bonheur (1822–1899) frequently wore men's clothes. She was one of the few nineteenth-century women to receive explicit permission to do so to enable her to execute her prize-winning animal studies. Bonheur had been educated by her liberal-minded father, the painter Raymond Bonheur (1796–1848). She was in her midthirties and an artist with an international reputation when the approximately eight-year-old Nahida met her. On Bonheur see Renate Berger, *Malerinnen auf dem Weg ins 20. Jahrhundert* (Cologne: DuMont, 1982); Berger and other feminist art historians agree that Bonheur was a lesbian (36).

The relationships between Germans and non-Germans, Christians and Jews, aristocrats and servants structure the distribution of insider and outsider positions in the early sections of *Ich suchte Dich!* In a scene that parallels the introduction of Veilchen as an outsider, young Nahida is reprimanded for letting a Jewish servant comb and kiss her blond hair, a violation of class divisions and religious boundaries. The bond of affection between the German girl and lower-class Jewish women in the countess's house signifies transgression and suggests that the foreign child from Germany and the Jewish servants formed a community of outsiders. "From that day on, a peculiar, quiet yet sympathetic relationship developed between the foreign child and the Jewish maid" (30). Contact with Jewish women offers Nahida a female role model her own mother could not provide. The Jewish servant woman Amalia supports her ill mother and her seven siblings with her labor in the countess's house, presumably in the absence of a male provider. Unlike Nahida's mother, the Jewish women in *Ich suchte Dich!* are capable of preserving the familial bond the young narrator so misses.

Religious reading confirms to the child that Christian and Jewish society differ in their treatment of mothers. Nahida discovers an old Bible on the countess's bookshelves, carefully wiping and caressing its torn cover. "In her heart the Holy Scripture took on a very personal quality. She saw in it a second mother" (50). The Jewish maid and the old Bible become surrogate mothers. Lazarus dedicates a separate chapter to the discovery of the Bible and her passionate reading of the Scripture. The memory of reading habits counts among the axiomatic narrative elements of autobiography, inviting the reader into the writer's inner world and the formation of her or his identity. Moreover, the intertextuality of a history of reading situates the autobiographer within an intellectual tradition and instructs the reader in how to interpret the narrative. Young Nahida immerses herself in the Old Testament because only there did she find the "comforting and the motherly element" for which she had "searched so eagerly" (52).[32] The world of biblical Judaism becomes the point of reference for Lazarus's assumptions about Jewish mother-child relationships. Referring to the stories of Hagar, Sarah, and Rebecca, she recalls that

> all of these and innumerable other moments in the Old Testament in which a trace of most tender affection between mother and child can be felt, these simply human, familiar qualities, touched a sympathetic chord in the heart of the lonely child with magical power and a long-lasting effect.

---

32. In the handwritten manuscript the word "mütterlich" is underlined.

The discouraging mysticism of the New Testament, on the other hand, she could not understand, and when she searched for the mother, she could not find her. Even harder to comprehend for the childlike soul than all mysticism: she found the figure of the mother, as such, disparaged and rejected. (52–53)

Lazarus identifies with the mother's abasement rather than with the abandoned child. The mother who has lost her revered position marks the dividing line between Christianity and Judaism. Jesus' repudiation of his mother when she informs him that the wine has run out at the wedding in Cana (John 2:4) serves as the central argument in Lazarus's autobiographical rejection of Christian religion and society:

On another occasion he addressed his parent like a stranger: "Woman, what does your concern have to do with me?"

That millions of people prayed to him who spoke thus as their "savior" and their God—Nahida knew this to be a historical fact, but she did not comprehend it and never would comprehend it. (53)

Lazarus's interpretation of Christian society as hostile to mothers on the one hand, and her experience of Jewish women as capable mother figures on the other, emerge as the primary impetus to her conversion to Judaism several decades later.

When Lazarus penned her autobiography in the second half of the 1890s she had already written extensively and with significant popular success on the history of Jewish women and mothers. Several years before her conversion and the appearance of her autobiography she published *The Jewish Woman,* her cultural history of the Jewish woman from biblical times to the present. With this book she contributed to the debate on the "Jewish woman" in which the Reform Jewish community had been engaged since the last decades of the nineteenth century.[33] These debates, which revolved around the figure of an "ideal Jewish woman," were an attempt to integrate Jews into modern national society while simultaneously preserving Jewish difference. In her primary function as mother and educator of her small children, the Jewish woman guaranteed the future of Judaism as a distinct religious culture. At the same time, her revered position within Jewish society and history confirmed the modernity of Judaism and its

---

33. The role of women in Reform Judaism was of interest not just to German-speaking communities. See Karla Goldman, "The Ambivalence of Reform Judaism: Kaufmann Kohler and the Ideal Jewish Woman," *American Jewish History* 79, no. 4 (summer 1990): 477–99, for the role of women in Reform Judaism in the United States.

rightful place in German society, demonstrating to the Christian-German majority that Jewish women were not oppressed by a patriarchal religion but, on the contrary, enjoyed high status within their families and in their religious culture. The dual function of the Jewish woman as a manifestation of difference and a connecting link to majority culture resurfaces in a variety of contexts. It placed Jewish women in a precarious position between tradition and modernity.

Meyer Kayserling's *Die jüdischen Frauen in der Geschichte, Literatur und Kunst* (Jewish women in history, literature, and art) is the best-known example of numerous books and pamphlets with similar titles.[34] Written in the manner of popular cultural histories *(Kulturgeschichten)*, Kayserling's book was pointedly addressed to Jewish women. It aimed, the historian and rabbi explained in his introduction, to bridge the gap between a secular "societal education" and the love for traditional Judaism.[35] Kayserling reiterated an often formulated assumption when he pronounced that the future of any religion depended on women much more than on men. He spoke not only for Jews with his insistence that "domesticity was and continues to be the most beautiful word of praise that can be bestowed on woman."[36] Emphasizing the high social value that Jewish tradition attaches to women's domestic work and pointing out the sympathetic understanding Judaism reserves even for women's negative qualities, like a penchant for gossiping, Kayserling suggests a privileged relationship between Jewishness and femininity. Literary historian and journalist Gustav Karpeles, in his 1871 lecture "Women in Jewish Literature," maintained that while "not a single Jewish woman" demanded the "aberrations" of "total female emancipation," Jewish women were among the leading activists claiming women's legitimate right to employment in all fields.[37] "Excellence of the Jewish spirit," Karpeles argued, enabled Jewish women to distinguish between rightful emancipation and the aberrant desire to eradicate the difference between women and men. Adolf Kurrein, rabbi and preacher in the Galician city of Bielitz, pushed the connection between Jewishness and female emancipation even further by reminding Jewish women of their privileged position. "The Jewish woman," he stated in a 1885 address to the local Israelite Women's Organization, has "inaugurated the modern position of women, emancipated all of womankind."

---

34. Meyer Kayserling, *Die jüdischen Frauen in der Geschichte, Literatur und Kunst* (Leipzig: Brockhaus, 1879). The bibliography of Lazarus's *The Jewish Woman* lists Kayserling's work.

35. Kayserling, *Jüdische Frauen*, vi.

36. Ibid., 6.

37. Gustav Karpeles, *Die Frauen der jüdischen Literatur: Ein Vortrag, gehalten zum Besten des Sefath-Emeth-Vereins in Berlin* (Berlin: Poppelauer, 1871), 23.

But, he hastened to add, "one must not understand emancipation to mean all those aberrations of female fantasy."[38] Bible and Talmud, Kurrein continued, carry within them the foundation for the emancipation not only for Jewish but also for Christian women. Judaism, these writers agree, is a tradition very much compatible with the demands of the women's movement in the second half of the nineteenth century. With what Karla Goldman has termed the "ambivalence of Reform Judaism" they also insisted that Judaism should serve as a bulwark against the "aberrations" of female emancipation that not only Jews feared.[39]

Both Jewish and women's emancipation challenged its proponents to weigh how equality could be achieved without loss of difference. Supporters of both projects needed to find an equilibrium between desirable modernization and the necessary abandonment of archaic restrictions on the one hand, and the preservation of positive traditions, on the other. Because Jewish and non-Jewish thinkers alike shared the concern about women's difference from men, the gender question united Jewish and majority culture and could be evoked to uphold Jewish difference at the same time.

The ideal Jewish woman combined nineteenth-century notions of femininity with definitions of Jewishness. Two related arguments resurface in these debates. First, the role of women in Jewish history as defenders of the faith; and second, the revered position of women in Judaism compared to other religions and societies. The history of Jewish persecution and resistance was evoked to construct a troubled yet genuinely Jewish past in which women heroically defended their religion. The Jewish women of the Bible and the Middle Ages were willing to die for their faith, the literature on the Jewish woman contended, as it presented historical heroines as role models to its nineteenth-century female readership. Their contemporary counterparts, these narratives implied, who were unwilling to defend their religion under less than life-threatening circumstances, were in danger of losing not only their Jewish but also their female identity. Jewish tradition honored its women more than other cultures, these texts claimed. It was now up to the women to preserve Judaism and their special position within

38. Adolf Kurrein, *Die Frau im jüdischen Volke: Vortrag gehalten zu Gunsten des israelitischen Frauenvereins in Bielitz* (Frankfurt am Main: Kauffmann, 1885), 3.

39. Goldman, "Ambivalence of Reform Judaism." Other texts on the Jewish woman are Hosea Jacobi, *Über die Stellung des Weibes im Judenthum: Mit besonderer Berücksichtigung der Eheschliessung, wie sie uns in den Schriften des Alten-Testaments vorliegt* (Berlin: Julius Sittenfeld, 1865); David Kaufmann, *Wie heben wir den religiösen Sinn unserer Mädchen und Frauen?* (Trier: Sigmund Mayer, 1893); Noëmi Banéth, *Soziale Hilfsarbeit der modernen Jüdin* (Berlin: Louis Lamm, 1907); and Fritz Wilke, *Das Frauenideal und die Schätzung des Weibes im Alten Testament: Eine Studie zur israelitischen Kultur- und Religionsgeschichte* (Leipzig: Dieterich'sche Verlagsbuchhandung, 1907).

it against the excesses of a modernity that threatened Jewishness and femininity alike.

Motherhood emerges as the single most important criterion of idealized Jewish female identity. In a slim volume from 1907 entitled *Aus dem Tagebuch einer jüdischen Studentin* (From the diary of a female Jewish student), the nameless narrator of this fictional diary, who introduces herself as an "aging girl" and university student, implores her "dear sisters" not to forgo the warmth and satisfaction of Jewish motherhood in favor of cold intellectualism.[40] The narrator laments that she "not only became no Moses but not even a Jochebed."[41] Women, in others words, cannot be male Jewish leaders, but they can be mothers of Jewish leaders and should not forgo this chance. This fictional diary, to be sure, says much about male anxieties and very little about the realities of Jewish women students. Yet it shows that in the minds of these commentators modernity, Jewish identity, and female gender identity were held in an intricate balance that was easily upset by an excess of emancipation. Jewish women, these texts impress upon their readers, cannot only secure their personal happiness by remaining Jewish but also help mitigate the ills of modern society. Viennese rabbi Max Grunwald ended a lecture delivered before the Austrian-Israelite Union in 1903 with the words,

> When an age seems decadent and small, its women must have sunken; the continuance and the future of a people relies on the nobility of its mothers. . . . If we succeed in renewing the noble tradition of the Jewish woman and the Jewish mother among ourselves, then our future generation will be preserved for Judaism, and Judaism will be preserved for our descendants.[42]

Judaism needs mothers to guarantee its future survival. At the same time, women need Judaism to remain women and mothers. Nahida Lazarus found in Judaism a religious culture that offered her an alternative to the sufferings of her motherless childhood. In writing the history of the Jewish woman, she assured herself of a world in which women were allowed to be mothers.

In keeping with nineteenth-century conventions of cultural history, Nahida Lazarus began *The Jewish Woman* by establishing a hierarchical order of world civilizations determined by the status of women from the

---

40. Raphael Breuer, *Aus dem Tagebuch einer jüdischen Studentin* (Frankfurt am Main: Knauer, 1907). German women won access to universities in 1908.

41. Breuer, *Tagebuch,* 13–14.

42. Max Grunwald, *Die moderne Frauenbewegung und das Judentum: Vortrag gehalten im Verein Oesterreichisch-Israelitische Union* (Vienna: Beck, 1903), 24–25.

"barbarous, semi- and three-fourth barbarous races" such as the "Australians" and the "Negroes," to the Greeks, Romans, Christians, and finally the Jews.[43] The assumption that "civilization" developed by a linear process can be found in nineteenth-century histories as diverse as August Bebel's 1879 *Woman under Socialism* and Richard von Krafft-Ebing's 1886 *Psychopathia Sexualis.* Krafft-Ebing, for instance, states in his introduction that it is "of great psychological interest to follow up the gradual development of civilization and the influence exerted by sexual life upon habits and morality."[44] August Bebel, whose voluminous study features three sections dedicated to the status of women in the past, present, and future, drew extensively on examples from primitive as well as historic societies to support his argument that only socialism guaranteed women equal rights.[45] Nahida Lazarus, writing in this same conceptual context, privileged the position of women in Jewish society over that of their Christian sisters. "In order to comprehend woman, one must study the history of slavery; to correctly judge the Jewish woman, one must compare her with the women of other nations," she argued in the opening chapter of her study.[46] Her discussions of the women of the Bible, Jewish queens, mothers, and artists, verify the outstanding status and accomplishments of Jewish woman through the ages; throughout history, Jewish women, Lazarus maintained, have been treated with honor and dignity, the conduct of Jewish mothers like Rebecca, biblical queens like Esther, and contemporary writers such as Emma Lazarus justifying their revered position.

Like her male counterparts who commented on "the Jewish woman," Nahida Lazarus addressed what she perceived to be a weakening link between Jewish women and their religion. While male writers like Karpeles and Kurrein warned Jewish women against excessive emancipation, Lazarus focused on Jewish conversion to Christianity. Titled "Apostates" ("Abtrünnige"), her chapter on female converts such as Henriette Herz, Dorothea Schlegel, and Rahel Varnhagen doubles as a discourse about sexuality. Drawing on nineteenth-century notions of decadence and degeneration, Lazarus characterized Dorothea Schlegel, daughter of the

---

    43. Lazarus, *The Jewish Woman,* 20.

    44. Richard von Krafft-Ebing, *Psychopathia Sexualis: A Medico-Forensic Study* (New York: Physicians and Surgeons Book Company, 1924), 2.

    45. August Bebel, *Woman under Socialism,* trans. by Daniel de Leon (New York: Schocken, 1971). Nineteenth-century cultural histories include Johannes Scherr, *Deutsche Kultur- und Sittengeschichte,* 5th ed. (Leipzig: Wiegand, 1873); and Gustav Friedrich Klemm, *Allgemeine Culturgeschichte der Menschheit,* 10 vols. (Leipzig: Teubner, 1843–52). Henrik Ibsen alludes to and satirizes the popularity of histories of civilization in *Hedda Gabler* (1890). Hedda Gabler's former lover, author of an acclaimed *history* of civilization, hopes to publish a sequel about the future of civilizations.

    46. Lazarus, *The Jewish Woman,* 15.

philosopher Moses Mendelssohn and wife of the Romantic writer and critic Friedrich Schlegel, as a "product of degeneracy," who became the "prototype" of Schlegel's scandalous *Lucinde* because she chose Schlegel's offer of "free love" over her first marriage with the Jewish banker Simon Veit.[47] Convert Henriette Herz, a friend of the theologian Schleiermacher, whose fondness for beautiful Jewish women earned him a reprimand of the Berlin clergy, could not love her husband because she lacked the love for her religion. "Henrietta's beauty, Rachel's genius, and Dorothea's liberality only gained for them a deplorable renown, where they could have attained glorious fame and the blessings of posterity if they had promoted liberal ideas and faithfulness to conviction."[48] The trope of the sexual licentiousness of the German Romantics and the gifted Jewish women associated with them, who chose sexual gratification over Judaism, signifies the impending chaos of modernity. According to *The Jewish Woman,* which is as much about the loss of female Jewish identity as the praise of outstanding Jewish women, the perceived breakdown of the family as the social institution that controls sexuality has its most troubling manifestation in the loss of Jewish family life. The Jewish woman Lazarus created in her study is either far better or far worse than her Christian counterpart. Her rejection of tradition thus connotes more than a waning of religious observance; it symbolizes the loss of sexual order and the demise of family relationships. In her autobiography, Nahida Lazarus told the story of her own painful experiences as a child born out of wedlock to a mother whom circumstances prevented from fulfilling her maternal role. In *The Jewish Woman* she assured herself and her readers of the existence, albeit precarious, of a better world.

In late-nineteenth-century Germany, "the Jewish family" enjoyed a somewhat legendary status as an intact institution in an age when modernization began to threaten the family as the "basic unit of the social order."[49] While *The Jewish Woman* refers Jewish women to the past as source of identity, Lazarus also drew on contemporary perceptions when she privileged the Jewish family as the locus of undamaged familial relationships. In this context, the image of the Jewish mother is as important as the notion of the Jewish husband and his presumably liberal (and nonviolent) relationship to his wife and children. In her *The Making of the Jewish Middle Class,* historian Marion Kaplan questions this blanket assumption about the Jewish family and calls for a careful comparative analysis of "the importance of the family to the Jews relative to their Ger-

---

47. Ibid., 183.
48. Ibid., 187.
49. Isabel Hull, "The Bourgeoisie and Its Discontent," *Journal of Contemporary History* 17, no. 2 (1982): 256.

man bourgeois counterparts, or the degree to which the centrality was a result of internal and external circumstances. . . . What is clear is that the *ideology* of the family was very important to all Jews, simultaneously proclaiming their Jewishness and their Germanness."[50] Lazarus's study on the Jewish woman in all likelihood was inspired by this self-image of middle-class Jews rather than the realities of Jewish family life, to which she had little exposure. Not surprisingly, her book on *The Jewish Woman* was welcomed by Jewish men who shared her concerns about the loss of Jewish family life.[51] Middle-class Jewish women might well have rejected it as not relevant to their experiences. Yet the desire to define Jewishness and Germanness as distinct yet mutually compatible categories—and the central importance of the family in this project—Lazarus shared with the majority of middle-class German Jews.

The central chapters of *Ich suchte Dich!* tell of Nahida's experience of Christian religious education. Lazarus does not present the reader with a sinful self before conversion; neither does she introduce her redeemed self as a model for the reader to emulate. Instead, society and its representatives are the sinners that victimize the future convert. Her critique of women's roles in the New Testament and her insistence on the base position of women in Christian society prepare the reader for the autobiographer's conversion to Judaism. The connection between religion and sexuality emerges as a decisive factor in her experience of victimization.

Nahida's stay in Pisa ends with her flight from the countess's house. Mother and daughter spend the early 1860s in Palermo and Naples. The revolutionary political events, Garibaldi's liberation of Palermo and Naples in the spring of 1860, his "Procession of Thousands" and the subsequent defeat of the Bourbons, are not mentioned. Nahida continues her education in a Catholic girls' school, where she receives instruction in "religion, needlework, and French" (77). She objects to her peers' bad pronunciation of French as much as to the Catholic devotional books with their stories of miracles and saints. More gravely, no minister "could move the student, who showed such mental and physical maturity, to accept the idea of a Trinity and other dogmas" (80). Isolated from her peers in church, she finds herself "alone! She knew well that she was alone among

---

50. Kaplan, *Jewish Middle Class*, 83.

51. Heymann Steinthal, "Giebt es noch Jüdinnen?" *AZJ*, October 16, 1891, 494–95; Eduard Bieberfeld, "Das jüdische Weib," *Israelitische Monatsschrift* 10 (1981): 37–38; see also "Das jüdische Weib," *Westermanns illustrierte deutsche Monats-Hefte* 37, no. 74 (1893): 717. In 1895, the *Allgemeine Zeitung des Judenthums* published a list of books recommended for purchase by Jewish community libraries. Nahida Remy's *Das jüdische Weib* was listed among the endorsed readings ("Eine jüdische Vereins-Bibliothek," February 15, 1895, 88).

the crowd!" (87). In a chapter titled "Struggles of the Soul" ("See-lenkämpfe"), Lazarus recalls a series of religious disputations with educators and peers, in which her younger self rejects fundamental principles of Christianity such as the Holy Trinity from the Jewish perspective of strict monotheism. *Ich suchte Dich!* presents the pubescent girl's religious opinions as the result of her own thoughts, suggesting that she was well versed in Jewish religious philosophy long before she had a name for it.

Young Nahida's assumption that Christian society does violence to women finds its proof in an incidence of sexual violence. At the age of fourteen, the physically mature girl is confronted by the sexual demands of an effeminate Protestant minister and teacher. "The [minister's] tall, exceptionally slim figure looked much too elegant, his hands were manicured with almost feminine vanity, his curly hair fell over his shoulders in a perfectly artistic manner" (95). After his class, the preacher lures Nahida back into the empty classroom, where he attempts to kiss her. The reader witnesses this incident through the dialogue that ensues between mother and daughter after the assault. The episode, which is narrated from the perspective of Nahida's mother, signals a loss of innocence. "Full of tenderness and smiling at the memory of delightful scenes of childhood, the mother looked to the girl at her side. But how it frightened her to see the lovely face streaming with tears. 'Child! What happened to you?'" (97). The mother's prodding questions and the daughter's halting narrative fill the next several pages. Slowly she reveals what transpired in the empty classroom. Her mother demands:

> "And you—?"
> "I looked at him disdainfully and said: shame on you."
> "And he?"
> She squeezed her quivering lips shut.
> "He violently wanted to kiss me, but I kept evading him." (102)

The dialogue form allows Lazarus to relate this incident in the first person, its halting pace heightening the dramatic tension with which the narrative fuses her experience of religious alienation and sexual victimization. The Christian male's androgynous appearance, his seductive rhetoric, and his brutish sexuality form a continuum of mental and physical corruptness. Nahida's mature and unambiguous femininity, by contrast, and her unalterable religious beliefs, authenticate her status of a superior victim. The "wound, which her virginal soul had received in this encounter with a conscienceless man," strengthens her rejection of Christianity on religious as well as sexual grounds (113). After the incidence she finds comfort in the Jewish world of the Bible. The sexual violence committed by the Christian male leaves a peculiar physical mark on the autobiographer's body. Her eyes change color over night, turning the young girl into a stranger to herself (114).

Religion and sexuality cannot be separated from one another. Lazarus's own as well as her mother's experience leads her to conclude that women are in danger of falling victim to either male sexual aggression or abandonment. Only Judaism protects women against these transgressions.[52] Moreover, the Christian religion fosters a sexually charged atmosphere that Lazarus rejects as frivolous. The central position of this incident within Lazarus's narrative and the conclusions she draws from it suggest that her journey toward conversion is also her attempt to come to terms with sexuality. While there is no reference to the autobiographer's out-of-wedlock birth, the negative accounts of male and female sexuality might also be a condemnation of her mother's sexual conduct.

Despite its numerical insignificance, conversion to Judaism was a topic of public interest in the pages of Jewish newspapers and family magazines in the second half of the nineteenth century. Between the years 1843 and 1875, the *Allgemeine Zeitung des Judenthums,* for instance, covered more than twenty cases of individual or group conversions to Judaism. Without exception the convert's motivation was of central interest to those who reported on these conversions. Strict observance of Jewish law, which in some cases was said to precede the actual act of conversion by decades, most persuasively indicated the convert's sincerity in becoming a Jew. The majority of these newsworthy "conversion narratives" focused on male converts, whose conduct during the "conversion operation" *(Bekehrungs-Operation)* became a standard narrative element intended to illustrate the new Jew's sincerity.[53] By comparison, reports on female conversions, which were commonly attributed to the convert's desire to marry a Jew, tended to discredit the conversions as less meritorious than male religious convictions. Later, from the mid-1880s into the first decade of the twentieth century, the stories of famous converts abounded in the weekend supplements of Jewish family journals and Jewish "house calendars" *(Haus-Kalender).* Scholarly journals also featured contributions on the topic. Countess Anna Constanze von Cosel (1680–1765), mistress and later prisoner of the Saxon elector August the Strong (1670–1733), ranks among the

---

52. In his review of *Ich suchte Dich!* the poet, art critic, and chief editor of the culture magazine *Die Gesellschaft* Ludwig Jacobowski (1868–1900) suggests that Lazarus's conclusions from a few unfortunate incidents with Christian ministers are too far-reaching, especially in the eyes of Christian readers. He ends his article with the question what would have happened had Lazarus met a Galician "Wunderrabbi" ("Nahida Ruth Lazarus," 235).

53. *AZJ,* March 27, 1866, 197.

famous converts to Judaism, as does the Polish count Joseph Steblicki.[54] Toward the end of the nineteenth century, as Jewish assimilation and German antisemitism grew in tandem, the interest in Christian conversion to Judaism marked a critical intersection between Jewish-German and Christian-German identity positions. The stories of exceptional converts no longer questioned the desirability of converts, nor did they ponder the requirements for conversion. Rather, the figure of the outstanding proselyte exemplified the attractiveness of Judaism in light of the obstacles and risks posed by the convert's particular historical context. Christian conversion to Judaism became a barometer for the legal and social position of Jews in European Christian society. Praise of eighteenth-century religious tolerance and enlightenment was also a condemnation of contemporary antisemitic prejudice.

Nahida Lazarus, a frequent contributor to *Allgemeine Zeitung des Judenthums* in the 1890s, must have been familiar with the debates on conversion to Judaism. Her *Ich suchte Dich!* is a response to the narratives about Christians who became Jews. Lewis Rambo's argument that "conversion is actively constructed by a religious group and by the wishes, expectations, and aspirations of the convert" also applies to Lazarus's late-nineteenth-century conversion autobiography.[55] In contrast to the Christian conversion narrative with its pivotal conversion experience, Lazarus tells a "Jewish" story of spiritual isolation, persecution, and resistance. She appropriated the model of conversion that the contributors to the *Allgemeine Zeitung des Judenthums* had reserved for male converts and demonstrates that it applies to her case as well. In strictly separating her resolve to marry Moritz Lazarus from her religious history, she distanced herself from the majority of female converts to Judaism and their supposedly inferior motivations and claimed the religious inspirations of male converts together with the positive reception they found in the Jewish community. Lazarus shared, however, the assumption that conversion to Judaism encompassed religious as well as gender identity. The hardships to which she found herself subjected as a religious outsider she also suffered as a woman.

In the mid-1860s, mother and daughter returned to their native West Prussian town of Flatow. A beloved aunt made a last attempt to provide Nahida, now about fifteen years old, with the appropriate religious instruction for her confirmation in the Protestant Church. This time, the adolescent girl was to receive individual instruction; as before in Italy, her

---

54. On converts to Judaism in the nineteenth century see Gerstenberger, "January 31, 1850."

55. Lewis R. Rambo, *Understanding Religious Conversion* (New Haven: Yale University Press, 1993), 7.

intellectual superiority sets "the young German" apart from her female peers, who attend classes in religious instruction only to enjoy the privilege of wearing nice clothes at the confirmation celebration and to participate in dancing parties afterward (109). The intellectually inferior and spiritually insincere female population of West Prussia that, like its Italian counterpart, conflates sexuality and religion, is no community for Nahida. In the next two chapters, titled "The Candidate for Confirmation" ("Die Konfirmandin") and "Without Confession" ("Confessionslos"), she asserts herself as an intelligent, eloquent, and educated young woman against older Christian males.

Turn-of-the-century Germany as well as traditional Judaism severely limited women's access to intellectual activities in the public sphere. Religion and religious disputation, however, are areas of expression on which women have traditionally relied to define themselves as thinking and speaking beings in both private and public contexts.[56] From the medieval mystics to the confessions of eighteenth-century Pietists, women have used their relationship to God to speak and act on their own accounts. Brereton, in her study of American women's conversion narratives, concludes that these texts are an "important part of women's literary heritage" and that they have "led in surprising ways to an expanded role for women in the world."[57] For Lazarus, religion became the intellectual battleground on which she fought the discrimination she faced, prior to conversion, as a Jew in spirit and as a woman.

The well-meaning attempts of the local minister in the village of Flatow who gives the young woman private lessons fail, for he cannot convince his student that the teachings of the New Testament supersede the beliefs of the Old Testament. Lazarus describes in great length and detail the dispute between herself and the minister over the question of the one true religion. Nahida dismisses the Christian dogma of the Holy Trinity as polytheism, rejects the command to love one's enemies as unnatural (128), and counters the idea that spiritual poverty is prerequisite to understanding Jesus Christ with the self-confident argument that God might have endowed her with intelligence instead (119). Unwilling to accept Jesus Christ as God's Son, she characterizes him as a "Jewish rabbi" (133) who depended on the kindness of others: "He himself did not possess anything. He was nourished and cared for by people willing to sacrifice themselves, and most of them were women" (131). The young woman not only challenges Christ's divinity but also his masculinity. Rejecting the "Jesuit"

---

56. See Jeanine Blackwell, "Herzensgespräche mit Gott. Bekenntnisse deutscher Pietistinnen im 17. und 18. Jahrhundert," in *Deutsche Literatur von Frauen,* ed. Gisela Brinker-Gabler, 2 vols. (Munich: Beck, 1988), 1:265–89.

57. Brereton, *From Sin to Salvation,* 120.

practice of "reservatio mentalis" (140), she finally exclaims: "'Do I not have the holy duty to be sincere and truthful?'"(138). Conversations like this between Lazarus's adolescent alter ego and pastors, preachers, and other church dignitaries make up a substantial portion of *Ich suchte Dich!* Predictably, none of the representatives of the Protestant Church can sway the young woman who time and again eloquently posits her truths against Christian beliefs. Religious conflict is carried out between decidedly uneven positions of power. Unlike most autobiographers of conversion, Lazarus did not relate episodes of internal religious struggles. Instead, she recounted her firm convictions in the dialogue form she had used so successfully in her dramas of the 1870s and 1880s. In reviving the tradition of the religious dispute she wrote a leading role for her younger self. Dramatic in both form and content, the theatrical interludes in Lazarus's third-person narrative give the autobiographer a voice. Lazarus becomes real to herself through her adolescent alter ego's controversial convictions and her ability to silence her adversaries in the first person.

Education and class privilege afforded Lazarus and her mother a degree of autonomy unavailable to the majority of women in nineteenth-century Germany. In the absence of male relatives or patriarchal husbands, both women led unconventional and independent lives. Unlike her mother, young Nahida Sturmhoefel did not associate herself with the women's movement and its demands for women's political and civil rights. Nor does she write about her extensive travels throughout Europe and her work as an actress. The autobiography simply announces matter-of-factly that Nahida, at the age of seventeen or eighteen, decided to "adopt a profession and to become independent, financially and otherwise" (150).

The majority of nineteenth-century women were unable to attain the economical and professional independence that apparently came so easily to Nahida Lazarus. The writer Fanny Lewald (1811–1889), for example, vividly described in her three-part autobiography *Meine Lebensgeschichte* the enormous difficulties she faced in achieving financial and professional autonomy against the wishes of her male relatives. Marie von Ebner-Eschenbach, the most famous woman writer in the German language of her time, recounted that she contended with her family's resistance to her career wishes in her autobiography, *Meine Kinderjahre.* Consistent with earlier sections of the narrative and in the absence of confrontations over access to education, money, and decision-making power, religion remains the arena of Lazarus's struggle. Upon her arrival in Berlin, a Jewish doctor and friend tries to persuade her to accept her confirmation into the Protestant Church. After a final attempt to be confirmed into the church fails, "She focused her thoughts and energies on acquiring a life profession suited to make her as independent as possible" (162). Socioeconomic sovereignty is an incidental result of the narrator's religious conflicts rather than a goal she sought for its own sake.

Nahida Lazarus belonged to the ranks of the "reluctant feminists," as Jean Quataert aptly described Germany's women socialists.[58] Her choices and arguments, however, in many ways echo those of the bourgeois women's movement and were possible only because of the activities of women's organizations. In 1866, about the year Nahida resolved to become independent, feminist activist and writer Luise Otto-Peters published her pamphlet *Das Recht der Frauen auf Erwerb* (Women's right to work). Focusing on the situation of middle-class women like Nahida Lazarus, Otto-Peters insisted on women's right to work for economic as well as moral reasons. Lack of education and the resulting inability to find suitable work, Otto-Peters argued, rendered women dependent on men, and, in extreme cases, forced them into prostitution.[59] Both Otto-Peters and Lazarus agreed that women's dependence on men heightened their sexual vulnerability, suggesting that women's right and ability to work would lead to a desirable desexualization of gender relationships.

Lazarus did not view her quest for religious freedom as a project of female emancipation, but without the women's movement it almost certainly would have taken a different form. Lazarus's emancipated life choices on the one hand, and the distance she kept from organized feminist efforts on the other, make sense if we keep in mind that the women's movement was blamed for many of the developments Lazarus criticized in modern society, in particular the demise of the family. She could therefore not identify with an ideology that questioned women's exclusive role as wives and mothers even as she exercised alternative options. As a woman and a Jew, Lazarus was confronted with both misogyny and antisemitism. Yet she found it easier to decry discrimination against Jews than to respond to the criticism her untraditional female conduct must have elicited.

Supporting herself with the small inheritance from her late aunt, eighteen-year-old Nahida Sturmhoefel was one of the first students to join the newly founded academy for women painters in Berlin. In the second half of the nineteenth century women painters in a number of different German cities organized separate institutions for female students. The Berlin Zeichen- und Malschule des Vereins der Künstlerinnen und Kunst-

---

58. Jean H. Quataert, *Reluctant Feminists in German Social Democracy, 1885–1917* (Princeton, N.J.: Princeton University Press, 1979).

59. Louise Otto-Peters, "Das Recht der Frauen auf Erwerb," in *Die Frauenfrage in Deutschland, 1865–1915: Texte und Dokumente,* ed. Elke Frederiksen (Stuttgart: Reclam, 1981), 303.

freundinnen (Drawing and Painting School of the Organization of Woman Artists and Female Friends of the Arts), for instance, was founded in January 1867 by a group of women who had met while sketching in the Dresden gallery.[60] In her study on European women artists, Renate Berger discusses the financial, legal, and ideological resistance that women artists encountered in the pursuit of their profession. While instruction in drawing and painting was considered appropriate for upper-class women for private purposes, professional women painters were a small minority with slim hope of decent remuneration or security. In addition to their presumed lack of talent, women were excluded from art academies because moral codes denied them one of the most important requirements of artistic training of the time, namely nude drawing.[61] Even more significantly, however, female artists posed a threat to gender difference:

> Where women become mannish, men must become effeminate. For one, because the degenerate woman, unwilling to bear children, sires a breed of men without resistance and of weak will power; and then, because the reign of woman in the arts is possible only in the midst of a generation of men who are incapable of putting a stop to it.[62]

These remarks, which are far from exceptional and can stand for analogous opinion not confined to women's entry into the arts, illustrate that women's professional advancement was not the economic and moral issue Otto-Peters had made it out to be but a fundamental challenge to gender difference. The very existence of woman artists posed a threat to masculinity in the general culture.

In light of these deterrents, young Nahida Sturmhoefel's resolve to gain financial independence as a professional painter must be considered an example of her remarkable courage and self-confidence. Her anatomical drawings elicited the admiration of her teachers, including the neoclas-

---

60. See Berger, *Malerinnen,* 91. Edith Krull, *Women in Art* (London: Studio Vista, 1989), describes women's art schools as a "stopgap" to protect women from exploitation by unqualified private teachers (14). The Berlin Malerinnenakademie opened in the presence of Adolf Lette, one of the supporters of women's vocational training and founder of a school of his own. His guidelines for the painter's academy stressed the subjects of perspective and anatomy, in both of which Lazarus says she excelled. By 1906 the *Handbuch der Frauenbewegung,* ed. Helene Lange and Gertrud Bäumer (Berlin: Moeser, 1906), could report that a few academies had opened their doors to women, who received instruction together with their male peers except in "nude drawing and modeling" (203). Women's exclusion from art academies persisted until after World War I.

61. Berger, *Malerinnen,* 103.

62. Karl Scheffler, quoted in ibid., 71. The quotation is from Scheffler's misogynist 1908 essay titled "Die Frau und die Kunst."

sicist painter Peter Cornelius (1783–1867). Every morning she visited the Berlin art museum before the doors opened to the public to make drawings of Greek sculptures; her reference to how easily she sketched bone structure and muscle placement of the human body suggests that she might well have had the opportunity to study life models (163).[63] In contrast to the male resistance to her spiritual quest, Lazarus does not mention any gender-based opposition to her artistic pursuits. However, with the exception of the painter Rosa Bonheur, who inspired her as a child, she mentions no female mentors. Lazarus apparently could not identify with the emancipatory program of the Berlin Zeichen- und Malschule and its goal, to further the artistic and financial autonomy of women. Her desire for independence remained personal.[64]

With the novelistic phrase "years passed by" (170), Lazarus glosses over the successful production of her first drama at the Burgtheater in Vienna in 1872.[65] In 1873, at the age of twenty-four, she married the journalist and art critic Max Remy (1839–1881). A chapter titled "A Strange Experience" ("Ein seltsames Erlebniß") emphasizes the religious implications that lead to Nahida's decision to marry a man whose appearance "carried the mark of a distinct, severe, and, as it turned out later, incurable ailment" (172). Lazarus integrates the story of her first marriage into her conversion narrative as a seven-year period of trial, retardation, and preparation. She reads Remy's name on his business card a few weeks after their first introduction, immediately knows by divine revelation that this man is to be her husband, and accepts God's will: "You want it, God, fine—then I also want it" (175). This passage parallels the episode of the Jewish butcher woman Veilchen in importance and in the absence of interpretative explanation, leaving to the reader the significance of the event and its connections to the rest of the story. The autobiographer's omitting to explain the importance of her first relationship with a Jewish woman or to elaborate why she thought of her first marriage as a result of divine command defers to an external power that assumes responsibility for her life course. Nahida's determination to marry an unattractive and ill man does not involve any will of her own: "And, after all—did she have a

---

63. Even in women's academies, however, male models posed with their genital area covered (Berger, *Malerinnen,* 143).

64. One can speculate that she included this relatively extensive discussion of her career as a painter as a negative tribute to her father, the art historian Max Schasler. Lazarus also mentions her mother's talents in the fine arts, which, however, never amounted to a career.

65. Lazarus noted on the title page of the handwritten manuscript of this play, the one-act drama *Rechnung ohne Wirth:* "etwa 12 Mal mit grossem Beifall gegeben." The manuscript is in the Jewish National and University Library, Jerusalem, Arc. Ms. Var. 298/138. According to *Burgtheater, 1776–1976,* the play was performed four times between January 9 and January 23, 1872.

choice, *since she knew so well that he, the suffering, uncomely man was the chosen one?"* (176). Even before Remy proposes to her, the young woman engages in fantasies of female adventure, sacrifice, and break with her previous life:

> As if she were planning a journey across the ocean, where dangers, perhaps even death, were waiting, she put all her affairs in order in her mind and said farewell to several things that had become dear to her, including farewell to her art, because she made clear to herself that a journalist, who furthermore was apparently ailing, had to find support in his wife. (175)

She also convinces herself that her mother, whose resistance she anticipates, will ultimately accept her decision.

Lazarus's narrative of a specifically female trial period—her "voyage across the ocean" taking place in the private sphere of her home—fulfills traditional gender expectations. The autobiographical rendition of this relationship draws upon the narrative model in which the individual undergoes a period of challenging trials and rites of purification to earn an outstanding reward. Nahida's "seven years of apprenticeship and suffering" (185) evoke Goethe's paradigmatic novel of education *Wilhelm Meister's Apprenticeship,* as well as the plot element common to fairy tales that requires the protagonists to render faithful and unquestioning service before their elevation by an eminent reward. Lazarus's narrative also recalls the biblical story of Jacob and his seven-year marriage to Lea, his uncle Laban's unattractive eldest daughter, as the precondition to marry Rahel, her beautiful younger sister and the woman of his choice. "Why," she asks herself, "since thousands of her gender in a similar position in life were leading a comfortable, limited existence, why had she, especially she, been chosen to go through such strange trials?" And she adds: "Perhaps to accomplish something different, better, higher? *Perhaps!"* (186). While it is uncertain to what degree this section of *Ich suchte Dich!* discloses twenty-four-year-old Nahida Sturmhoefel's motivations in marrying Max Remy, it impresses upon the reader that the autobiographer's life is guided by divine destiny. In revealing to her that the name on the calling card is that of her future husband, God for the first time speaks to her. In accepting God's choice of a husband, she also accepts that God had chosen her. While the power to make decisions, which she had asserted so confidently only a few pages earlier, is no longer hers, God's will enables Lazarus to counter any resistance with which her mother, who wished for her daughter to join her in Italy, or other people might have confronted her.

In the story of her first marriage, the autobiographer fulfills the con-

ventional role of woman as caregiver while at the same reversing the traditional gender polarization. Nahida retains her agency by providing her
invalid husband with unfailing care and subverts the female role from
within by asserting a male position of strength. The healthy young woman
and her ill husband form an "uneven pair—she, young, flourishing,
strong—he, grayed too early, bent down in his wheelchair" (183). Both
mother and husband suffer from poor health. Nahida Sturmhoefel's illness had a psychologically damaging effect on her daughter; Max Remy's
illness, by contrast, allows the autobiographer to feel her youthful strength
and her beauty. Inserted between the narration of the religious sufferings
of her childhood and her adult life as scholar of Judaism, the episode of
Lazarus's first marriage, who is thirty-two years old when her husband
dies, serves a transitory function in her autobiographical narrative. It
marks the end of childhood and, importantly, the psychological separation from her mother. Nahida's sexualized religious trials and her marriage to an unattractive, physically impaired man have a common trait in
that they are both attempts to come to terms with sexuality. The section on
her marriage ends with the words, "Now she had become a widow, almost
without knowing that she had been married," suggesting the absence of a
sexual relationship between the marriage partners (184).

Men in this autobiography appear either as sexual aggressors or as
asexual. In the context of a conversation with Max Remy's mother,
Nahida relates the story of her unusual first name. Her maternal grandfather, a true Prussian soldier in his professional life but a "gentle, feeling
nature" in private, had named his daughter after the virtuous heroine of a
novel (178–79). Nahida's mother had passed on her first and last names to
her daughter, thus establishing a female genealogy. The grandfather is the
only positive male figure in the autobiographer's family. Her father, who
did not give his daughter his name, remains unnamed and unnamable: "I
never speak about my father . . . he made my mother very unhappy" (180).
Male sexuality either inflicts disease upon women, as Nahida experienced
in the cases of her father and the effeminate priest, or disease results in the
loss of masculinity, as in the case of her first husband. The Jewish family
with its traditional gender roles becomes the only legitimate and secure
space for female sexuality because it is capable of controlling male sexuality.

The final chapter of *Ich suchte Dich!* relates the autobiographer's public
affirmation of her Jewish identity and marks the end of Nahida's existence
as an isolated yet eloquent religious outsider. The chapter's title, "Die neue
Ruth" ("The New Ruth"), promises the narrative's arrival at the identity
featured on the autobiography's front page: "Nahida Ruth Lazarus." In

the tradition of the "first" female convert to Judaism, Lazarus adopted the name of the biblical Ruth, the Moabite woman who, after the death of her husband, followed her widowed mother-in-law to the land of Judah. The parallel between the modern convert Nahida Lazarus and her biblical ancestor thus extends to the loss of a husband before their conversion.

The last chapter covers the years from 1881 to 1895, from the time of her husband's death to her conversion to Judaism. Nahida Remy, now in her thirties, spent the 1880s in Berlin. The rise of political antisemitism, which she encountered in the public sphere as well as in her family, had a profound impact on her. The assault on the religious culture with whose philosophical foundations and gender arrangements she so strongly identified was an important impetus to immerse herself in Judaism and to defend it against its German critics. During this period, she came in contact with middle-class Jewish men and women, whose indifference to religious observance she soon felt competent to condemn. Antisemitism, on the one hand, and secularization among Berlin's Jews, on the other, appear as the issues that occupied Lazarus during the next one and a half decades. Through conversations with Jews and extensive reading on the subject of Jews and Judaism, she acquired the information necessary to counter antisemitic prejudice with scholarly exactitude. Empowered by her new knowledge, she began to assert herself as a scholar of Judaism and a public advocate against antisemitism. Insufficient appreciation of Jewish culture among Christian and Jewish Germans, in Lazarus's mind, was responsible for both antisemitism and the secularization of Germany's Jews.

"So far, Nahida . . . had had no contact with Jews" is the opening line of this final chapter. The lower-class women of the autobiographer's childhood are replaced by the Jewish middle class of Berlin, whose members attract Nahida's critical curiosity in theaters and other public places, "in particular the Jewish ladies with their preference for jewelry and sparkling diamonds" (188). Perhaps unwittingly, Lazarus here repeats the "anti-Semites' image of the middle-class Jew with cultural pretensions."[66] In contrast to the antisemitic contention that Jews could never fully participate in German high culture, Lazarus criticized the women in the theaters for having relinquished their Jewishness. It is no coincidence, however, that for her the negative image of the Jewish upstart becomes doubly negative in its female manifestation. In *The Jewish Woman* and *Ich suchte Dich!* the newly rich Jewish woman is the negative mirror image of the figure of the "good Jewess" (207), whose activities center around the

---

66. Sander Gilman, *Jewish Self-Hatred: Anti-Semitism and the Hidden Language of the Jew* (Baltimore: Johns Hopkins University Press, 1986), 223.

observant Jewish home. Lazarus's criticism of middle-class Jewish women as inadequate Jews and preposterous representatives of their sex illustrates the proximity of misogyny and antisemitism. Yet she is correct in identifying the middle class and its values as a goal of German Jews as they assimilated into German culture.[67] Public spaces such as theaters and opera houses allowed the Jewish middle class to show its appreciation of the *Bildung* that was so central to bourgeois culture. What Lazarus "saw" in the bejeweled Jewish women in the theater was a loss of Jewishness. Her criticism of the ostentatious display of wealth also reflects the tensions between economic achievement and education as competing concepts in the self-definition of the middle class.

Several of Lazarus's dramas feature Jewish characters from different classes and national backgrounds. Her 1884 drama *Nationale Gegensätze* (National opposites), for instance, tells the love story of a German man and a Hungarian woman unfolding against a background of antagonistic relationships between Germans, Hungarians, Gypsies, and Jews.[68] Ewald, the upper-class German protagonist, brings culture and commerce, the two fundamental values of the bourgeoisie, to an underdeveloped region in Hungary against the stubborn nationalist resistance of his Hungarian counterpart. In this drama, the Gypsies' language identifies them as outsiders, whereas the German protagonist reveals his Jewish identity only in the end. His Germanic name, his class affiliation, and his command of German culture had rendered him invisible as a Jew. In *Schicksalswege* (Paths of destiny), her 1880 drama about young lovers, a stereotypical lower-class Jewish merchant of eastern European descent, readily identifiable as a Jew by his name and his "Jewish" language, cheats an unsuspecting German out of his only coat.[69] Her depiction of the lower-class Jew with his deficient language and his stereotypical profession shows that the status of Lazarus's Jewish figures is determined by gender, class, and national identity. Unlike their male counterparts in the plays, the lower-class Jewish women of *Ich suchte Dich!* are positive figures who share the loneliness of the German child. The upper-class Jewish women of the Berlin theaters, by contrast, signify an unsuccessful attempt at bringing together German and Jewish culture. The male protagonist of *Nationale Gegensätze*, finally, demonstrates what a successful symbiosis might look like. To become a Jew, Lazarus needs to assume that Germanness and Jewishness are compatible. Yet in much of her work she excludes

---

67. See Kaplan, *Jewish Middle Class,* 8ff.

68. Remy, *Nationale Gegensätze,* Jewish National and University Library, Jerusalem, Arc. Ms. Var. 124a.

69. Remy, *Schicksalswege,* 21, Jewish National and University Library, Jerusalem, Arc. Ms. Var. 298/124a.

Jewish figures from this dual identity and privileges the upper-class male Jew as the one who can assimilate into German culture without losing his Jewishness. Lazarus praised the observant Jewish woman as an ideal, but she knew from her own experiences that men faced fewer obstacles as they crossed traditional boundaries.

Toward the end of the 1870s, antisemitism, the "shame of the century" as emperor Friedrich III described it, began to spread in Berlin like a disease. Conversations with Jews, whose "education and sensitivity" Lazarus acknowledges to have surprised her (190), motivated the autobiographer to devour the current literature on Jewish cultural accomplishments, including the Jewish historian Heinrich Graetz's eleven-volume *Geschichte der Juden von den ältesten Zeiten bis auf die Gegenwart* (History of the Jews from antiquity to the present) and Protestant theologian Franz Delitzsch's *Handwerkerleben zur Zeit Jesu* (Jewish artisan life at the time of Jesus). Heinrich Graetz's work counts among the outstanding examples of *Wissenschaft des Judentums* (science of Judaism), a movement that "emerged in the second decade of the nineteenth century among young Jewish intellectuals who had been exposed to the ideal of an impartial, scholarly, and developmental approach to the past during their studies in German universities."[70] Lazarus's desire to familiarize herself with "modern data and figures" (193) about Judaism echoes the agenda of the young Jewish intellectuals more than fifty years earlier who employed scholarly methods to create a bridge between the traditional Judaism of their upbringing and the modern German society that they aspired to join. Lazarus, toward the end of the nineteenth century, studied Jewish culture to refute antisemitic prejudice and the new divisions it created between Germans and Jews.

By the second half of the nineteenth century a number of non-Jewish Germans like Nahida Lazarus began to publish scholarly contributions to Jewish history with the intent to educate their readership and, in some cases, to atone for past sins. The biologist Mathias Jacob Schleiden, for instance, justified his hundred-page scientific treatise *Die Bedeutung der Juden für Erhaltung und Wiederbelebung der Wissenschaften im Mittelalter* (The importance of the Jews for the preservation and revival of the sciences in the Middle Ages) with his desire "to begin at least to make amends for some of the unspeakable wrongs Christians inflicted upon Jews."[71] Both Schleiden and Lazarus relied on the persuasive power of scholarship as they illustrated and defended Jewish religious and cultural achieve-

---

70. Meyer, *Response to Modernity,* 75.

71. Mathias Jacob Schleiden, *Die Bedeutung der Juden für Erhaltung und Wiederbelebung der Wissenschaften im Mittelalter* (Leipzig: Commissionsverlag von Baumgaertner's Buchhandlung, 1877), 1.

ments. Such books, which tended to disregard the racial, economic, and populist aspects of antisemitism, were well received by Jews who tried to preserve and further the knowledge of Jewish culture among Jews. Not surprisingly, they found less of an audience among the non-Jewish Germans they hoped to reach.

Lazarus's readings in Jewish history and her contacts with Jews in the Berlin of the 1880s and 1890s provided her with a community whose values and beliefs she shared. The narrative, however, does not relate the autobiographer's entry into these new social circles to the religious battles of her childhood and early adulthood, nor are these contacts and conversations presented as a prelude to her conversion. Moreover, *Ich suchte Dich!* does not describe any encounters with antisemites, which would have allowed the autobiographer to put her new knowledge to the test. There is no mention of events such as Bernhard Förster's 1880 "antisemite petition," whose goal it was to curb immigration of foreign Jews, to exclude Jews from governments office, and to reduce the number of Jewish professors at German universities. Overall, Lazarus's rendition of these years remains somewhat ahistorical. She refrains from offering an analysis of antisemitism as an organized political movement with economic, racial, and national implications.[72] Instead, she stresses her acceptance as a non-Jew into the Jewish community. Most important, she won the close friendship of Zerline Meyer, an elderly Jewish woman in Berlin who on her deathbed bequeathed her most valuable Jewish writings to her Christian friend.[73]

Moritz Lazarus, whom the autobiographer probably met at the same time she befriended Meyer in the early 1880s, appears toward the very end of *Ich suchte Dich!* She first meets the founder of ethnopsychology as the "president of the Berlin branch of the Schiller foundation, . . . unaware that he was a Jew" yet familiar with his some of his writings. Moritz Lazarus is introduced not as a Jew but as a prominent intellectual and representative of German high culture. The acquaintanceship between the "famous professor" and the "modest young woman" grows into a teacher-student relationship that is to last more than ten years before the two decide to marry (199). Phrases such as "the young woman" or the "young scholar" instead of the narrator's first name linguistically mark the transi-

---

72. Neither Moritz nor Nahida Lazarus joined the Verein zur Abwehr des Antisemitismus (Kratz-Ritter, "Konversion," 15).

73. Lazarus, *Ich suchte Dich!* 209. Zerline Meyer died on May 4, 1894, less than a year before Lazarus's conversion. The obituary in the *Allgemeine Zeitung des Judenthums* states that Meyer maintained close contact with a good number of Jewish intellectuals and rabbis. It is likely that she introduced Lazarus into her circles. David Rosin, "Zerline Meyer," *AZJ*, June 15, 1894, 278–80.

tion from child to adult scholar. Enduring the double burden of the "Cinderella existence" she associates with running her own household—despite her relatives' pleas to join a pension for unmarried or widowed women—Lazarus spends her days with her "learned studies" of Jewish religion, history, and, at the suggestion of Moritz Lazarus, the Hebrew language (197).

Lazarus dedicates a "full decade quietly and industriously to her work," withdrawn from the public eye (200). She interprets the seven years she spent caring for her ailing first husband in the 1870s, as well as the ten years of arduous study from the 1880s to the 1890s, as periods of preparation for a greater but as yet unrevealed goal. This goal was her study *The Jewish Woman.* Neither her promising career as a painter nor her achievements as a playwright and novelist are the material of this autobiography. Instead, the writing of *The Jewish Woman,* at the initiative and under the guidance of Moritz Lazarus, emerges as the work that she considers to be her most important contribution to her time and the fruits of long years of preparation. After her mother's death in 1889, she writes, she was ready to undertake the task she had understood to be her "life's work" (211), the fight against anti-Jewish prejudices among Christians and the promotion of self-confidence among Jews.

The overwhelmingly positive reception of *The Jewish Woman* among Reform Jews explains why she considered this book her lifetime achievement.[74] The community she was about to join approved of her ideas on a topic that had occupied German Jews since the first two decades of the nineteenth century. There is no evidence that she persuaded antisemites to examine their prejudices or that she convinced Jewish women to return to the old ways. But she had made a name for herself as a Christian and as a woman with deep admiration for what she understood to be the merits of Judaism. Lazarus formulated one answer to two of the most pressing issues of late-nineteenth-century culture: the changing roles of women and the position of Jews in modern German society. Her reflections on the Jewish woman as a keeper of tradition delighted those who worried about gender difference as much as Jewish difference.

In 1895, at the age of forty-six, Lazarus converted to Judaism and immediately thereafter married Moritz Lazarus. On her way from Berlin to Geneva, where the conversion was to take place, she passed through Freiburg to visit Moritz. Finding him to be ill, she spent the next six weeks

---

74. See Bieberfeld, "Das jüdische Weib"; and Steinthal, "Giebt es noch Jüdinnen?" The majority of reviewers were men. In an article titled "Was sollen unsere Töchter lesen?" Regina Neisser states with regret that Christian women such as Nahida Remy and Bertha von Suttner have a more profound understanding of Judaism than their Jewish contemporaries (*AZJ,* September 22, 1893, 452).

taking care of the seventy-one-year old man. When a doctor suggested a trip to Italy to further his recovery, the need for a travel companion and a nurse prompted student and teacher to get married. *Ich suchte Dich!* does not contain a description of the conversion ceremony, nor does the auto-biographer reveal her emotional responses to this event. After years of religious struggles and intellectual labor, Lazarus had no need for a conversion experience, and her resolve to become a Jew presents itself as the necessary outcome of her life story. In converting to Judaism, Lazarus did not change her identity. She merely confirmed the self-definition she had possessed since early childhood.

The relationship between Nahida Lazarus and her mother, the writer and feminist Nahida Sturmhoefel, shows perhaps most clearly the contradictions that run through the autobiographer's self-understanding as a woman in late-nineteenth-century Germany. Despite its apparent absence from large sections of the narrative, the relationship between mother and daughter permeates all aspects of the autobiography. In the daughter's rendition, Nahida Sturmhoefel appears as the victim of an unspeakable and tragic fate. Her death in 1889 in a remote Italian fisher village marks the end of a relationship whose memory proves to be unbearable to the daughter:

> The life and the end of this noble, ingenious, but, against her will, oh so restless woman were of such an unspeakably melancholy kind . . . that the daughter could never dwell on the memory if she wanted to retain her composure.
> Silence is comforting when one has too much to say! (210)

In a reversal of the opening scene, in which the young narrator was silenced by her mother, the autobiographer now chooses not to speak to maintain her own emotional stability. The daughter's silence, however, obscures Nahida Sturmhoefel's activities as a writer, feminist and socialist, and pacifist. She reduces the unusual career of her mother to her suffering, thus denying her the agency that she possessed as an educated and independent woman who lived in several countries, traveled extensively throughout Europe, and earned her livelihood as a writer and as a manual worker. In the final scene of the autobiography, immediately following the narrator's conversion and marriage, Lazarus portrays herself on the grave of the "noble dreamer, who also spent her whole life searching" (223). In contrast to her mother's ceaseless but unsuccessful search, the autobiographer has brought her quest to a closure. On her mother's Italian grave she emphatically exclaims: "I sought you, my God—and I found you. I sought you, my Judaism, and I found you" (223). The characterization of the mother as a beloved but disempowered alter ego and the narrative positioning of her death as the necessary precondition for the daughter's successful completion of the search for an identity implies that what Nahida Sturmhoefel stood for—her participation in the women's movement and her support for the working-class movement—did not provide her daughter with a workable example of a female life. Yet the daughter's independence and her unconventional choices support the speculation that her mother was perhaps more of a role model than the autobiography concedes.

Nahida Lazarus's life and writing encompasses modern possibilities and the longing for tradition. In the end, she created several versions of her story to accommodate the paradoxes that shaped her life. Her most prominent texts, her writings on the Jewish woman and the story of her conversion, do not form a continuous narrative, that of someone who first wrote about the Jewish woman and then became one herself. In *Ich suchte Dich!* Lazarus told what led to her conversion, but she denies the reader a glimpse at her daily practice as a Jewish woman. In her work on the Jewish woman, by contrast, she created an ideal whose gender conservatism is not easily reconciled with her own remarkably emancipated life.[75] The reasons for the incongruity between Lazarus's lived realities and the ideal she so successfully promoted lie not only in her ambivalence toward feminism and the losses she experienced because of women's changing roles, but in the anxieties about gender difference in late-nineteenth-century Germany. The existence of masculinity and femininity as each other's natural opposites was the yardstick that measured the health or pathology of society. Female emancipation and the challenge it posed to gender difference came at considerable psychological and social cost to the individual woman, and Lazarus tried to protect herself from some of the consequences by inventing her conservative utopia. In her last creative phase she found a way of telling a version of German-Jewish life in which gender did not seem to be a problem.

As early as 1884 the widowed Nahida Remy had persuaded Moritz Lazarus to dictate to her the story of his life. She was undoubtedly motivated by her deep admiration for her teacher but also because his story resonated with hers. As Moritz Lazarus's auto/biographer, she could tell the story of a successful German-Jewish life and illustrate the compatibility of

---

75. Her case, however, is more complicated than Alan Levenson acknowledges when he claims that Lazarus's "philo-semitism subverted her proto-feminism." See Alan T. Levenson, "An Adventure in Otherness: Nahida Remy-Ruth Lazarus (1849–1928)," in *Gender and Judaism: The Transformation of Tradition,* ed. T. M. Rudavsky (New York: New York University Press, 1995), 100.

Germanness and Jewishness. The autobiographies of Moritz Lazarus, raised in an orthodox Jewish family in a small town in western Prussia, chronicle his ascent into the German cultural and intellectual elite. Moritz Lazarus never denied his traditional upbringing, yet he felt it necessary to transcend what he perceived to be his Jewish particularity in favor of an identity defined by German high culture. Mastery of the German language provided his entrance into German culture and society. In *Aus meiner Jugend,* the volume he dictated in the early 1880s, he describes his successful efforts to shed his Yiddish dialect and to acquire standard high German.[76] His memoirs continue in *Ein deutscher Professor in der Schweiz* and *Lebenserinnerungen,* the two volumes Nahida compiled after his death from her husband's narratives, papers, and letters, as well as her own recollections of her life with him. Here Moritz Lazarus emerges as a revered scholar among the Jewish and non-Jewish German-speaking cultural elite and a central figure in nineteenth-century intellectual life. As a teacher, colleague, and friend of prominent Germans, Moritz Lazarus himself became a German whose Jewishness was no longer immediately apparent. *Ein deutscher Professor* includes a letter to Lazarus from 1898 in which the writer, implicitly refuting antisemitism, asserts that in the 1860s he and his fellow students "barely realized that you are a Jew. So completely were we focused on the generally human and the philosophical that we did not at all sense these divisions."[77] Despite such assurances, antisemitism had in fact a significant impact on Moritz Lazarus's life and academic career. As a Jew, he was denied an appointment at a German university, forcing him to teach at the university of Bern from 1860 to 1866. Nahida Lazarus's compilations of her husband's life make no mention of such difficulties. Instead, they illustrate a successful German-Jewish symbiosis.[78] Through her husband's autobiographies Nahida Lazarus told another conversion narrative that complements her own story of the Christian-born German woman who became a Jew: the story of the male Jew who became a German intellectual.

Ich suchte Dich! was published five years prior to Georg Misch's attempt at the first scholarly definition of autobiography. As an "inappropriate subject of autobiography,"[79] Nahida Lazarus could not synthesize

---

76. Lazarus, *Aus meiner Jugend,* 22.

77. Lazarus, *Deutscher Professor,* 189. The title of this volume, most likely Nahida's choice, indicates that in her mind Moritz was most of all a German academic.

78. Michael Meyer confirms this perception when he writes about Moritz Lazarus's role at the 1869 synod in Leipzig: "Its elected president was the noted ethnologist and knowledgeable Jew, Professor Moritz Lazarus, symbolizing Jewish achievement in general culture" (*Response to Modernity,* 189).

79. Smith, "Construing Truths," 159.

the story of her life as a woman, as a Jew, and as an intellectual into one narrative. In *The Jewish Woman* she created a traditional female ideal. In her autobiography she related her sufferings in the absence of this ideal. In Moritz Lazarus's auto/biographies, finally, she told the story of a German intellectual life denied to her as a woman. Gender and Jewishness are the two categories of difference that shaped Lazarus's life. She was unable to incorporate women's changing roles into her thinking in a progressive way. Instead, she focused on Jewish difference to mitigate the consequences of modernization. She spoke out against antisemitism, but she did not acknowledge its effects on her husband's life, nor did she see herself as a potential target after her conversion. She relied on a cultural model of Christian-Jewish difference and ignored the racial aspects of antisemitism.

Nahida Lazarus's response to modernity is unique. Her blind spots and her insights into a society that defined itself through the differences that also shaped her own life and work show the profound impact of gender and race on late-nineteenth-century culture and the project of modernity. To put these differences into words, she abstained from becoming an autobiographical "I" throughout the majority of her autobiographical works. Before the modernist writers of the early twentieth century began to problematize the self, Nahida Lazarus experimented with the autobiographical form to express her experience of the modern age and the crisis of the self it brought on.

interesting mix of the autob. + the story of
the Jewish woman
but I am not convinced that the "crisis of
the self" is the focus of all this -
how much was conscious?
leaving Lazarus out till near end - perhaps
her need to separate conversion experience
from love exp. ?
more on mother / daughter
was Lazarus the missing father?

CHAPTER 2

The Autobiography of a White Woman: Margarethe von Eckenbrecher's Colonial Memoir

German colonialism officially began in 1884, little more than a decade after unification. By 1900 Germany had acquired possessions in Africa, the Pacific, and China, but never seriously challenged the predominance of Britain and France as colonial powers. The stipulations of the Treaty of Versailles in 1919 formally ended Germany's colonial rule. German colonies did not yield the anticipated economic rewards, and at no point were there more than twenty thousand Germans in Africa.[1] Settlement in the colonies paled compared to the seven million Germans who emigrated to the United States in the nineteenth century. These facts have led to the assumption that German colonialism was both a minor and a belated occurrence. As a result, it has only recently become the subject of study.[2] Yet Germans created a sizable body of colonial fiction and autobiogra-

---

1. Sara Friedrichsmeyer, Sara Lennox, and Susanne Zantop, eds., *The Imperialist Imagination: German Colonialism and Its Legacy* (Ann Arbor: University of Michigan Press, 1998), 11.

2. Recent books on German colonialism in addition to Friedrichsmeyer, Lennox, and Zantop, *The Imperialist Imagination,* are Russell A. Berman, *Enlightenment or Empire: Colonial Discourse and German Culture* (Lincoln: Nebraska University Press, 1998); Susanne Zantop, *Colonial Fantasies: Conquest, Family, and Nation in Precolonial Germany, 1770–1870* (Durham: Duke University Press, 1997); Nina Berman, *Orientalismus, Kolonialismus und Moderne: Zum Bild des Orients in der deutschen Kultur um 1900* (Stuttgart: Metzler, 1997); and John Noyes, *Colonial Space: Spatiality in the Discourse of German South West Africa, 1884–1915* (Chur: Harwood, 1992). The study of German colonial literature goes back to the 1980s; Joachim Warmbold, *"Ein Stückchen neudeutsche Erd' . . .": Deutsche Kolonial-Literatur: Aspekte ihrer Geschichte, Eigenart und Wirkung, dargestellt am Beispiel Afrikas* (Frankfurt am Main: Haag + Herchen, 1982), translated as *Germania in Africa: Germany's Colonial Literature* (New York: Peter Lang, 1989) (Warmbold's bibliography of primary sources comprises approximately six hundred entries); Amadou Booker Sadji, *Das Bild des Negro-*

phy; they promoted the colonial enterprise in magazines and journals and depicted colonial landscapes in paintings and photography. The "imperialist imagination" comprised fantasies of national glory, notions of racial superiority, and anxieties about racial mixing. For many, the idea of rural life in the colonies offered an alternative to the decadence of Germany's urban centers and the accompanying ills of modernity. Lure of prosperity and rebirth of tradition, fear of miscegenation and individual desire for freedom are some of the competing meanings of German colonialism. Colonialism was an antidote to the consequences of modernization, but it also raised fears of transgression.

Inspired by Benedict Anderson's seminal *Imagined Communities,* recent studies on German colonialism have emphasized fantasy and imagination as important ingredients of the colonial enterprise.[3] Susanne Zantop first examined colonial fantasies in her 1997 study of the century preceding German unification and the period of formal colonialism.[4] The contributors to the 1998 anthology *The Imperialist Imagination* trace the power of colonial discourse from the late eighteenth century to contemporary Germany, arguing that fantasies exist with or without the existence of colonies. Late-nineteenth-century colonial fantasies envisioned German settlers transforming uncultivated spaces into flourishing agricultural landscapes.[5] Competing economic interests, natural disasters, and resistant native populations, however, challenged the idea of the German farmer. Colonial fantasies rubbed against the realities of colonial life and, more important, had to compete for attention in Germany. "In Germany . . . nobody talks about us" was a common complaint among Germans in the colonies.[6] Colonial autobiographers appealed to the Germans who

---

Afrikaners in der deutschen Kolonialliteratur (1884–1945): Ein Beitrag zur literarischen Imagologie Schwarzafrikas (Berlin: Reimer, 1985). For the history of German colonialism see Jürgen Osterhammel, *Kolonialismus: Geschichte, Formen, Folgen* (Munich: Beck, 1995); W. O. Henderson, *The German Colonial Empire, 1884–1919* (London: Frank Cass, 1993); Arthur J. Knoll and Lewis H. Gann, eds., *Germans in the Tropics: Essays in German Colonial History* (New York: Greenwood, 1987); and Woodrow Smith, *The German Colonial Empire* (Chapel Hill: University of North Carolina Press, 1978).

3. See also Jacqueline Rose, *States of Fantasy* (New York: Oxford University Press, 1996).

4. Zantop, *Colonial Fantasies;* Hans Peter Herrmann, Hans-Martin Blitz, and Susanna Moßmann, eds., *Machtphantasie Deutschland: Nationalismus, Männlichkeit und Fremdenhaß im Vaterlandsdiskurs deutscher Schriftsteller des 18. Jahrhunderts* (Frankfurt am Main: Suhrkamp, 1996); and Klaus Theweleit, *Male Fantasies,* trans. Erica Carter and Chris Turner, 2 vols. (Minneapolis: University of Minnesota Press, 1989).

5. Zantop points out that settlement ideology has had a stronghold in German colonial fantasies since the seventeenth century (*Colonial Fantasies,* 9).

6. Gustav Frenssen, *Peter Moors Fahrt nach Südwest: Ein Feldzugsbericht* (Berlin: Grote, 1906), 105.

stayed behind on behalf of those who had left home to undertake the nation's colonizing work. Formal colonialism forced Germans to rethink their fantasies and to conceive of the position of the German overseas and the meanings of Germanness in new ways. Margarethe von Eckenbrecher, whose autobiography is the subject of this chapter, enticed readers with her fantasy of a German home in Africa.

As women began to join the German colonial enterprise in the 1890s, the imperialist imagination had to accommodate their presence in the colonial setting. The majority of them traveled to the colonies as nurses and as settlers' wives.[7] Female colonizers crossed geographical as well as social boundaries as they set up homes in territories often considered "no place for a white woman." As white women in a dark continent they were seen alternately as intruders in "virgin" territories that were awaiting penetration by men and as traditional helpmates who had their place by their white male counterparts.[8] In the colonial context European women became "white women." Their race placed them above dark-skinned men and women, while their sexuality strategically positioned them between white men and dark-skinned women. Women were participants, commentators, and icons in the social, economic, and sexual hierarchies produced by colonialism's system of race and gender. Their presence in the colonies gave rise to a debate about what kind of woman should be permitted to represent Germanness in the foreign landscapes yet to be transformed into German spaces.

The greater freedom of frontier conditions in the colonies allowed women to lead lives they could not have led at home and enabled them to write autobiographies they otherwise could not have written. Sidonie Smith described their situation: "At the margins of the empire, far from the European center's hold, they could as white women break through the borderland of female embodiment and achieve a mobility of autobiographical script unavailable to them in the 'home' country."[9]

---

7. On German colonial women see Lora Joyce Wildenthal, "Colonizers and Citizens: Bourgeois Women and the Woman Question in the German Colonial Movement, 1886–1914," Ph.D. diss., University of Michigan, 1994; and Martha Mamozai, *Schwarze Frau, weiße Herrin: Frauenleben in den deutschen Kolonien* (Reinbek bei Hamburg: Rowohlt, 1982).

8. For a discussion of the ambiguous roles of European women in colonial settings see Margaret Strobel, "Gender and Race in the Nineteenth- and Twentieth-Century British Empire," in *Becoming Visible: Women in European History,* ed. Renate Bridenthal, Claudia Koonz, and Susan Stuart (Boston: Houghton Mifflin, 1987), 375–95. Also see Patricia W. Romero, ed., *Women's Voices on Africa: A Century of Travel Writings* (Princeton, N.J.: Wiener, 1992).

9. Sidonie Smith, "The Other Woman and the Racial Politics of Gender: Isak Dinesen and Beryl Markham in Kenya," in Smith and Watson, *Del Colonizing the Subject,* 413.

German women's active involvement in the colonial enterprise began in the 1890s. Autobiography was one place where women worked out their position within the German colonial imagination. These narratives often lack individuality and reiterate shared assumptions about gender, race, and culture. But they also press against the roles assigned to women both in Germany and in the colonial setting. Women's colonial memoirs contribute to the turn-of-the-century debates about women's changing roles in contemporary society as well as Germany's changing role in the world.

Margarethe von Eckenbrecher (1875–1955) is the best known among the twenty German female colonial autobiographers and travel writers.[10] First published in 1907, her 240-page narrative *Was Afrika mir gab und nahm: Erlebnisse einer deutschen Ansiedlerfrau in Südwestafrika* (What Africa gave me and took from me: Experiences of a German settler's wife in Southwest Africa) went into eight editions, the last two revised and considerably expanded.[11] The memoir is divided into three equal parts. In the first section, von Eckenbrecher describes the journey by ship to German Southwest Africa (present-day Namibia). The second part is about the two years she spent in a remote village as a settler's wife, raising livestock and engaging in modest farming. In the final section, she recounts her experiences during the anticolonial war of the Herero and Nama, the loss of her property, and her forced return to Germany in 1904. Von Eckenbrecher's memoir appeared a year after Gustav Frenssen's best-selling novel *Peter Moors Fahrt nach Südwest* (Peter Moor's journey to Southwest Africa), the story of a volunteer from Germany's northernmost province who joined German troops against the

---

10. Figure based on Warmbold, *Ein Stückchen neudeutsche Erd'*. Other colonial memoirs by women include Helene von Falkenhausen, *Ansiedlerschicksale: Elf Jahre in Deutsch-Südwestafrika, 1893–1904* (Berlin: Reimer, 1905); Else Sonnenberg, *Wie es am Waterberg zuging: Ein Beitrag zur Geschichte des Hereoaufstandes* (Braunschweig: Wollermann, 1906); and Clara Brockmann, *Briefe eines deutschen Mädchens aus Südwest* (Berlin: Mittler, 1910).

11. An expanded and updated version appeared in 1937 with a slightly altered subtitle: *Erlebnisse einer deutschen Frau in Südwestafrika, 1902–1936*. Von Eckenbrecher's other publications include a travel account titled "Padleben in Südwest-Afrika," published in the collection *Deutsch-Südwestafrika. Kriegs- und Friedensbilder: Selbsterlebnisse geschildert von Frau Margarethe von Eckenbrecher, Frau Helene von Falkenhausen, Stabsarzt Dr. Kuhn, Oberleutnant Stuhlmann* (Leipzig: Weicher, 1907). Kurd Schwabe's *Der Krieg in Deutsch-Südwestafrika* (Berlin: Weller, 1907) includes a letter by von Eckenbrecher in which she details the last days of Fort Okombahe (101–4). The inclusion of this letter by a "brave German lady" (100) emphasizes the importance of female presence in the German colonies. In 1912 von Eckenbrecher brought out a second autobiographical narrative, *Im dichten Pori: Reise- und Jagdbilder aus Deutsch-Ostafrika* (Berlin: Mittler, 1912), an account of a big-game hunting expedition in the East African grassland, the "Pori." None of these publications enjoyed the success of *Afrika*.

Herero in faraway Southwest Africa.[12] It can be assumed that many of von Eckenbrecher's readers were familiar with Frenssen's text. She now offered a female version of this war and, unlike Frenssen, an eyewitness account. Moreover, her memoir appeared at a time when the Reich's involvement in Southwest Africa had come under intense scrutiny in Germany itself. The autobiography defends the colonial project against both the insurgent Africans and its critics at home.[13]

As is the case with many women writers, the biographical facts about Margarethe von Eckenbrecher are sparse. She was born Margarethe Hopfer in 1875 Bernburg, Saxony. The information she provides in the introduction to *Afrika* adds little to what we know about her. The brevity of her biographical sketch hints that she considered her life in Germany as a mere prelude to her experiences as a German woman in Africa. The opening sentence, "Already as a very small tot I got around in the world quite a bit," attests to the autobiographer's predisposition for travel at an early age and explains her desire to set up in Africa the home she never had in Germany.[14] Owing to unexplained "sad family circumstances," she spent her teen years in a Protestant boarding school. Encouraged by her mother, she passed a "number" of examinations that permitted her to obtain a teaching position at an upper-division girls' school *(höhere Mäd-chenschule)* in the western part of Berlin in 1893 at the age of eighteen.[15] She was driven "to work and to learn in order to become independent," and she left Germany for England in 1897 to continue her own education (iii). Wilhelmine Germany apparently did not offer von Eckenbrecher the independence she longed for. Marriage, the most common option for middle-class women, was either not available to her in her early twenties or she

---

12. See John Noyes, "National Identity, Nomadism, and Narration in Gustav Frenssen's 'Peter Moor's Journey to Southwest Africa,'" in Friedrichsmeyer, Lennox, and Zantop, *The Imperialist Imagination,* 87–105, for a discussion of this novel.

13. On the German opposition to colonialism see Helmuth Stoecker and Peter Sebald, "Enemies of the Colonial Idea," in Knoll and Gann, *Germans in the Tropics,* 59–72. The Social Democratic Party opposed colonialism from a Marxist position; the Catholic Center Party demanded a more humanitarian treatment of native populations but did not altogether reject colonialism. For a critical analysis of the Reichstag debates concerning German colonial policy and the centrality of racial thinking see Helmut Walser Smith, "The Talk of Genocide, the Rhetoric of Miscegenation: Notes on the Debates in the German Reichstag concerning Southwest Africa, 1904–14," in Friedrichsmeyer, Lennox, and Zantop, *The Imperialist Imagination,* 107–23.

14. Margarethe von Eckenbrecher, *Was Afrika mir gab und nahm. Erlebnisse einer deutschen Ansiedlerfrau in Südwestafrika* (Berlin: Mittler, 1907), iii. Subsequent references are given in the text. All translations are mine.

15. In 1887 Helene Lange petitioned the Berlin assembly with her famous "Yellow Brochure" to permit women to educate girls. On the higher education of girls by female teachers see Ute Gerhard, *Unerhört: Die Geschichte der Frauenbewegung* (Reinbek bei Hamburg: Rowohlt, 1991), 140.

did not consider it a viable choice. When she returned to Berlin around 1900, she audited lectures in philosophy and theology at Berlin's Friedrich-Wilhelms-Universität.[16] Von Eckenbrecher took advantage of the educational and professional opportunities made possible by the advances of the bourgeois women's movement, but she did not join its ranks. Leading women's rightists like the pedagogue Helene Lange (1848–1930) and the economist Alice Salomon (1872–1948) had turned late-nineteenth-century Berlin into a center of women's struggle for access to higher education and unrestricted admittance to the university. Teaching at a girls' school, the young Margarethe Hopfer must have been aware of these efforts to expand women's education; the limitations imposed on her generation led her to seek her independence elsewhere.

In 1902 Margarethe Hopfer married her cousin, Gustav Heinrich Themistokles von Eckenbrecher (1876–1935), the oldest son of the landscape painter Themistokles von Eckenbrecher (1842–1921), and left with him for Southwest Africa a few weeks after the wedding. In 1903 she gave birth to her first son, Bitz. After their return to Germany in 1904 the couple settled in Weimar, where their second son, Hans-Henning, was born 1905. Von Eckenbrecher later moved to Braunschweig, presumably without her estranged husband, where she taught English, French, economics, and geography at a women's business school *(Höhere Handelsschule für Damen)*. During this time she lectured extensively on colonial questions; between 1910 and 1914, several local chapters of the Frauenbund der Deutschen Kolonialgesellschaft (Women's Auxiliary of the German Colonial Society) were founded as a result of her presentations.[17] Shortly after her divorce in 1913, she returned to Southwest Africa with her two underage sons. She did not resume her life as farmer; instead, she supported her family as a teacher at a German high school in Windhoek.[18] Margarethe von Eckenbrecher died in Windhoek in 1955.[19]

In German Southwest Africa, the colony that von Eckenbrecher attempted to make her home, missionaries, trading companies, and individual settlers paved the way for formal imperialism. Following British and Dutch colonizers, the first Germans to arrive in larger numbers in southwest Africa in 1839 were the members of the Protestant Rheinische

---

16. Women had been granted a nondegree status at some German universities, including Berlin and Leipzig, since the mid-1890s. They gained regular admittance to German universities in 1908 (Gerhard, *Unerhört*, 157).

17. Else Frobenius, *Zehn Jahre Frauenbund der Deutschen Kolonialgesellschaft* (Berlin: Kolonie und Heimat, 1918), 49, 65, 68, 69, 71, 72, 81.

18. The area around Okombahe, where von Eckenbrecher's farm was located, became one of the few territories reserved for indigenous groups after 1907.

19. I thank Jochen Kutzner of the National Archives of Namibia for this information.

Mission (Rhenish Missionary Society). Shortly thereafter, trading companies staked their claims in southwest Africa by negotiating individual contracts with indigenous rulers for substantial amounts of tribal lands. In 1883 the Bremen tobacco merchant Adolf Lüderitz acquired some land around the bay of Angra Pequena and renamed the area Lüderitzbucht (Lüderitz Bay). Prompted by British threats to annex large parts of southwest Africa, including Lüderitzbucht, Bismarck declared German Southwest Africa a "protectorate" *(Schutzgebiet)* on April 24, 1884, and thus inaugurated Germany's twenty-five-year period of colonial rule in Africa.[20] Neither the missionary societies, whose members proselytized among the native populations, nor the large trading companies, who pursued economic interests, created an efficient colonial administration. Even after the German government had declared its willingness to protect German interests in Southwest Africa, its actual involvement remained hesitant. German settlers like von Eckenbrecher and her husband had to assert themselves against other colonizers, such as the Dutch and the British, as well as the indigenous population without the full legal and military support of the German government. Von Eckenbrecher's account exposes the vulnerable position of middle-class farmers in Southwest Africa and inadvertently reveals the discrepancies between the ideology of the "German farm" in Africa and its realities.[21]

When von Eckenbrecher published her memoir in 1907, colonial literature was a well-established genre, much of it written with the intent to stir up enthusiasm for the Reich's fledgling overseas empire. Frenssen's *Peter Moor* had just come out; Frieda von Bülow, the "founding mother of German colonial literature," had promoted colonialism in her novels since the early 1890s.[22] Colonial literature opened up new territories to which Germans could transport their dreams of economic prosperity together with their notions of racial and cultural superiority. These novels stressed the hardships of colonial life but also showed how German industriousness and aptitude could transform "unused" land into German landscapes and homes. Native populations served as a labor force at best in

---

20. The term *protectorate* implied that the German government offered "protection" to individual indigenous rulers against British influences as well as against each other. For a detailed account of German diplomacy in Southwest Africa see J. H. Esterhuyse, *South West Africa, 1880–1894: The Establishment of German Authority in South West Africa* (Cape Town: Struik, 1968); also Helmut Bley, *South-West Africa under German Rule, 1894–1914* (London: Heinemann, 1971).

21. Smith (*The German Colonial Empire,* 60) confirms the "colonial administration's lack of sympathy with settlement colonialism" described by von Eckenbrecher.

22. Friederike Eigler, "Engendering German Nationalism: Gender and Race in Frieda von Bülow's Colonial Writings," in Friedrichsmeyer, Lennox, and Zantop, *The Imperialist Imagination,* 69.

these scenarios. The success of colonialism, these novels cautioned, was threatened by the possibility of miscegenation. The inclusion of German male figures who gave in to the temptation of interracial sex emphasized that it was the responsibility of the German colonial community to preserve its racial purity.[23]

Autobiographies played a vital role in shaping and proliferating the fantasies of German life overseas. Presumably realistic accounts of life in the colonies, memoirs such as von Eckenbrecher's allowed readers back home to witness the creation of German farms and family life under severe circumstances. Colonial autobiographies by women constitute a small but significant subset within German colonial literature. In the context of the aggressive publicity campaigns waged by the colonial societies in Germany to stimulate financial and military support for the colonies, women's authentic reports from German Africa proved that the success of the German colonialist enterprise depended on the presence of women who were capable of enduring the hardships of foreign climates and continents. Women's memoirs of colonial war, in particular, confirmed the true meaning of German femininity. It took the colonial war, exclaimed an enthusiastic reviewer of von Eckenbrecher's autobiography, not only to renew the nation's faith in "men's ancient Germanic loyalty" (altdeutsche Männertreue), but also to prove that the "ordeals of torturous privation and lurking death brought to the fore again the German woman's Teutonic qualities of heroic courage . . . and her fiery fervor for the preservation and propagation of national glory in the present and the future."[24] Colonialism was the battlefield on which the Germanic character rejuvenated itself and reached new heights. Under the extreme conditions of the colonial combat zone the German woman resurrected Germany's tribal past, and its future as a nation issued forth.

Women colonizers pursued various agendas and adopted a multiplicity of strategies to fulfill their fantasies, yet the majority assumed a privileged relationship to the nation. A study on German colonial literature from the mid-1980s overlooked the differences among these narratives when it summarily described women's colonial memoirs as "housewives' literature."[25] More recent feminist work analyzes the daily interaction between German women and Africans in the colonial household to

---

23. Frenssen's hero Peter Moor, for instance, repeatedly criticizes the conduct of his fellow soldiers. Observing "enemy wenches," he comments that "it displeased me that some of us approached them right away and . . . trifled with them" (*Peter Moors Fahrt*, 46).

24. Richter, "Die Südwesterin im Kriegssturm," *Deutsche Kolonialzeitung* 19 (1907): 190. *Deutsche Kolonialzeitung* was published by Mittler Verlag, which also brought out von Eckenbrecher's autobiography.

25. Sadji, *Das Bild des Negro-Afrikaners*, 226.

explore exactly how these women relied on their identity as "white woman" as a source of empowerment and to understand what they hoped to achieve in the colonial setting.[26] The subjectivity of colonial women is shaped by the supremacist construct of the white woman as much as by the anxieties many of them experienced as they acted out this role.

Margarethe von Eckenbrecher's autobiography appeals to her German readers who remained in the home country with the image of a domestic idyll. Upon opening the cover of *Afrika,* the reader sees a photograph of a woman standing in front of a dark doorway with an unusually high arch; the door frame separates the dimly visible interior space of the house from an outside space with a paved floor and lush garden vegetation (fig. 2). The woman carries a small child of about ten months in her arms. The caption underneath reads: "Frau v. Eckenbrecher in the veranda of the house at Okombahe," encouraging the viewer to identify the woman in the picture as the autobiographer in front of her African home. Frau v. Eckenbrecher, clad in a long-sleeved belted white dress with a wide, floor-length skirt, occupies the center of the picture. The doorway, the walls of the house, and the smooth floor situate the female figure firmly within her domestic environment. Von Eckenbrecher focuses her gaze on the child, heightening the impression of self-contained family life and motherhood. In the absence of Africans, the architecture of the house and the exoticism of the plants signify "Afrika." The autobiographer introduces herself as a recognizably German woman in the foreign yet reassuringly domestic setting of "Okombahe." A byline credits the photograph to the autobiographer's husband. The man behind the camera and the woman posing in front of it together created an image of German domesticity in Africa.[27]

Opposite the photograph, on the same page, we find the words "What Africa gave me and took from me." Von Eckenbrecher's contemporaries would have known to interpret the title as a reference to the Herero war and the temporary eviction of German settlers from the Hereros' territories. The idyll in the photograph, they understood, no longer existed, yet the image confirmed its existence in the past, and it appealed to them to

---

26. For instance, Marcia Klotz, "Memoirs from a German Colony: What Do White Women Want?" in *Eroticism and Containment: Notes from the Flood Plain,* ed. Carol Siegel and Ann Kibbey (New York: New York University Press, 1994), 154–87; Laura Wildenthal, "She Is the Victor": Bourgeois Women, Nationalist Identities, and the Ideal of the Independent Woman Farmer in German Southwest Africa," *Social Analysis* 33 (1993): 68–88.

27. The photograph could well be an illustration of a scene witnessed by Gustav Frenssen's protagonist Peter Moor: "With wide eyes we gazed into the garden, which in former years the colonists had laid out with great care. . . . And there in the shade of the veranda stood a German woman; she held a little child on her arm" (*Peter Moors Fahrt,* 111). The powerful image of the "white woman" remains unique in the novel. Moor otherwise has little contact with the settlers he came to defend.

Fig. 2. Margarethe von Eckenbrecher. (Reproduced from Margarethe von Eckenbrecher, *Was Afrika mir gab und nahm* [Berlin: Mittler, 1907]. Every effort has
been made to contact the copyright owners of the photograph and to secure permission for its use.)

fight for its resurrection in the future. The gains and the losses were not only von Eckenbrecher's but those of all turn-of-the-century readers who wanted to assure themselves of a domestic ideal that was vanishing in Germany as well. The opening page thus suggests that the colonial war against the Herero was fought to preserve the German family. The successful establishment of her African Arcadia, its loss, and the promise of its renewed existence form the parameters of von Eckenbrecher's autobiographical project. The grammatical structure of the title positions the autobiographer in an object relationship to a personified continent in the role of an omnipotent giver and taker. In her case, "Africa" is not a continent waiting to be taken by the male colonizer but an agent that acts upon the autobiographer. From the beginning, von Eckenbrecher offers her reader a female version of the colonial experience.

Photography accompanied colonialism and colonialist ethnography from the late nineteenth century, quickly replacing ethnographic drawings.[28] Countless examples of colonial photography illustrate how colonizers used the camera to insert themselves into colonial landscapes, often occupying center stage within a group of colonized people. Von Eckenbrecher's pictures are largely informal portraits, intended to show everyday life and to illustrate the autobiographer's influence on her African environment rather than the exoticism of a foreign country.[29] The photographs blend the strange with the familiar, presenting to the viewer a rendition of Germany with a difference, or, put another way, an Africa in which the German eye could recognize familiar elements. About one-third show interior and exterior domestic scenes; nine of them allow the viewer

---

28. Christraud M. Geary, *Images from Bamum: German Colonial Photography at the Court of King Njoya, Cameroon, West Africa, 1902–1915* (Washington: Smithsonian Institution Press, 1988), 10; Uwe Timm, *Deutsche Kolonien* (Cologne: Kiepenheuer & Witsch, 1986), a collection of photographs from the German colonies; Norbert Aas and Werena Rosenke, eds., *Kolonialgeschichte im Familienalbum: Frühe Fotos aus der Kolonie Deutsch-Ostafrika* (Münster: Unrast, 1992); John Pultz, *The Body and the Lens: Photography, 1839 to the Present* (New York: Abrams, 1995), especially the section "Colonialism, Race, and the 'Other.'" Camera manufacturers advertised the suitability of their products for use in tropical climates in newspapers such as *Deutsches Kolonialblatt*.

29. *Afrika* includes sixteen plates with thirty-three individual photographs, six of them taken by the autobiographer herself and four of them showing her. By the time she traveled to German East Africa in 1909, von Eckenbrecher had turned herself into a semiprofessional photographer. In the opening paragraphs of *Im dichten Pori* she describes the preparations necessary for a hunting expedition to Africa. In addition to money, tents, and guns she packs a "Universal-Palmos-Kamera mit Teleobjektiv," donated by Zeiß, the Jena producer of lenses and optical equipment, and 720 photographic plates to test them under tropical conditions. Most colonial autobiographies include visual aides such as photographs, drawings, and maps to authenticate the experience; for instance Mary H. Kingsley, *Travels in West Africa: Congo Français, Corisco, and Cameroons* (London: Macmillan, 1897).

to identify von Eckenbrecher's house. A picture captioned "Morning coffee in the patio" perhaps most vividly reproduces Germany in Africa: It shows the autobiographer and her husband sitting at a table, complete with tablecloth, European china, and a baby bottle, while an African female servant is carrying a calabash on a tray.[30] The baby son's cradle can be seen next to the table. All three figures look directly into the camera. The African woman with the exotic vessel on the familiar tray is dressed in the clothes of a German female servant, testifying to the success of von Eckenbrecher's domesticating mission. The Africans in these photographs are for the most part linked to von Eckenbrecher's household as servants, either directly through their activities, such as the servant with the tray, or attending to her young son. In five pictures nameless Africans support settlers in activities such as hunting or travel. The only image coded as "negative" (her plate 9) shows the autobiographer's house after the war and is captioned "Our deserted house in Okombahe." The photographs are not intended to show Africa to the German viewers. They are meant to show the autobiographer in Africa and her success as a female colonizer.

Like most colonial women, von Eckenbrecher went to Africa as a settler's wife to carry out the domestic and domesticating work of the female colonizer. Her interest in Africa began with a male fantasy rather than any desires of her own. In her adolescence, she relates in the foreword to *Afrika,* her brother and her cousin had shared with her their vision of Africa as the "land of their dreams" (iii). Later, under the influence of her cousin, who by then had become her husband, these dreams would become hers. Married to a colonizer, von Eckenbrecher enjoyed more freedom than the average Wilhelmine woman without having to give up the respectability so central to her middle-class identity.

Themistokles von Eckenbrecher plays a remarkably marginal role in the autobiography. He had spent 1897 to 1900 in Southwest Africa, serving in the German military during part of these three years (122). When he returned with his wife in 1902, he could take her to a place where he had acquired some property and had established connections with Southwest Africa's German and African population. Von Eckenbrecher's position as a married white woman is defined by her husband's previous status as an unmarried settler who has taken a German wife and brought her back to Africa. She comes into an existing network of relationships, the particulars of which, however, remain vague. Passages like the following reveal that her presence introduced significant change into her husband's life. "But that you would bring with you a white woman none of us would have

---

30. Eckenbrecher, *Africa,* plate 10. Helmut Bley reproduced this image in his *South-West Africa* (plate 17) as "an example of German colonial life."

thought," she quotes members of Okombahe's native population telling her husband upon his return (102). She does not speculate about why the Africans doubted that "Mr. von Eckenbrecher" would return with a white woman, but they may well have been referring to her husband's attitudes toward marriage and possibly to his earlier sexual conduct. Marriage gives both partners respectability. Beyond that, von Eckenbrecher chose to tell the story of the white woman rather than the Wilhelmine wife.[31]

"Colonial experience was prefigured as a process of self-endangering and self-renewal," David Trotter writes about the subjectivity of the male colonizing subject.[32] Von Eckenbrecher understood this necessity when she dedicated the first seventy pages of *Afrika,* about a third of the narrative, to the journey from Germany to Southwest Africa. The voyage away from the old home to an as yet unbuilt new home is not only a physical act but also a test of the traveler's psychological aptitude as a future colonizer. The five-week journey from the sodden port of Hamburg to the heat of the Namib desert demonstrates von Eckenbrecher's suitability for her duties in the colony as wife, homemaker, and mother of future "Africans." Willing to suffer seasickness and severe headaches, the damp cold of the British Channel and the torrid African coast, she proves herself capable of enduring physical hardship even before she sets foot on African soil and refutes contemporary assumptions that middle-class European women were weaker than their male counterparts and were prone to specifically female illnesses. Von Eckenbrecher's first activities on the ship are to arrange her and her husband's belongings in her cabin, although she is continuously thwarted by the rolling sea. The difficult circumstances under which the autobiographer assumes her domestic duties as a housewife as well as her persistence foreshadow the challenges she is about to encounter in Africa. These opening passages illustrate that being female is not an obstacle to undertaking the work of the colonizer but also convey that not everyone can be a colonizer. The ability to cope with adverse conditions distinguishes von Eckenbrecher from the average woman and the majority of men.

---

31. According to Siegfried Gehrecke's bibliography of the landscape painter Themistokles von Eckenbrecher, the father of the autobiographer's husband, the younger von Eckenbrecher was a gifted but "unsteady" character who traveled restlessly and lost large sums of money in unsound business deals. The 1937 edition of *Afrika* confirms this view. Themistokles' refusal to return to Southwest Africa might have contributed to the failure of the marriage (155). He remarried and emigrated to Paraguay, where he died in 1935. Gehrecke suggests that after 1905 the couple had a third son who died at birth. Von Eckenbrecher makes no mention of this. Siegried Gehrecke, *Themistokles von Eckenbrecher, 1842–1921* (Goslar: Museumsverein Goslar, 1985), 18–19.

32. David Trotter, "Colonial Subjects," *Critical Quarterly* 32, no. 3 (1990): 5.

The ship that carries von Eckenbrecher and her husband from Germany to the Southwest African port of Swakopmund is a microcosm of the gender and class relations of colonial life. United by a shared racial and class identity, the first-class passengers on the *Eduard* are doctors and businessmen who possess both money and education.[33] Unlike German peasants, prospective farmers like von Eckenbrecher and her husband shared the education, the financial means, and the values of the middle class. Von Eckenbrecher's portrait of the passengers on the ship circumscribes the socioeconomic makeup of desirable colonizers, distinguishing her peer group from mere adventurers as well as from those too timid to leave home. Colonization is the work of only the most self-sacrificing and determined members of the middle class. Propelled by individualism and restrained by their adherence to middle-class norms—the ladies do not sleep on deck even in the greatest heat—von Eckenbrecher and her fellow travelers set out to do the colonizing work for those Germans who could not join them.

The majority of women in Southwest Africa were wives of settlers or missionaries who supported their husbands as homemakers and mothers of their children. In 1901, the year before von Eckenbrecher left for Africa, one hundred "white women" and 1,763 men lived in Southwest Africa, Germany's only colony that was relatively free from malaria.[34] The most powerful argument in favor of women in the colonies was that their presence prevented sexual relationships between German men and African women and helped avert the threat of miscegenation.[35] Lora Wildenthal's study of bourgeois women in the colonial movement lists numerous passages from women's colonial autobiographies showing that female colonizers indeed saw as one of their primary functions reining in the sexuality of German men.[36] Von Eckenbrecher's memoir is no exception: Two brides-to-be, accompanied by a male chaperon, make the journey to Africa, a newly married woman who, like von Eckenbrecher, traveled with her husband, and an energetic wife returning to Africa from a fund-raising trip to Germany during which she had left her children in her husband's care. The "traffic in women" between Germany and Southwest Africa confirms their function in the colony as wives of German men. Gazing at the ocean waves, von Eckenbrecher recalls Hans Christian Andersen's "blissful" fairy tale of the little mermaid: "Is it not as if in the distance the unfortunate mermaid was bouncing on the waves? Out of love for the

---

33. Von Eckenbrecher traveled on a ship that belonged to the Woermann Steamship Line, founded by the Hamburg Woermann concern in the 1880s.

34. Klotz, "Memoirs from a German Colony," 155.

35. Wildenthal, "Colonizers and Citizens," 146.

36. Ibid., 172.

prince she swallowed the dreadful potion and became human. But . . . she could not acquire a soul because she did not find love, and thus she dissolved into foam" (6). While the ship's female passengers look forward to a future as wives and colonizers, the fairy tale serves as a—perhaps unintentional—reminder that female sacrifice is not always rewarded.

Also among the passengers on the *Eduard* is an "old maid," a self-effacing teacher whose fate von Eckenbrecher might have shared had she continued her own teaching career. Since German law forced female government employees to choose between marriage and profession, von Eckenbrecher's "spinster" might well have sacrificed her livelihood in Germany for the chance of finding a husband in the statistically favorable environment of Southwest Africa. A representative of the so-called surplus of women in Germany, the unmarried woman is the sociosexual opposite of the newlywed narrator. Unlike the autobiographer, whose marital status commands dignity, the unmarried teacher is the object of distasteful jokes during the journey. "She did get married after all," von Eckenbrecher reports on her female fellow traveler's fate in Africa, "but she too fell, one of the first victims of the uprising, murdered in the lowest, most brutal fashion" (9). Presumably raped and killed by Africans, the spinster did not live to tell her story of the white woman in Africa. The educated spinster hoping to be married, the brides, the newlyweds, and the wife of many years represent the range of legitimate female positions in the colony.

In reality, not all female colonizers conformed to the norms of middle-class respectability, some of whom emigrated to the colonies to escape the confines of Wilhelmine society. The Women's Auxiliary of the German Colonial Society, founded in 1908 by the conservative Prussian aristocrat Freifrau Adda von Liliencron, responded to this development by processing female emigrees through a selection committee. "Women who wanted to get away from their husbands . . . and finally those who have the lust for adventure of all kinds written plainly all over their face" were rejected.[37] Lower-class women were often placed under the tutelage of their bourgeois counterparts in the hope of increasing the number of "suitable" women in the colonies and to realize the Auxiliary's declared goal of "strengthening family life, education of adolescents and women, and the preservation of German girls in the colonies."[38] Colonial life required perseverance and sacrifice, but it was not to be a mere adventure or an opportunity to leave behind the values of middle-class culture. The Auxiliary

---

37. Quoted in Wildenthal, "Colonizers and Citizens," 219.
38. Frobenius, *Zehn Jahre Frauenbund,* 11.

expected women to renounce individual desires and to make the colonies a better version of Germany without replicating its ills.

The Spanish island of Las Palmas off the North African coast is the ship's first stop. As if to emphasize the color of their skin, the travelers, who had neglected their wardrobes on the ship, don their white tropical attire (10). The group is thus outfitted to represent racial difference in the sexualized southern environment they are about to encounter; lush tropical vegetation, brown people from various national origins in bright clothes, and dirty streets. "Here one could study them," von Eckenbrecher says of her first contact with the inhabitants of Las Palmas, "the brown, pitiful sons of the South. Spaniards, Portuguese, Indians, Negroes, everyone yelled and charged about at once, seeking to draw attention with smatterings of English, German, or French to negotiate some kind of an advantageous deal" (11). "Race" presents itself to von Eckenbrecher as an amalgam of people of various origins. It is inseparably intertwined with commerce and finds its expression in the "abuse" of the languages of the colonizers. The narrator differentiates between the people she meets according to national and racial background, yet these distinctions get lost in the overall commotion and noise of the commercial situation. "A veritable stream of these crooks" poured over the passengers, trying to sell their merchandise (11).

The first encounter occurs between two groups separated by race rather than between individuals. Von Eckenbrecher's narrative thus confirms Robert Young's suggestion that racism as well as colonial discourse is a "group fantasy" that is socially produced rather than conceived by individuals.[39] Von Eckenbrecher and her group "see" but they do not "understand." The island's languages are either incomprehensible or bad imitations of European languages. The natives have the uncanny ability immediately to recognize the group as German, suggesting that the travelers might not be as foreign to them as the exoticism of Las Palmas is to the travelers (12). "Small, bronze-colored boys with limbs that seemed to be cast out of ore stood naked in the boats, begging for coins after which they wanted to dive," arousing the narrator's voyeuristic desires (12).[40] Von Eckenbrecher and her fellow travelers participate in the sexualized economy of Las Palmas as paying onlookers, whose coins buy the spectacle of

---

39. Robert J. C. Young, *Colonial Desire: Hybridity in Theory, Culture, and Race* (London: Routledge, 1995), 169.

40. Von Eckenbrecher's remarks echo Susan R. Horton's observation, *Difficult Women, Artful Lives: Olive Schreiner and Isak Dinesen, in and out of Africa* (Baltimore: Johns Hopkins University Press, 1995), about Olive Schreiner's novels, in which "'Kaffir' children gambol everywhere, the adjective *naked* attaching to them like a second skin" (155).

naked boys diving. The travelers scrupulously avoid physical contact with the inhabitants of Las Palmas, throwing alms and cigarettes into the dust for the natives to pick up. A "dark-eyed beauty" looking from her window and soldiers with "eyes bright as buttons" cast sexual glances for von Eckenbrecher to "see" (13). As she is drawn into the exchange of glances, coins, and souvenirs, the "alluring South" begins to permeate her subjectivity, her fantasies, and her desire. The colorfully dressed soldiers, "handsome little fellows despite their listlessness," are "made for love," but, she speculates, they could not stand up to the arduous demands of a war (13). The soldiers' masculinity promises sexual virility without true manliness.

Sexuality not only permeates all aspects of native life but transgresses the boundaries between the local population and the foreign visitors. The narrator observes how a peasant girl, making her confession in church, smiles invitingly at Themistokles von Eckenbrecher (13). Von Eckenbrecher makes no mention of her husband's response. "Nineteenth-century theories of race," Robert Young argues, "did not just consist of essentializing differentiations between self and other: they were also about a fascination with people having sex—interminable, adulterating, aleatory, illicit, inter-racial sex."[41] Von Eckenbrecher's narration of her first exposure to "race" doubles as a discourse about sexuality.

Von Eckenbrecher's racialized fantasies of sexuality reserve a special position for the "white woman." From the deck of the ship she sees enormous clouds of smoke that rise from vast bushfires on the African mainland, reminding her of the "Indian tomes" [Indianerschmöker] of her youth. She imagines "how the Indian [i.e., Native American] lifts the white girl onto his horse and races against fire and storm!" (17). Von Eckenbrecher transfers a sexual fantasy across oceans and cultures and peoples the African coast with German literature's version of the noble savage to imagine a sexualized scene between a white woman and a dark-skinned man.

Von Eckenbrecher's sexualized orient produces abundance without value. The fecund southern nature resists the transformation into the meaningful commodities of capitalist economy. The caged birds in the market, she notes, are more expensive than the ones at home, but they do not sing. The travelers are continually assaulted by street vendors with their cheap souvenirs; begging children force themselves upon the narrator and her fellow travelers. The sexualized abundance of Las Palmas, with its colorful people, animals, and plants, expresses the fear and fascination of racial and cultural hybridity that underlies colonial discourse. The ever-present half-naked dirty children, staple figures in every colonial text, are

---

41. Young, *Colonial Desire,* 181.

symbols of unrestrained sexuality and a threatening fertility that results in a population of "brown" people. In the "false" economy of the South, goods and people of inferior value circulate, forever reproducing themselves. Von Eckenbrecher's Las Palmas is what Mary Louise Pratt has termed a "contact zone," defined by the "spatial and temporal copresence of subjects previously separated by geographic and historical disjuncture."[42] Von Eckenbrecher's description of the voyage to Southwest Africa serves as more than a chronological function. The hardships of travel usher in the labor of colonization, and contact with "brown" peoples precedes life among the Hottentots and the sexual and economic chaos awaiting the systematizing energy of the female colonizer.[43]

Colonial autobiography produces the autobiographical subject as colonial subject. Von Eckenbrecher's memoir, however, lacks the individual qualities one might expect from a narrative that relates an extraordinary experience. She makes sparse use of the first-person pronoun and subordinates her individuality to the group. In a few passages the autobiographer substitutes the language of German romanticism for the colonial group fantasy to express a subjectivity presumably free from the particularities of gender and race. One night, as she attempts to escape the "merrymaking" of her fellow passengers, the sleepless narrator "sent her gaze to the stars . . . and more than ever I perceived in this silent tropical night the powerful, soul-penetrating language of the ocean" (32). Poetic lines like these are among the more intimate passages of the autobiography. Confronted with her insignificance in the vastness of the universe, she reveals her subjectivity through one of romanticism's most celebrated images, that of the solitary male self and the poetic baring of his soul. In these passages, von Eckenbrecher claims the universal humanity of the autonomous male subject. The African ocean far from home empowers the German soul to express its innermost depth in the universal language of German romanticism and to shed its gendered particularity. Von Eckenbrecher's reluctance to say "I" cautions us to rethink the assumption that the colonial experience opens new spaces for female subjectivity. Her hesitation to assume the position of what Nancy L. Paxton has described as the "Imperial I" might well reflect her insight that as a "white woman" she is participating in a collective enterprise in which the roles and the desires have been assigned.

---

42. Mary Louise Pratt, *Imperial Eyes: Travel Writing and Transculturation* (New York: Routledge, 1992), 7.

43. Von Eckenbrecher's voyage in many ways resembles that of Frenssen's protagonist Peter Moor. He, too, suffers the hardships of seasickness, is dazzled by the natural beauty of the South, marvels at its brown inhabitants and their colorful merchandise before he reaches torrid Southwest Africa.

The last stop before the travelers reach their destination is Port Alexander in the Portuguese colony of Angola. The economic transactions that have accompanied the entire journey shift from the "flood" of cheap goods to the colonizers' desire for rare authentic African cult objects. Recalling the displays in Berlin's Museum für Völkerkunde, von Eckenbrecher and her fellow travelers set out to acquire a *Götze,* a West African idol endowed with miraculous healing powers. The West African fetish is perhaps the object that best embodies the encounter between European and African culture. Portuguese sailors brought the first *feitiços* to Europe in the fifteenth century, where they were displayed in curio cabinets as strange objects with magical powers.[44] By the late nineteenth century, West African fetishes had entered the European conscious as either objects of art, whose "ugliness" confirmed to Europeans the primitive nature of African aesthetics, or as items of anthropological interest. Ethnographers like Felix von Luschan (1854–1924), director of the Museum für Völkerkunde in Berlin during the first decade of the twentieth century, systematically enlarged their collections with African art and cult objects.[45] Authentic fetishes, as the narrator repeats hearsay, had become increasingly rare and fetched a good price on the European markets. With the help of a Portuguese doctor the group sets out to find a fetish, systematically searching every hut along the way until they discover one in a remote dwelling with a low door, located "between two large sand hills" (37). The landscape evokes the female body as the source and the realization of fetishistic desire; the fetish is located inside the womblike hut whose low opening forces the group members to stoop as they enter its interior. Covered with nails, the fetish looks like a "rusty porcupine" (37).

The object that von Eckenbrecher and her companions were after was most likely one of the "famous Kongo nail fetishes" William Pietz described in his philosophical essays on fetishism.[46] Pietz argues against the assumption that a fetish is a "proper object with its own singular significance."[47] Instead, the fetish must be located in its historical and its cross-cultural context in the encounter between Europeans and Africans. "The fetish, then, not only originated from, but remains specific to, the problematic of the social value of material objects as revealed in situations formed by the encounter of radically heterogeneous social systems."[48] The

---

44. V. Y. Mudimbe, *The Invention of Africa: Gnosis, Philosophy, and the Order of Knowledge* (Bloomington: Indiana University Press, 1988), 9–10.

45. Geary, *Images from Bamum,* 92–93.

46. William Pietz, "The Problem of the Fetish, I," *Res* 9 (spring 1985): 16. Von Eckenbrecher describes the object as both "Götze" and "Fetisch."

47. Ibid., 5.

48. Ibid., 7.

negotiations between the inhabitants of the hut and the travelers entail such an encounter between two systems. The owners' initial refusal to hand over their fetish falters when a "gentleman" in von Eckenbrecher's party holds up a "glittering" ten-mark coin. The "craving" in the Africans' eyes matches the groups' desire to possess the fetish. Gold, von Eckenbrecher concludes disdainfully, is the most powerful of all fetishes. She assumes that the shimmering of the coin rather than its monetary value attracts the Africans, like the "first encounter" between Africans and Europeans, when worthless trinkets sufficed to exchange goods of value. The fact that the group offers "real" money, however, suggests that the African and the European value systems have come to share the same currency.

Only men on both sides engage in the transaction. The native women try to prevent the sale, crying and screaming hysterically and bloodying their bodies on the statue's nails until the fetish is soaked by the women's tears and blood. Their reluctance to relinquish the statue indicates that they retained a closer relationship to an African belief system than their male counterparts. In trying to protect their fetish, the African women do what is expected of their European counterparts as well, namely to defend tradition against change. Von Eckenbrecher identifies with the women, regretting that the deal cannot be called off because of the native men's greed (37–39). The struggle between the inferior African magic—the fetish does not help its owners—and the Europeans' successful persistence occurs along the racial divide as well as gender lines. The narrator's sympathies in this cultural encounter gone awry shift from race to gender. The scene haunted her for a long time, von Eckenbrecher recalls in one of the more compassionate passages of *Afrika*.

Fetishism, according to Sigmund Freud, has its origin in the little boy's insistence that his mother possesses a penis. The fetishized object, such as a shoe or a piece of female underwear, enables the adult fetishist to fantasize something he knows not to exist. If male fetishistic desire is suspended between knowing and not wanting to acknowledge, von Eckenbrecher's narrative desire oscillates between wanting and not wanting to possess the fetish. The exchange of the two fetishes—the wooden statue and the gold coins—results in the breakdown of rational capitalist economy. What was supposed to have been a capitalist transaction between men became an eruption of female resistance beyond the control of the Europeans as well as the African men.

The trade is tainted by tears, blood, and slime. After the acquisition of the statue the travelers, perhaps instinctively, search for a way to cleanse themselves. To that purpose, they inspect and immediately reject the villagers' water source, a "disgusting hole" that is both a source of drinking water and a laundry tub (38). The demarcation between male and female, white and black, health and pathology, self and Other, this episode shows, is unstable and permeable. As befits the treatment of a fetish, the returning travelers place their bounty in the center of the ship's dining hall and celebrate its arrival with champagne. The wooden statue resists its transformation into a "rational" commodity and has the power to turn those who desired to possess it into fetishists who dance around their golden calf. A "quantity of negative value . . . ultimately enables fetishism to undermine monolithic belief structures from Christianity and Enlightenment philosophy to the 'rational' laws of capitalist exchange," Emily Apter writes in her study of fetishism in turn-of-the-century French culture.[49] Margarethe von Eckenbrecher's encounter in the hut between the sand dunes confirms fetishism's ability to undermine the laws of capitalist exchange and its power to destabilize the subject position of the colonizer. The journey functions to transform the autobiographer into a colonizer. The fetish-episode interrupts and decenters this identity-in-progress.

German colonial fantasies were about rural life away from the city and its social and moral ills. The selection of suitable women by the colonial societies reflects this ideology of healthy farm life as well as the dream of economic autonomy away from the capitalist exchange mechanisms of the urban centers. Farm life in Africa was the antidote to high capitalism and the changes in class and gender relations it had brought about in Germany. The ideal colonists belonged to the middle class, whose willingness to undertake physical labor on the one hand, and familiarity with high culture on the other, differentiated them from their lower-class counterparts as well as the financial elites. Margarethe von Eckenbrecher, who shared this dream of the middle-class farmer, had to find out that not all Europeans who made their living in a colony were indeed good colonists. In Southwest Africa, German settlers competed not only against the Dutch Boers, reputed to be slovenly and lacking colonizing energy, but also against Germans who ignored the colonial imperative to create a new Germany in Africa.

After they arrived in Swakopmund, von Eckenbrecher and her husband traveled into the north of German Southwest Africa, where they were to spend the next two years, until the war expelled them from their home. Their destination is Okombahe, a small village of about eight hundred African inhabitants and fourteen other Germans, with a Christian mission station, a church, a cemetery, at least one store, and a fortress,

49. Emily Apter, *Feminizing the Fetish: Psychoanalysis and Narrative Obsession in Turn-of-the-Century France* (Ithaca: Cornell University Press, 1991), 5.

where von Eckenbrecher's husband owns property.[50] The couple stop to buy supplies in Karibib, a city founded in 1902 at the northernmost point of the railroad line between the port city of Swakopmund and Windhoek, Southwest Africa's capital. A commercial center that owes its origins to railroad speculation, Karibib attracts a "dubious" white underclass intent on cheating gullible newcomers out of their possessions (56). Karibib has succumbed to urban decadence, its economy set up to enrich the specula- tor and the thief at the settler's expense. The real colonizer's Africa is the rural idyll, where hard work promises economic prosperity and autonomy to the self-sufficient individual. The Karibib episode illustrates the fragility of the farmer's antimodern idyll in a setting that ultimately was not immune to modernity.

Von Eckenbrecher's desire to live the "myth of the white farmer" ren- dered her African experience significantly different from the stories of those colonial women accompanying husbands who were employed in the colonial administration, and decidedly less glamorous and affluent than, say, Karen Blixen's life on her Kenyan coffee plantation. Namibia, according to historian Wolfe Schmokel, was "perhaps the most extreme case of an economically unviable, politically dependent settler agricultural system."[51] A careful reading of von Eckenbrecher's account of her strug- gles reveals that the story of her African farm is not one of unmitigated success. In their two-year stay in Southwest Africa she and her husband did not succeed in buying suitable farmland. The combination of an inefficient government bureaucracy, which she describes in some detail, and the unwillingness of large landowning companies to sell the couple farmable land prevented them from establishing a farm of their own (120). Instead, they cultivated the land allotted to them by "Häuptling Cor- nelius," the leader of the Bergdamara. Local workers performed most of the farm labor. Oversupply of livestock made it difficult to sell cattle profitably nearby, forcing von Eckenbrecher and her husband to under- take long journeys to sell. The autobiographer confirmed to herself and her readers that hard work could yield German-style farms in the Namib desert, but her livelihood depended to a large degree on African labor, trade, and benevolence. "Settler agriculture," in the words of Schmokel, was an "essentially parasitical phenomenon."[52] The ideology of farm life in Africa and the "curious politico-cultural activity" it propelled was the

---

50. Number of Germans from Bley, *South-West Africa,* 86–87 n. 39. Okombahe was founded as a mission station in 1871 by the Rhenish Mission.

51. Wolfe Schmokel, "The Myth of the White Farmer: Commercial Agriculture in Namibia, 1900–1983," *International Journal of African Historical Studies* 18, no. 1 (1985): 93.

52. Ibid., 93–94.

founding narrative of German colonialism.[53] Its antimodern essence is a response to modernization in Germany itself.

"Before I go into the details of life in Okombahe," von Eckenbrecher introduces the second part of her autobiography, "I would like to preface them with a brief description of the peculiarities of the peoples with whom we came in contact there" (72).[54] The colonialist's story depends on the natives with whom she "came in touch," but this presence must be kept separate from the real story. Predictably, von Eckenbrecher "sees" what has been "seen" by many before, her introductory ethnography another version of what J. M. Coetzee describes as the "Discourse of the Cape."[55] European writing about southern Africa, Coetzee found, has recycled the rhetoric of the Hottentot's "idleness, indolence, sloth, laziness, torpor" since it was first developed in fifteenth-century travel accounts.[56] Von Eckenbrecher offers her own derogatory descriptions of physical features, culinary customs, and dress, ridiculing African imitations of European dress while criticizing the absence of "proper" garments. Her observation that women perform all the work while men sit idle as well as her insistence that Africans do not know how to ration their food over the course of a year echoes a century-old tradition of European travel writing about southern Africa.

The preface about the natives, presumably for the benefit of readers unfamiliar with Africa, serves to situate the autobiographer and her fellow farmers in the colonial setting. Von Eckenbrecher's discourse of the cape with its descriptions of Africans and their customs has the rambling quality of gossip. She indiscriminately mixes hearsay with her own experiences, interspersing the stories of other settlers with her own and inserting herself into accounts of events she did not witness, while hiding behind passive constructions in stories she did experience firsthand. The African experience is a collective narrative shared by the white farmer community. "African gossip," writes Susan Horton, assures a "community's cohesion and stasis."[57] Von Eckenbrecher repeatedly describes how she, her husband, and a few white friends sat in their comfortable house around the fireplace, telling the old stories of their German *Heimat* and the new sto-

---

53. Ibid., 94.

54. An anonymous reviewer of von Eckenbrecher's autobiography remarked in his otherwise positive evaluation that she should have omitted these passages altogether. "Eine Frau, die sich in und ausser dem Haus, in friedlicher Arbeit und in Stunden kriegerischer Gefahr so bewährt hat, hat es wahrlich nicht nötig, hin und wieder mit gelehrtem Wissen zu prunken." *Blätter für Volksbibliotheken und Lesehallen* (1907): 33.

55. J. M. Coetzee, *White Writing: On the Culture of Letters in South Africa* (New Haven: Yale University Press, 1988), 16.

56. Ibid., 18.

57. Horton, *Difficult Women, Artful Lives*, 195.

ries of their African home. Narrative confirms the settler's legitimacy in Africa and reaffirms the connection to the homeland. The domestic setting illustrates that Africa is now the home of Germans.

Like most gossip, von Eckenbrecher's is lengthy and contradictory. Her descriptions of the African populations oscillate between the certainty of absolute knowledge ("The main characteristics of the Herero are insolence, cruelty, and laziness") and the impossibility of knowing them ("Little is known about the Ovambos") (77). The natives are both visible ("The Hottentots are generally small, scrawny, and wrinkled") (72) and invisible to the European eye ("When one hunts in the Kalahari and believes oneself all alone in this endless desert, all of a sudden, here and there, a head crops up") (90). The native spoils the settler's "romance" with the land and places the observer in the position of the observed.[58] Much of von Eckenbrecher's ethnography is an attempt to re-create a southwest Africa before the "first contact" between Europeans and Africans occurred and to portray the natives in their "natural" state. More troubling than the encounters in the desert, therefore, are the results of cross-cultural contact between whites and blacks in the settlements where the decadence of the colonial city threatens to encroach upon the pristine quality of the colony's rural areas. "In fact I found that the Herero who lived near the big settlements seemed unnerved" (76).

Contact between the two races who occupy opposite poles in the hierarchy of civilizations does not raise African culture to a higher level; instead, it confronts European culture with a distorting mirror. Clothing is one such example. Von Eckenbrecher remarks that the Herero men childishly flaunt white European suits and their women parade about in elaborate wardrobes that often outshine the settlers' wives. The image of black men in white suits serves von Eckenbrecher to fantasize a sexual encounter between a white-clad male Herero and a "heathen" Herero woman who still follows the native custom of greasing her body with reddish fat. After the tryst, which takes place only in the narrator's imagination, the Herero man has sex written all over his white suit, her "nature" having stained his "culture." The white suit dirtied with red grease reflects the precarious nature of colonialism's civilizing mission. A Herero in a white suit not only will never be the equal of a white man, he also relinquishes his natural connection to the "heathen" Herero woman. Trapped between the loss of his "nature" and the impossibility of achieving "culture," the "unnerved" Herero loses both his nativeness and his masculinity. The fantasy of the "intercultural" sex act is about the breakdown of difference in the contact zone. The stains on the rightful garment of the white settler allow von Eck-

---

58. Friedrichsmeyer, Lennox, and Zantop, *The Imperialist Imagination,* 23.

enbrecher to make visible the illicit nature of sexual intercourse between a white man and a black woman without having to put the possibility into words. The white suit smeared with the "traces of miscegenation" is a metonymic displacement of illicit sex between white men and black women.[59]

The colonial experience, however, fundamentally depends on the contact with the colonized. Von Eckenbrecher concludes her observations of the natives with what she acknowledges to be an often-repeated tale about the most "elusive" of Southwest Africa's inhabitants, the Bushmen. A military officer, von Eckenbrecher's gossip goes, pitched his tent near a Bushman village during a hunting trip in the Kalahari. Refusing to hand out gifts in excess of the customary quantity, he shrugged off the village sorcerer's threat of an impending illness and went to bed. After a few hours of sleep, the officer awoke with a terrible stomachache that neither his own potion, a bottle of cognac, nor the massage administered by his African servant could cure. "As his pains reached their peak," he called the sorcerer, who performed his magic by burning so much incense inside the tent that "one imagined one was suffocating" (92). Von Eckenbrecher, it seems, fears choking on her breath-taking gossip. The feminized medicine man, a "monster" with the thin arms and spindly fingers of the European witch, shrieks hysterically as he dances around the fire and finally delivers the officer from his bellyache. His power, the shaman explains, "extends to the white man" (93). The ceremony leaves the witch doctor "fatigued to the point of exhaustion" and the officer "newly born." "To become a 'colonizing subject' was to be born again," David Trotter has argued, "the same but different; the more hideous the picture, the more authentic the rebirth."[60] To be reborn, the officer, a member of the most manly of professions, had to relinquish his white male superiority. As this story circulates among the colony's settler community, promise of rebirth extends to all its members.

Von Eckenbrecher's prefatory gossip has a universal quality but includes few personal responses to her African environment. The female colonizer can recount the stories that bind, but she cannot undergo a symbolic rebirth for the entire community. She therefore introduces herself as a colonial subject who negotiates her autobiographical rebirth through her daily struggles as a homemaker. The German home in Africa is a colonial fantasy, to be sure, but is one that von Eckenbrecher can fill with her own content. "Housewives' worries" *(Hausfrauensorgen)* such as von Ecken-

---

59. Young, *Colonial Desire,* 174.
60. Trotter, "Colonial Subjects," 19.

brecher's are central to most women's colonial narratives. But to be a housewife in Africa von Eckenbrecher must reinvent the activities of a German housewife. Detailed descriptions of cooking and baking practices, food preparation and preservation, furniture making and sleeping arrangements, baby care and after-dinner scenes in front of the fire place with her pipe-smoking husband illustrate her perseverance in creating a German-style domesticity under African circumstances. Von Eckenbrecher's efforts, which by far exceed the demands on an ordinary German homemaker, secure her identity as a female colonizer long after the experience has ended.

The housewife's story takes place in the contact zone of the settlement, where von Eckenbrecher interacts with Africans in two capacities: as a supervisor of the black servants in her household and on her farm, and as a provider of medical care, food, and advice. Von Eckenbrecher's household is her private empire in which she creates and enforces the law. In a section on animal husbandry she includes a detailed description of "her" shepherds' practice of allowing an animal to die slowly in the hope of receiving its meat. She prohibits this custom and enforces her law by having the expiring animal slaughtered in her presence and, if she determines its death was deliberate, having the meat fed to the dogs. "Slowly," she reports with satisfaction, "the shepherds got used to the new fashion of the white woman" (130). More important than her victory over the shepherds is that the Africans initiate von Eckenbrecher into her identity as a "white woman." She becomes "real to herself by seeing her reflection in their eyes."[61] The challenges of the colonial household as a female contact zone complete the autobiographer's transformation into a colonial subject.

The "Discourse of the Cape," the endless reiteration of the natives' lack of cleanliness and their reluctance to work, resurfaces in von Eckenbrecher's "housewives' worries." The native servants do not clean properly, they carry "vermin" on their bodies into the house, and they steal whenever they can. She gives her workers the "quintessential colonizing commodity, cloth," but they do not make the use of it she had intended.[62] Like most colonialists, von Eckenbrecher does not shy away from physical punishment. "Every once in a while my riding crop had to arbitrate successfully," she writes, because "the young people simply went too far" (108). On her African farm, she makes and enforces the law.

In the colonial context the traditional female domain of creating and maintaining domestic order takes on new meanings. The white woman's

---

61. Horton, *Difficult Women, Artful Lives,* 195.
62. Pratt, *Imperial Eyes,* 23.

ability to reproduce the domesticity of the homeland and thus to provide for her husband's domestic and sexual needs separates white men from black women. The importance of female domesticity, however, reaches beyond her own family unit, because her efforts help to sustain the unity of the predominantly male white community. Colonial domesticity expands the private sphere of the home toward a more public function. "The lonely bachelors especially enjoyed the comfortable domesticity," von Eckenbrecher confirms, celebrating the success of her domestic enterprise (163). Her minority status as a white woman gives the autobiographer, certainly in her own mind, additional responsibilities for those with whom she has race and class values in common. Hoping to safeguard the future of her race, she deploys her femininity and performs domesticity for "all" white men in the colony, imagining herself to possess the social position and the domestic skills to prevent illicit sex between white men and African women.

"The European imagination," writes Megan Vaughan, "is easily captured by the image of the white doctor in a dark Africa."[63] As a provider of medical care and advice von Eckenbrecher establishes her own network of relationships with the colony's native population. An untrained woman, she appropriates the image and the power of the white male doctor. In her study on German colonial women Marcia Klotz argues that doctoring, an occupation denied to women in turn-of-the-century Germany, was one of the activities von Eckenbrecher could undertake without help or interference from her husband.[64] "I became a rather famous doctor in the area," von Eckenbrecher asserts with confidence. Her patients' veneration is central to the autobiographer's self-image as doctor. "I never went voluntarily or offered my services; instead I let the people come and fetch me" (168). Von Eckenbrecher's successful medical practice depends on her whiteness and her superior potions on the one hand, and the Africans' confidence in her powers on the other. With the help of "quinine, calomel, and opium," she asserts, "one can make rather nice cures" (168).[65] Fever can be cured by "any white" in Africa. An episode of reluctant doctoring illustrates the relationship von Eckenbrecher imagined she had with her patients. She agrees to treat an epileptic child only after a messenger implores her with these words: "Come and let yourself simply be looked at, that will cure the child" (168). The use of direct speech illus-

---

63. Megan Vaughan, *Curing Their Ills: Colonial Power and African Illness* (Stanford, Calif.: Stanford University Press, 1991), 1.

64. Klotz, "Memoirs from a German Colony," 161.

65. Chinin is used to combat fever, and calomel is a laxative; opium, of course, sedates rather than cures a patient. Von Eckenbrecher continued her medical practice in East Africa during her hunting expedition (*Im dichten Pori,* 57, 69).

trates the black man's respect for the white woman doctor; his appeal to the imaginary powers of the narrator's white skin reveals his shrewd understanding of her self-identity. Deeply moved, von Eckenbrecher consents. Even though she modestly dismisses it as "coincidence," the child recovers after three months with the help of the bromine she had prescribed.

Von Eckenbrecher's fame as a doctor is, however, not uncontested among the African population, whose native healers delimit the autobiographer's sphere of influence. She recounts an episode involving a badly burned child. As the story unfolds, a contest ensues between the narrator's medicine, which consists of an "artfully wrapped gauze," and the native woman healer with her ointments and her incense. Suspicious of one another's powers, each doctor destroys the work of her predecessor. The African healer removes the gauze von Eckenbrecher had applied to the child's wounds and replaces it with an ointment made of "rancid butter, cow dung, and a pulverized type of root," while the narrator in turn extinguishes the fire her rival had lit inside the *pontok* with the dying child (171). The child's body becomes the battleground on which the two doctors compete for the loyalties of the native women without whose faith their powers are impotent. The burned child's grandmother confirms von Eckenbrecher's medical might by taking her side against the native healer's: "No, your art is greater than hers, you must help" (170). In the end the child dies, which von Eckenbrecher attributes to the African healer's interference and the "superstition" of the child's relatives.[66] Shortly after the African child's death, the four-year-old daughter of a fellow settler succumbs to an unspecified illness. In this case, von Eckenbrecher is not invited to apply her medical expertise; instead, the white community sends for a male doctor from the neighboring town. The white woman's ability to practice medicine is delimited by African magic as well as by European patriarchy. The child dies before the doctor arrives (175). The autobiographer's grief for this child is perhaps also an expression of remorse over the loss of the young African.

Von Eckenbrecher's attempts at doctoring as well as the charity she bestows on the inhabitants of Okombahe reflects the colonialist conviction that Frantz Fanon has summarized thus: "if it were not for me they would be worse off."[67] Toward the end of 1903, a few months before the uprising, the African population of the village is threatened by starvation. The autobiographer does not ask why the native inhabitants are hit so much harder

---

66. For a more extensive reading of this scene, see Klotz, "Memoirs from a German Colony," 161ff.

67. Quoted in Horton, *Difficult Women, Artful Lives,* 163.

by the dry season than the settler community. The drought and the von Eckenbrechers' "sizable profit" (174) gives her ample opportunity to do good: "I myself distributed the food." She describes herself standing at the cauldron, apportioning "sweet porridge" first to the "children, then to the old people, the women, and finally to the men" (175). Together with the food, von Eckenbrecher seeks to impose her notion of order, structure, and social hierarchy on the native population.

Her narrative, by contrast, lacks structure and moves from one topic to the next without transition. Her response to the hunger epidemic is interspersed with the story of the first and only Christmas she celebrated in her African home; domestic worries like the near impossibility of obtaining an appropriate Christmas tree are related side by side with the death of the settler's child and the lack of gratitude on the part of the natives who had received alms and Christmas presents. In her meandering narrative style von Eckenbrecher maps out an autobiographical self in the making. She interweaves the constant threats to the civilization she helps build with the successes she can celebrate in domesticating both the harsh land and its inhabitants.

The Herero war of 1904 was a result of the diverging interests of the colonial companies, the German government, and the settlers.[68] The colonial administration, backed by the German government, aimed to protect the interests of the mining and railroad companies by brokering peace agreements between the rival Herero and Nama. The settlers, by contrast, who were in direct competition with the Herero over land and cattle, demanded more land for their own use and largely disregarded the native policies of the colonial administration. "The settlers, an economic element in the colony that could not be accommodated within the political system established by the authorities, brought the clash between Europeans and Africans to a head."[69] At the beginning of the war, which caught the colonial administration under governor Theodor Leutwein by surprise, over a hundred Europeans, the majority of them German farmers, were killed. The German government sent troops and machinery. Under the leadership of General Lothar von Trotha the Herero were beaten during the decisive battle at Waterberg on August 11, 1904. After the military victory von Trotha issued his infamous order to kill or exile every Herero man, woman, and child. Approximately 80 percent of the Herero population, about sixty thousand people, lost their lives during this genocidal war. Most of the surviving Herero were imprisoned in concentration camps to

---

68. Smith, *The German Colonial Empire,* 60ff.
69. Ibid., 62.

be used as cheap labor. German casualties numbered about two thousand.[70]

A good number of the colonial autobiographies from Southwest Africa narrate women's experiences during this war, describing the loss of property and, in some cases, the death of a husband. Many settler's wives had to flee the country under physically and psychologically devastating conditions, often with small children.[71] Their narratives confirmed to the German public women's ability to withstand the ardors of war as well as the necessity of female presence for the reconstruction of what had been lost. Women's memoirs of Wilhelmine Germany's first war, the first military engagement since Bismarck's wars of unification, were eyewitness accounts of white women in distress. The German farmer's wife threatened by African insurgents was a powerful image in the service of the settler ideology and the colonial societies who propagated it in Germany.

Titled "The Uprising," the last third of *Afrika* chronicles von Eckenbrecher's experience of the war and the loss of her African home. As a civilian and a woman, she was not directly involved in any war action. Instead, her narrative merges elements of the female story of war, the "home front" experience, with male narratives that reached her from the "battlefield." The section on the war is von Eckenbrecher's most passionate narrative engagement with Africa. Her pastiche of war stories is a frenzied compilation of gossip, breathlessly recounting strategic movements across the African landscape and trying to achieve linguistic mastery over the forbidding space of the Namib desert and the hostile Herero warriors that populate it. The intense engagement with territory, the attempts to overcome the resistance of the colonial space, and the appreciation of its beauty are vital to the unfolding of the colonizer's subjectivity. "Theories of spatiality," according to John Noyes, are "explanatory models for the relations between subjectivity and the world."[72] Von Eckenbrecher's autobiographical engagement with colonial space is most concentrated in her rendition of the war; her colonial subjectivity culminates in her female war stories and her ability to control the flow of language across space.

In a detailed, almost day-to-day account, von Eckenbrecher covers events between January and early March 1904, the beginning of the uprising and her departure for Germany. Around the middle of January 1904, she was forced to abandon her house. She spent the next three weeks in the

---

70. On the Herero war see Horst Drechsler, *"Let Us Die Fighting": The Struggle of the Herero and Nama against German Imperialism (1884–1915)* (London: Zed Press, 1980); also Bley, *South-West Africa,* 150–52; Smith, *The German Colonial Empire,* 64–65.

71. For instance Sonnenberg, *Waterberg;* for an overview see Wildenthal, "Colonizers and Citizens," 155–66.

72. Noyes, *Colonial Space,* 11.

small military station of her village, Okombahe. An attack during this time would have been fatal, according to the autobiographer's estimate, because the seven armed men stationed in Okombahe could not have defended the fort (198). During the second week of February, a larger contingent of troops under the leadership of Colonel Viktor Franke reached Okombahe and the next day evacuated von Eckenbrecher and her son to Omaruru, a village with a larger military station about seventy kilometers to the east. Von Eckenbrecher spent the next two weeks in Omaruru waiting for safe passage to the coastal city of Swakopmund. She traveled by ox-cart under military protection to Karibib and by train to Swakopmund. On March 7 she boarded a ship and left for Germany with her small son, leaving behind her husband.

Survival in a foreign landscape depends on the colonizer's ability to decipher and interpret it. Von Eckenbrecher narrates colonial war as a semiotic war in which she must rely on her ability to correctly read its signs. The war is foreshadowed in a sequence of cryptic remarks made by the narrator's African acquaintances and servants. Asked to explain why he inquired when von Eckenbrecher's husband intended to send his wife back to Germany, the Herero chief's son, Justus Hongera, elaborates: "Africa is not suitable for her. It is a country for men who love the war . . . you can stay . . . but if you love your wife, send her away" (184). Using the language of romantic love and patriarchy, von Eckenbrecher's Herero not only predicts war but also excludes the "white woman" from a conflict between the men of the two races. Her husband, however, claims to be at a loss over "what to make of it." Von Eckenbrecher overhears the washerwoman's song about the "poor whites" who will "perish in this country" only to dismiss it as equally incomprehensible. The white community's initial inability to understand the semantic precursors of war conveys a sense of security in the absence of any feelings of "wrongdoing" on its part. But von Eckenbrecher's African interlocutors perceive the impending uprising as a "race war" that will pit black against white in an existential battle. "You whites should not think that you are safe here in the land of the blacks," she quotes a tribal leader (184). While it is not clear to what degree this reflects the opinions of the Africans, von Eckenbrecher and many other women memoirists of the war were convinced that race rather than economics was the central factor in this conflict.

A change in the colonists' relationships with the Herero, finally, alerts the settlers to the impending danger. The Herero, who used to greet their white visitors "joyfully" in their villages, all of a sudden turned "icy." Only then was the "possibility of an uprising considered" (185). Couriers are dispatched and messages begin to circulate, entangling colonizers and colonized in an intricate network of communication and interpretation across the colonial space.

The military station in Okombahe, von Eckenbrecher's temporary home after she is forced to abandon her house, becomes the hub from which messages are sent and received. From this position of relative safety her activities radiate out into the dangerous desert environment, situating the autobiographer in the center of a constant flow of messages across enemy territories. People and horses, clothes and ammunition, hidden letters and false reports move across the landscape. Von Eckenbrecher deploys messengers with letters and ammunition to warn and arm fellow white settlers; she sends clothes and letters to her husband; she receives communications whose accuracy she must establish. She dismisses news of her husband's death: "The matter didn't seem quite credible to me" (192). Rumors about rumors fly wildly across the landscape: "There was hearsay about large gatherings, secret messages, and constant interchange between the places" (186). Spies are dispatched and enemy agents captured and tortured until they divulge information (216, 221). An African seer throws his granite dice to predict the settlers' fate. Von Eckenbrecher dismisses his powers as nonsense, but she hastens to include what she—and the reader—want to hear: "Were we going to die? No, not anymore," the three stones divined assuringly (220). Relief finally comes in the form of a message. A newspaper that reaches the group by coincidence informs the defenders of the Okombahe military station that fresh troops have arrived from Germany (218). Even before the troops actually get there, the settlers celebrate the end of the siege by hoisting the German flag on the roof. The power of the message surpasses the implementation of its content.

Exotic place-names—Otjimpane, Okarundu, Kawab—draw a linguistic map of the colonial space across which messages and people move. While most of von Eckenbrecher's readers would not have been able to correlate her maps with images of familiar places, they create order in the chaos of war and suggest narrative control over the territory. "Writing and map making," John Noyes contends, "are complex interplays between [the] dual tendency inherent in all knowledge—to inform and to disperse, to systematize relationships, and to chart the breakdown of this systematization."[73] Von Eckenbrecher's messages fuse mapmaking and writing in a final attempt to appropriate the colonial space she is about to lose.

The interpretation of statements and the systematization of relationships reach the most important stage with the war diplomacy that von Eckenbrecher initiates to determine the loyalty of the different tribal

---

73. Ibid., 285.

groups she has discussed in her ethnographic preface to her farm life. She quotes at length an interview she conducted with "Kapitän Cornelius," the leader of the Bergdamara. Unlike in previous conversations, the missionary is called upon to translate the dialogue, "so there wouldn't be any misunderstanding" (194). Once the fact of an uprising has been established, von Eckenbrecher cannot afford not to understand.

> "Are you inclined to side with the whites?"
> "Yes, I will try to protect them."
> "Are you thinking of making common cause with the Herero?"
> "No."
> "Which reasons keep you on the side of the Germans?"
> "I and my kaffirs, we remember the slave services we had to perform for the Herero. . . ."
> "Do you think, then, that the Germans will reward you for your loyalty?"
> "I do not know, but they are the masters and they will punish us if we defect." (194)

This conversation provides the model for communication between German questioners and African respondents. The words of the African confirm the Germans as the masters and the preferred rulers. In contrast to the Herero, the instigators of the uprising, the Bergdamara are the ideal natives who accept German rule as the more enlightened rule. Von Eckenbrecher considers her politics of divide-and-conquer a crucial contribution to the war effort. "Thanks to our diplomacy we succeeded in keeping the tribe of the mountain kaffirs permanently government-friendly" (219).[74] The autobiographer enjoys the highest degree of agency during the war, making decisions on her own, saving lives with her foresight, and insisting that her strategic plans be carried out against the opinions of the men in her group. Faced with the loss of her home and the temporary absence of her husband, von Eckenbrecher leaves behind the role of housewife; her war narrative suggests that what she really wanted in Africa was this freedom.

The threat of rape turns the "white woman" into the most sensational and a highly symbolic victim of colonial war. The image of the sexually violated white female body testifies to the failure of white colonial rule. In her analysis of the rhetoric of rape in colonial India, Jenny Sharpe cautions us not to assume that the image of the dark-skinned man raping a

---

74. Bley confirms that the Bergdamara indeed remained neutral, but he stresses that this was not as inevitable as von Eckenbrecher describes it (*South-West Africa,* 93).

white woman is an a priori element of all narratives of native rebellion. Reversing the causal chain of the argument, Sharpe suggests that the "crisis in British authority is managed through the circulation of the violated bodies of English women as a sign for the violation of colonialism."[75] Stories of rape, Sharpe argues, are circulated during times of instability to illustrate the crisis of colonial rule itself. German colonial literature has not brought forth "stories of rape" such as E. M. Forster's *Passage to India* or Paul Scott's *The Jewel in the Crown*. But newspapers reported on German women raped and "butchered" by Herero men and images of violated female bodies were used repeatedly in the debates in the Reichstag.[76]

Margarethe von Eckenbrecher's autobiography does not include an actual rape scene, but the text alludes to rape of white women by African men. The spinster on the boat that carried von Eckenbrecher from Hamburg to Swakopmund became one of the first victims of the uprising, "murdered in the lowest, most brutal fashion" (9). At the very beginning of the autobiography, this hint at rape foreshadows the impending crisis of German colonialism. The victim, an aging woman who travels to the colony to find a husband, plays no further role in the narrative. Her brief appearance, however, evokes the crisis of German colonial domination in Africa. Toward the end of the autobiography, von Eckenbrecher returns to the issue of rape in a scene involving herself and two Herero men with their servants. The incident happens on January 13 around noon. The precise date underscores its importance and veracity, as it coincides with the beginning of the uprising on January 12. Geert Afrika, the spokesman for the group of six Africans, follows von Eckenbrecher into her house, pretending to want to trade with her. Because trade between settlers and Africans is common, the "unsuspecting" narrator's innocence only emphasizes the Africans' cunning. Von Eckenbrecher, conducting business as usual, clings to the notion that German colonial rule and her own position as a white woman cannot be challenged. Once inside the house, Geert Afrika asks her opinion about the war. She answers truthfully that she thought it foolish because the "white man" was sure to punish the African insurgents. At Geert Afrika's signal, the servants block the doors, trapping the autobiographer inside her house. "Now comes the real conversation about the war, that you will see!" (188). In the absence of the white man whose disciplinary power the narrator had just invoked, the "real" conversation takes place between the white woman and the black

---

75. Jenny Sharpe, *Allegories of Empire: The Figure of Woman in the Colonial Text* (Minneapolis: University of Minnesota Press, 1993), 4.

76. According to Drechsler only three white women and not a single child were killed by the Herero (*Let Us Die Fighting,* 150). For an analysis of the rhetoric of Herero brutality in the Reichstag debates see Smith, "Talk of Genocide," 113.

man. Each other's opposite in terms of race and gender, von Eckenbrecher and Geert Africa symbolize the colonial war: If she is raped, the act is also a transgression against Germany's colonial enterprise. If not, the autobiographer has confirmed the legitimacy of German women in the colonies.

Out of all the conversations that circulate through von Eckenbrecher's war, this is one she refuses to have. "You come to trade with me and do not know how to treat the white woman? Make way, you scoundrel!" (188). She bursts past the men blocking the door, catching them by surprise, and escapes into the open. Her husband, she surmises, would have been killed under the same circumstances. When her evocation of the white man's punishment fails to deter the African men, she takes the power by reminding him, herself, and her reader, of her status as "the white woman." Von Eckenbrecher does not speculate which course the "real" conversation between Geert Afrika, the quintessential African man, and herself might haven taken. She acknowledges, however, that she was prepared for a blow with a *kirri,* a blunt, phallic-shaped weapon. While she is spared, her narrative suggests that she was, in Jenny Sharpe's term, "rapable."[77] Acknowledging that there were "other women who had fared much much worse than I had," the narrator reminds the reader of the white woman's fate in a "race war."[78]

The progression from colonial self-confidence—the narrator is unsuspecting—to colonialism under duress—a white woman trapped by six black men—is condensed into one page. The outcome, however, allows her to offer to the female reader a "gift" of identification with her whiteness.[79] "But in my case they must have felt at least some inhibition, and they thought better of carrying out their plan" (189). Colonial rhetoric of rape is a "discourse of power capable of coding anticolonial struggle as the violation of white women."[80] Even more significant than her successful escape from potential rape is von Eckenbrecher's refusal to become a symbol in the male-dominated rhetoric of colonial rule. The colonial hierarchy is reinstated as soon as she bursts out of her house. The loyal Bergdamara outside, she is certain, offer her protection against Geert Africa and his fellow Hereros. In the end, von Eckenbrecher reestablishes a colonial condition that rules out the possibility of rape based on her own relationship with the loyal natives in the absence of white men. The white woman, whose part she performs here so successfully, possesses colonizing power of her own.

Margarethe von Eckenbrecher defined herself as a settler's wife who

---

77. Sharpe, *Allegories of Empire,* 74.
78. Ibid., 240.
79. Klotz, "Memoirs from a German Colony," 159.
80. Sharpe, *Allegories of Empire,* 130.

contributed her physical labor as well as her reproductive capabilities to the creation of Germanness in a setting defined by racial, cultural, geographical, and climatic otherness. She was careful not to subsume her own story to her husband's, attributing her victories over adverse circumstances and resistant Africans to her identity as a white woman. Von Eckenbrecher did not achieve psychological depth in her memoir. Instead, she tried to determine the meanings and the possibilities of her own position as "white woman" by playing off race and gender against one another. She possessed the highest degree of agency in the absence of white men and experienced herself at her most powerful vis-à-vis black men. Black women appeared as rival healers in her narrative or as inadequate housekeepers, and white women play hardly any role at all. The destruction of her colonial life by the war allowed von Eckenbrecher to claim agency beyond the role of the German housewife in Africa. In those moments of disruption she comes closest to fulfilling her fantasies of colonial power.

Both Margarethe von Eckenbrecher and Nahida Lazarus created conservative utopias outside of German majority culture as they searched for alternatives to a society they found lacking. Both of them responded to the changing roles of women in a culture that looked to "woman" as it assessed its health or pathology. Their quests sent them in very different directions. In leaving the environment into which they were born they transported fundamental components of German self-definition into their chosen cultures and attempted to rework these ideas into viable identities. Lazarus held fast to her belief in German high culture, a notion that von Eckenbrecher shared, while von Eckenbrecher confirmed her views on German racial supremacy, an attitude that Lazarus rejected. Both of them sensed that their elected groups were not immune to the ills of modernity and accepted the idea that women had considerable responsibility in defending these utopias. The blend of conservatism and progressiveness they offered in their autobiographies reflects the ambiguities inherent in their self-image as women in the modern age. It is no coincidence that they reserved the autobiographical "I" for the exceptional moments in their memoirs in which they most closely approximated the identity they desired for themselves.

[Handwritten annotations:]

this feels more like history than autobiography
interesting account of Ger women in SW Africa
but autobiography is almost unproblematically
equated w/ historical fact

more, perhaps, on whole phenomenon of
the colonial project: they (Germans) as the
other — but not accepting that role — no
sense of the pleasure of the traveler — just
the re-creation of Germany in Africa
also more on class question ??

CHAPTER 3

From Suffering to Salvation: Adelheid Popp's *Autobiography of a Working Woman*

"One of the most effective means of illustrating certain social developments is the life stories of individual personalities who embody these developments in a particularly powerful and decisive fashion," Marxist literary critic Karl Kautsky maintained in his review of the anonymous *Die Jugendgeschichte einer Arbeiterin, von ihr selbst erzählt.*[1] The slim volume before him, which chronicled the impoverished youth of a weaver's daughter and her gradual rise within Austrian Social Democracy, did just that: it depicted the socioeconomic struggle of the working class through the life story of an outstanding individual. The unnamed autobiographer so highly praised was the Austrian Social Democratic leader Adelheid Popp (1869–1939). Her *Working Woman* was so successful that a second printing became necessary within the first year of its publication; by 1922, the fourth edition appeared on the German market and translations appeared in several European countries as well as the United States. Contemporaries could not recommend the book "warmly enough,"[2] and the modern reception continues to promote it as a "timely provocation" even today.[3]

---

1. Karl Kautsky, "Der Werdegang einer kämpfenden Proletarierin," *Die Neue Zeit* 27, no. 2 (1909): 314. Popp's autobiography was first published as *Die Jugendgeschichte einer Arbeiterin, von ihr selbst erzählt: Mit einführenden Worten von August Bebel* (Munich: Reinhardt, 1909). Popp's autobiography was republished in 1983 as *Jugend einer Arbeiterin* (Bonn: Dietz). Unless indicated otherwise, all references in this chapter are to the English edition, *The Autobiography of a Working Woman*, trans. E. C. Harvey (1913; reprint, Westport, Conn.: Hyperion, 1983). Subsequent references are given in the text.

2. Julius Deutsch, quoted in Michael Vogtmeier, *Die proletarische Autobiographie, 1903–1914* (Frankfurt am Main: Lang, 1984), 234.

3. Hans J. Schütz, introduction to Popp, *Jugend einer Arbeiterin*, 13.

Endorsed by its Marxist reviewers, Popp's life story became a paradigmatic working-class autobiography.

Adelheid Popp's contemporaries experienced the social developments whose documentation Kautsky saluted in manifold ways. For Popp's middle-class counterparts Nahida Lazarus and Margarethe von Eckenbrecher modernization signified loss of tradition and sent the autobiographers searching for ways to revive social structures of an imagined past. Popp, by contrast, embraced the idea of change as a political agenda and interpreted her working-class childhood with an eye toward a socialist society of the future. "Class formation is one of the most important markers of the economic and social transformation of nineteenth-century Europe, of the dissolution of the feudal state society and the rise of a modern, industrial urban society," Kathleen Canning has argued.[4] Popp's narrative records and contributes to this process of modernization. Its declared intention is to further the formation of the working class as a political unit and to integrate women workers into Social Democracy. It is therefore also about gender and about how the two categories should relate to one another. Popp's understanding of class is determined by her experience of family, femininity, and sexuality. She feared the sexualized atmosphere among female factory workers, but she also insisted that women's presence in the public did not need to violate moral codes. The anxieties of turn-of-the-century culture are felt in Popp's autobiography as well. Her investment in the modernization process through "class" made her see progress where others experienced loss.

By the time Popp's *Working Woman* came out in 1909, life stories from members of the lower classes had emerged as a genre that enjoyed widespread popularity among readers who did not necessarily share the experiences related in these texts.[5] Autobiographies of class-conscious workers appeared side by side with reports of middle-class reformers who had worked in factories for a certain period of time, memoirs of maid servants, and life stories of prostitutes. Despite their differences, these narratives were often reviewed in comparison to one another because they were thought to shed light on burning issues of the time and to document nec-

---

4. Kathleen Canning, "Gender and the Politics of Class Formation: Rethinking German Labor History," in Eley, *Society, Culture, and State,* 105.

5. For a discussion of audience see Mary Jo Maynes, *Taking the Hard Road: Life Course in French and German Workers' Autobiographies in the Era of Industrialization* (Chapel Hill: University of North Carolina Press, 1995), 50–53. Vogtmeier, *Die Proletarische Autobiographie,* lists more than eighty lower-class autobiographies published between 1843 and 1929. The majority of these texts came out between 1900 and 1914.

Fig. 3. Adelheid Popp. (Courtesy of Bildarchiv der Österreichischen National-bibliothek, Vienna.)

essary social reform.[6] Critics across the ideological spectrum debated whether such autobiographies should appear at all, who was qualified to write them, who should publish them, who should read them and which purpose they should serve.

The majority of working-class autobiographies were brought out by middle-class publishers who considered them profitable investments because they catered to the desire of bourgeois audiences to read about "foreign" cultures. August Bebel, for instance, endorsed the anonymous first edition of Popp's *Working Woman* with an introduction that speaks to the sense of foreignness the upper classes harbored for the lower classes. He agreed with a bourgeois newspaper's contention that the reading public knows more about the "half savage African tribes" than about the lower classes in their own countries. Class was permeated by images of race and sexuality, as this construction of the worker as Europe's exotic other suggests. Sexuality, in particular the issue of prostitution and its relation to class, played a central role in the debates about lower-class autobiographies and the cultural work they could be expected to do. Standards of moral as well as literary decency were at stake, as some welcomed these narratives as culture for the masses while others condemned them as mass literature. Bourgeois and Marxist critics alike considered lower-class autobiographies an important factor in the politics of class formation and the interpretation of social change.

The connection between descriptions of workers' lives and the formation of class occupied critics ever since the first workers' autobiographies came out in the 1890s. Socialist cultural theorists such as Kautsky and Franz Mehring hailed personal accounts of working-class life as harbingers of a distinct socialist literature with a readership and a literary practice of its own.[7] In their efforts to define and promote working-class culture, Kautsky and Mehring praised Popp's ninety-three-page narrative as a paradigm of class-conscious writing.[8] The working-class autobiography for Kautsky functions as an instrument of political agitation that generates class solidarity through identification. Contrasting Popp's narration

---

6. On autobiographies of maidservants and waitresses see Eda Sagarra, "Dienstboten-autobiographien der Jahrhundertwende," in Heuser, *Autobiographien von Frauen,* 318–29. Sagarra shows that these memoirs appealed to readers across class lines.

7. Members of the Social Democratic Party spent one and a half days discussing this issue during the Gotha convention of 1896. The worker's autobiography played a role in the so-called naturalism debate in which Marxists like Mehring criticized the works of naturalist artists such as Arno Holtz and others as decadent and averse to social change.

8. The majority of Social Democratic newspapers and magazines welcomed Popp's autobiography as an important tool in their political struggle. See Vogtmeier, *Die Proletarische Autobiographie,* 234–39; for a bibliography of review articles, see 365–66.

of a "proletarian ascent" with the "poor people's prose" *(Armeleutedich-tung)* of naturalism, Kautsky rejects the lengthy descriptions of misery devoid of revolutionary optimism that he considered characteristic of exoticizing renditions of lower-class life for a bourgeois audience.[9] Kautsky concluded his review of Popp's autobiography:

> Its revolutionary ending in particular gives this story of a proletarian youth its distinct value. It is useful and uplifting to read not only for adolescents but also for old people, not only for women but also for men.[10]

In his appraisal of Popp's narrative, Kautsky stressed the importance of a revolutionary agenda in forming a group of people of diverse ages and different genders into a coherent class. The working class, he suggested, is united not simply by the economic conditions depicted by "bourgeois naturalism," but by the determination to implement change. Incidentally, the identity of the anonymous author of *Working Woman* was known to both reviewers, and they disclosed her proper name. With their indiscretion, Kautsky and Mehring redesignated an "Anonymous Life" into the model autobiography of a functionary of the Austrian Social Democratic Party.[11]

In his critique of Wenzel Holek's 1909 autobiography *Lebensgang eines deutsch-tschechischen Handarbeiters* (Life of a German-Czech manual laborer), also published in *Die neue Zeit,* Mehring favorably contrasted Popp's text with Holek's. Mehring emphasized that the manageable length and the affordable price of Popp's text met the needs of a working-class audience, whereas Holek's longer and more expensive work catered to a nonproletarian readership.

> In other words, the memoirs of comrade Popp will make their way into the working class, the memoirs of Holek will not. This is a book for the bourgeoisie, and this is, then, what we have to criticize about it; or, to be more precise, about its literary presentation.[12]

With his critique of Holek's memoir Mehring also attacked Paul Göhre, a former Protestant minister and Social Democratic member of parliament who had published and prefaced the narrative. Göhre, author

---

9. Kautsky, "Werdegang einer kämpfenden Proletarierin," 315, 314.

10. Ibid., 316.

11. *Jugendgeschichte einer Arbeiterin* appeared in Ernst Reinhardt's series Lebensschicksale in Selbstschilderungen Ungenannter.

12. Franz Mehring, "Bücherschau," *Die Neue Zeit* 27, no. 2 (1909): 763.

of *Drei Monate als Fabrikarbeiter und Handwerksbursche* (Three months as a factory worker and journeyman [1891]) and thus himself a working-class autobiographer of sorts, hoped to justify the demand for social justice with reference to Christian values.[13] In his earlier publications of Carl Fischer's *Reminiscences and Memories of a Worker* and Moritz Bromme's *Life Story of a Modern Factory Worker* Göhre had initiated a literary tradition with humanitarian intentions directed mainly at a sympathetic bourgeois audience. Mehring denounced Göhre's editorship for his choice of authors, who had either never become outspoken socialists or whose involvement in the socialist movement Göhre de-emphasized, according to Mehring's verdict, in order to make these narratives palatable to a middle-class readership. Contesting what they perceived as the depoliticizing tendency of bourgeois literary practice, both Mehring and Kautsky read literature through the lens of class, aiming to anchor its critical and liberating potential within the project of an independent socialist culture. Consequentially, in order to develop an interpretative framework that affirmed the primacy of class in the construction of a socialist identity, they had to reject naturalism's ostentatious depictions of poverty as much as Göhre's appeals to middle-class sympathies. Mehring concluded his article by saying that "workers who wish to publish their life story are well advised to follow the example of Adelheid Popp and not the tutelage of Göhre."[14] From its inception, the working-class autobiography was an embattled territory between the two classes whose struggle their authors experienced and described.

Mehring's critical response to Paul Göhre's activities as a publisher of workers' autobiographies hints at the conflict over a literary genre and its often ambiguous relationship to the writer's and reader's class identity.[15] Literary depictions and theatrical stagings of working-class suffering, Marxist critics knew, could be produced and consumed without transforming the reading and viewing public into class-consciousness workers. The instrumentalization of literature for the political project of socialism, as proposed by Kautsky and Mehring, shaped the reception of working-class autobiographies in both East and West Germany into the 1980s. In

---

13. Others followed Göhre's example. The reformer Minna Wettstein-Adelt published a similarly titled report *3½ Monate Fabrikarbeiterin* (Berlin: Leiser, 1893).

14. Mehring, "Bücherschau," 764.

15. In her study of early working-class autobiographies, *Frühe deutsche Arbeiterautobiographie* (Berlin: Akademie Verlag, 1973), GDR scholar Ursula Münchow sees the contribution of Göhre, who after all was a member of the Social Democratic Party, in a more positive light than Mehring (25). West Berlin Germanist Bernd Neumann, in "Nachwort zu Brommes Lebensgeschichte," his afterword to the reprint of Bromme's narrative, stresses the vital importance of Göhre's role, arguing that bourgeois interest in working-class life descriptions created the market for these texts in the first place (370).

the introduction to his 1974 anthology *Proletarische Lebensläufe* Wolfgang Emmerich observes that Nazi fascism and the political conservatism of the Federal Republic have obscured the literary tradition of the working-class.[16] For Emmerich, the difference between bourgeois and working-class autobiographies lies in the writer's relationship to the self that is mediated by his or her class. A worker's self-identity is by political necessity collective rather than individualistic. The "best autobiographies of class-conscious workers" fulfill a political function, working toward the constitution of working-class culture as a "second culture" that is substantially different from bourgeois culture. He acknowledges, however, that not all workers' autobiographies accurately reflect the point of view of their class.[17] In a more recent contribution to the discussion of working-class autobiographies, the American historian Mary Jo Maynes revisits the question of class identity and points out that workers who wrote autobiographies often left the working class for the middle class. "Class ambiguity," she argues, "is, in fact, typical of worker autobiographers," referring to the writers' occupational status rather than their political opinions.[18] The working-class autobiographer's self-identity not only reflects the writer's economic "base" in multiple ways, but illustrates the multiple meanings of "class."

The traditional Marxist focus on class-consciousness relegates questions of gender to a status of secondary contradiction. In her 1966 collection *Aus dem Schaffen früher sozialistischer Schriftstellerinnen* GDR literary critic Cäcilia Friedrich explicitly rejects feminist appropriations of her collection, situating Popp's and other female working-class autobiographies within a materialist tradition of socialist thinking and creative writing.[19] The primacy of class as an evaluative tool still characterizes later works that focus exclusively on women's autobiographies, such as Richard Klucsarits and Friedrich Kürbisch's 1981 anthology *Arbeiterinnen kämpfen um ihr Recht*. Making the argument that women's autobiographies are particularly instructive illustrations of class struggle, the editors look to female gender identity in support of their interest in the autobiographers' class consciousness.[20]

16. Wolfgang Emmerich, ed., *Proletarische Lebensläufe: Autobiographische Dokumente zur Entstehung der Zweiten Kultur in Deutschland*, vol. 1, *Anfänge bis 1914* (Reinbek bei Hamburg: Rowohlt, 1974).

17. Ibid., 26.

18. Maynes, *Taking the Hard Road*, 4.

19. Cäcilia Friedrich, ed., *Aus dem Schaffen früher sozialistischer Schriftstellerinnen* (Berlin: Akademie-Verlag, 1966), xi.

20. Richard Klucsarits and Friedrich G. Kürbisch, *Arbeiterinnen kämpfen um ihr Recht: Autobiographische Texte rechtloser und entrechteter 'Frauenspersonen' in Deutschland, Österreich und der Schweiz des 19. und 20. Jahrhunderts* (Wuppertal: Hammer, 1975), 239.

The focus on class as a monolithic and all-subsuming entity obscures the view of gender difference and sexuality, blocking out their meanings in the writers' lives. Since the mid-1980s, American feminist critics have begun to shift emphasis from the primacy of class to readings that explore the interplay between class and female gender identity and the ways in which lower-class women have put these conjunctions into writing.[21] Katherine Goodman looked at the models of self-identity available to these writers and found that female working-class autobiographers negotiated their identity through the generic paradigms and traditions that define the subject as male.[22] Here gender rather than class becomes the oppressive category that forces women to adapt their story to a male plot whose lines they can never quite match. A more provocative challenge to "class" as a rigidly defined category is Carolyn Steedman's *Landscape for a Good Woman.* In this autobiographical account Steedman takes a "defiant pleasure" in subverting the master narrative of the class-conscious worker by telling the story of her mother's "envy" for the material things that life withheld from her.[23] For Steedman, her mother's "false" consciousness is not a failure but the lever with which she pries open the category of class to achieve psychological depth in working-class life and to make room for a broader range of working-class experience.

The story of the deprived working-class life and the subject's rise to class-consciousness as the master narrative that Marxist theorists adopted at the expense of other plots emerged when Popp's *Working Woman* was first published. Steedman, writing about mid-twentieth-century Britain, points out that many working-class childhoods were "simply not bad enough to be worthy of attention" and therefore could not be told.[24] Turn-of-the-century lower-class autobiography, however, was not the monolithic genre Marxist critics wanted it to be. Many of these life stories were products of mass culture and contributed significantly to the "flood" of memoirs that so disturbed the critics of the bourgeois press. The true story of hardship and suffering whose stranglehold Steedman rightfully critiques appealed to readers' emotions across class

---

21. See Goodman, *Dis/Closures;* Juliane Jacobi-Dittrich, "Working-Class Autobiography by Women in Nineteenth Century Germany," in *German Women in the Eighteenth and Nineteenth Centuries: A Social and Literary History,* ed. Ruth-Ellen Joeres (Bloomington: Indiana University Press, 1986); and Mary Jo Maynes, "Childhood Memories, Political Visions, and Working-Class Formation in Imperial Germany, 1871–1914," in Eley, *Society, Culture, and State,* 143–62.

22. Goodman, *Dis/Closures,* iii.

23. Carolyn Kay Steedman, *Landscape for a Good Woman: A Story of Two Lives* (New Brunswick, N.J.: Rutgers University Press, 1986).

24. Ibid., 9.

boundaries. It connected the story of class with the plot of sexuality and gender foreclosed by the Marxist imperative of class formation. The writer's desire to effect social change often stood side by side with the need to earn money and the pleasure of telling a gripping story. Stories of lower-class lives served to demand reform or to illustrate the dangers of modernization.

Perhaps the most notorious and certainly the commercially most successful autobiographical narrative of the early twentieth century was *Tagebuch einer Verlorenen* (Diary of a lost one).[25] Published in 1905, *Diary of a Lost One* is the story of a young prostitute. The 250-page narrative chronicles the protagonist's seduction and pregnancy at the age of fifteen, her subsequent life as a prostitute, and her untimely death of tuberculosis only a few years later. Margarete Böhme, whose name appeared on the title page as the editor, stated in her preface that this diary is no more and no less than an "authentic contribution to a burning social question of our time," referring to prostitution.[26] The majority of reviewers—whose ranks included journalists, psychologists, and Social Democrats—hailed the diary as a document that provided insights into a life "full of deepest tragedy," simultaneously condemning the society that allowed this catastrophe to happen and applauding the undistorted glimpses into the psychology of the prostitute.[27] The protagonist is a victim of circumstances, the scandal is as much society's as her own, and the reader can weep over the young diarist's fate. *Lost One* tells a story of sexuality, class, and social change in the modern world. Its extraordinary success underscores the predominance of these topics in turn-of-the-century culture.

The triumph of *Lost One* triggered a wave of lower-class female autobiographies. In *Mieze Biedenbachs Erlebnisse* (Mieze Biedenbach's adventures [1906]) the waitress Maria Biedenbach recalls how her most recent admirer, a "little journalist," encouraged her to write an autobiography in the style of *Lost One* because, he asserted, "the public has a great deal of

---

25. More than thirty thousand copies were sold in the first four months of publication.

26. Margarete Böhme, *Tagebuch einer Verlorenen: Von einer Toten,* ed. Hanne Kulessa, (Frankfurt am Main: Suhrkamp, 1988), 7. A heated debate ensued about the diary's genuineness. While the majority of critics believed that it was an authentic document, it is more than likely that Böhme wrote rather than edited the volume. For a detailed documentation of Böhme's life and work see Arno Bammé, ed., *Margarete Böhme: Die Erfolgsschriftstellerin aus Husum* (Munich: Profil, 1994); and Vogtmeier, *Die Proletarische Autobiographie,* 130. On the debates about prostitution see Karin J. Jusek, *Auf der Suche nach der Verlorenen: Die Prostitutionsdebatten im Wien der Jahrhundertwende* (Vienna: Löcker, 1994).

27. Franz Diederich, cultural editor of the "Sächsische Arbeiter-Zeitung," quoted in Bammé, *Margarete Böhme,* 135.

interest in this sort of reading, and rightfully so."[28] There can be no doubt that first-person narratives about female sexuality, suffering, and the underside of society were the "sort of reading" that indeed received a great deal of attention, affording readers insights into the illicit goings-on that transpired invisibly in their midst. The waitress, too, had a story to tell that was more exotic than Bebel's African tribes. Prostitutes and maidservants were not the autobiographers that critics like Kautsky and Mehring had in mind because they failed to produce class-conscious subjects. For many readers, these autobiographies put a human face to the crisis of turn-of-the-century culture.

The life story of Adelheid Popp, to be sure, is not a confessional in the vein of *Lost One*. In Popp's autobiography, a political leader and a future member of the Austrian parliament describes her lower-class childhood and adolescence in Vienna and the beginnings of her career as a public speaker and journalist. Yet, with its descriptions of innocent suffering, it was the "sort of reading" in which a broad public took a great deal of interest. Popp's narrative focuses predominantly on class, whereas the confessional memoir tells a story about sexuality, but they share certain features that explain their popular appeal. In both cases the innocent protagonist's suffering is caused by social circumstances rather than individual fault and can thus elicit an emotional response. Margarete Böhme urged the reader of *Lost One* not to view hard luck "with loveless contempt"; similarly, August Bebel stated that he read Popp's *Working Woman* "with deep compassion." The reader's sympathy across and beyond class distinctions was considered an important first step toward social change.

Popp's *Working Woman* was the inaugural volume of Ernst Reinhardt's series *Anonymous Lives in Self-Descriptions*. Subsequent autobiographies in the series included titles such as *Erinnerungen eines Waisenknaben* (Memoirs of an orphan boy [1910]) and *Ich suche meine Mutter* (*I am searching for my mother* [1910]). These emotionally charged titles appealed to the middle-class social reformer rather than the socialist

---

28. Mieze Biedenbach, *Erlebnisse: Erinnerungen einer Kellnerin* (Berlin: Fontane, 1906), quoted in Maynes, *Taking the Hard Road,* 52. Incidentally, "Mieze Biedenbach" was Margarete Böhme's literary invention; see Bammé, *Margarete Böhme,* 739. The authenticity of several lower-class autobiographies has come under scrutiny. Sagarra, "Dienstbotenautobiographien der Jahrhundertwende," argues that Doris Viersbeck's *Erlebnisse eines Hamburger Dienstmädchens* (Munich: Ernst Reinhardt, 1910) provides an authentic insight into the life of a female servant but was most likely written by an author who belonged to the middle class. On the connection between maidservants and prostitution see Karin Walser, *Dienstmädchen: Frauenarbeit und Weiblichkeitsbilder um 1900* (Frankfurt am Main: Neue Kritik, 1985).

revolutionary, their anonymity underscoring their general human perti-
nence. Both titles, moreover, emphasized that the absence of a traditional
family determined the unnamed author's fate. In his introduction to *Memoirs of an Orphan Boy,* Swiss sexologist August Forel (1848–1931) referred
to the spectacular success of Böhme's *Lost One* in his assessment that the
"tragedy of reality" can "arouse our soul in a more healthy fashion than
. . . the unnatural products of fantasy of the usual novelistic trade."[29] Forel
assumed a connection between the reality content of an autobiography,
the emotional response of the reader, and social change. Heinrich
Herkner, writing in the liberal-conservative *Prussian Yearbooks* echoed
this position in his review of workers' autobiographies. In "drastic descriptions of workers' misery," he maintained, "the personal directly touches
the sympathetic human soul. Here all things human, even if they cannot be
grasped in numbers, can be shared. And the imponderables might just be
the most important aspect of all."[30] Arguing from a middle-class perspective, Herkner stressed the universality of human experience, while critics
like Kautsky emphasized the specifics of class. Herkner, whose article
spanned the gamut of workers' autobiographies published by 1910, admits
to having been moved most deeply by the accounts of women like Adelheid Popp. Authentic and stirring reports of suffering, both Forel and
Herkner knew, were effective tools in the fight for social change, the credibility of the narrative determining its success.

The true story makes visible the social conditions that caused the protagonist's suffering and thus hints at possible solutions. In *Mixed Feelings,*
her study on Victorian mass culture, Ann Cvetkovich compares female
suffering in nineteenth-century British sensationalist novels with Karl
Marx's images of the (male) worker's body in pain.[31] *Capital,* she insists,
"is a sensational melodrama, in which the worker is the victim and the capitalist is the villain."[32] To document the realities that produce social violence, Marx sensationalizes its effects on the worker's body and dramatically unveils the social relationships responsible for the worker's
exploitation. Class in the worker's autobiography is as sensational as sex
in the confessional memoir. In *Working Woman,* Popp draws on the narrative techniques of the sensational novel to tell the suffering of her childhood self. In this case, it is the autobiographer's own body that suffers the
violence of child labor and overwork, and the writer herself gradually
uncovers the "mysteries" behind capitalist exploitation. *Working Woman*

---

29. Quoted in Vogtmeier, *Die Proletarische Autobiographie,* 151.
30. Herkner, "Seelenleben und Lebenslauf," 393.
31. Ann Cvetkovich, *Mixed Feelings: Feminism, Mass Culture, and Victorian Sensationalism* (New Brunswick, N.J.: Rutgers University Press, 1992).
32. Ibid., 11.

is a document of working-class suffering whose use of sensationalism as a narrative strategy is as affective as it is effective.

Sensational novels, which counted among the young Popp's favorite reading material, and confessional memoirs both tell stories about bodily and emotional "sensational suffering." Sensational literature shares the stigma of mass culture as a feminized and therefore inferior form of artistic expression.[33] Some feminist scholars have attributed subversive qualities to mass culture,[34] while others, among them Cvetkovich and Rita Felski, agree that mass literature is not by definition subversive, and, moreover, that it does not need to be subversive to merit interpretation. "Rather than either reproducing or heroically resisting a univocal dominant ideology," Felski suggests in *The Gender of Modernity,* "popular fiction can more usefully be read as comprising a variety of ideological strands that cohere to or contradict each other in diverse ways."[35] Though not a work of fiction, Popp's popular autobiography, too, comprises a variety of ideological strands. While the Marxist reception has secured *Working Woman* continuous readership ever since its first publication, it has obscured the text's complicated identity politics. *Working Woman*'s affinity to popular literature is a reflection of Popp's attempts to grapple with turn-of-the-century ideologies of gender and sexuality. In this, she draws on conservative and progressive ideologies. In sensationalist literature Popp found the model that enabled her to narrate her story of class, gender, and sexuality.

Adelheid Popp, born in 1869 as Adelheid Dworschak in Inzersdorf, Austria, was the youngest of five surviving children out of fifteen. Her father, an impoverished weaver, was fettered by the semifeudal home industry system that kept the worker in a position of material and psychological dependency on the patron. He died of cancer when Popp was six years old. In her autobiography, Popp characterizes her father as a physically abusive and emotionally distant alcoholic. Popp's illiterate mother, like the father a native of Czech-speaking Bohemia, supported her family as a washerwoman and street vendor. Economic necessity forced the young Adelheid to leave school at the age of ten, after only three years of formal education, in defiance of the law that decreed compulsory school attendance. She added to her family's income first as a domestic worker, then became a seamstress's apprentice, and at about age fifteen a factory

---

33. Andreas Huyssen, "Mass Culture as Woman: Modernism's Other," in *After the Great Divide,* 50.

34. For instance Janice Radway, *Reading the Romance: Women, Patriarchy, and Popular Literature* (Chapel Hill: University of North Carolina Press, 1985).

35. Felski, *The Gender of Modernity,* 142.

worker. She joined the Social Democratic Party around 1890 and supported the struggle for May 1 as an international workers' holiday. In the same year, she was instrumental in establishing the first Arbeiterinnen-Bildungsverein (Women Workers' Education Association). In 1892 Popp left the factory to become one of the founding editors of the *Arbeiterinnen-Zeitung* (Women workers' newspaper), which grew into the leading paper of the Austrian socialist women's movement.[36] In 1894 she married the Social Democrat and owner of the *Arbeiter-Zeitung* (Workers' newspaper) Julius Popp, with whom she had two children. Her husband died after nine years of marriage. Ideologically, Popp was a supporter of Victor Adler, cofounder of the Second International and revisionist leader of Austrian Social Democracy. In 1918, when women had gained the right to vote in Austria, Popp was elected an executive of the Social Democratic Party and became a member of the Austrian parliament and the Viennese district council. She succeeded Clara Zetkin as chair of the International Women's Committee. Popp died in Vienna in 1939.[37]

Adelheid Popp's realist narrative of less than one hundred pages spans the years from the early 1870s to 1893, recounting the hardships of her childhood and her experiences as a domestic worker, a factory worker, and a public agitator for the socialist movement. As the title indicates, the narrative does not continue beyond the autobiographer's initial successes as a political activist, omitting her role as a leader in Austrian socialism. The text usually referred to as Popp's autobiography is the somewhat expanded third edition of 1910, in which Popp officially disclosed her identity and included an account of her marriage to Julius Popp as well as a more detailed rendition of the relationship with her mother.[38] In 1915 Popp put out a sequel to her autobiography, a small volume named *Erinnerungen aus meinen Kindheits- und Mädchenjahren* (Memories from my

---

36. *Arbeiterinnen-Zeitung* was inspired by *Arbeiter-Zeitung,* which was first published in 1889.

37. This biographical sketch is based on the information provided by Schütz, introduction to *Jugend einer Arbeiterin,* 5–13; Frederiksen, *Die Frauenfrage in Deutschland,* 487–90; and Marie Juchacz, *Sie lebten für eine bessere Welt: Lebensbilder führender Frauen des 19. und 20. Jahrhunderts* (Berlin: Dietz, 1955), 75–80.

38. Between 1909 and 1930 Popp's autobiography went through six editions; starting with the fourth edition it was published by J. H. W. Dietz, the Social Democratic "Parteiverlag." Excerpts of Popp's text are included in several anthologies under various headings, including Friedrich, *Schaffen;* Emmerich, *Proletarische Lebensläufe;* and Klucsarits and Kürbisch, *Arbeiterinnen.* See also Georg Eckert, ed., *Aus den Lebensberichten deutscher Fabrikarbeiter: Zur Sozialgeschichte des ausgehenden 19. Jahrhunderts* (Braunschweig: Limbach, 1953). Passages from Popp's text are included in Alfred Kelly's English-language anthology *The German Worker: Working-Class Autobiographies from the Age of Industrialization* (Berkeley and Los Angeles: University of California Press, 1987).

years of childhood and girlhood).[39] The subtitle *Aus der Agitation und anderes* (Of political agitation and other issues) indicates that Popp intended the twenty-seven short thematic sketches of childhood memories and early political activities to further the political education of the readership rather than provide insights into her development as an individual. With the publication of *Memories* Popp explicitly put her story into the service of her political agenda.

In addition to her autobiographical works, Popp published extensively on issues of women and socialism, insisting on the legitimacy of gender-specific concerns within the general project of class struggle. Three years prior to the *Memories,* in commemoration of twenty years of the Austrian women workers' movement, Popp had edited the *Gedenkbuch* (Memorial book), a collection of autobiographical texts written by the "pioneers" of the movement.[40] In her introductory contribution to the slim volume, Popp refers to the women workers' movement as a collective working to include women in the project of class struggle, and she asserts that women's emancipation does not automatically and without women's active involvement coincide with the emancipation of the working class. In 1929, Popp put out a small pamphlet entitled *Der Weg zur Höhe* (The upward path) in honor of the international women's movement.[41] Again drawing on the narrative technique of using the personal to illustrate the political, Popp inserts her own story as a first-person narrative into a larger account of the women's movement.

In *Working Woman* and *Memories* Popp interprets her personal story through the social and economic marginalization of the working class. Narrating her individual development from a socialist position, Popp anchored her story within the history of the socialist movement and thus endowed it with the legitimacy provided by the discourse of class struggle. With *Memorial Book* and *The Upward Path* she strategically employed autobiography to construct a sense of collective identity among the women in the socialist movement; in the context of class the personal narrative acquires political validity and can then be used to create a female public sphere as an integrated and yet distinct realm within the working-class public sphere. In addition to her work as a journalist, Popp's publications include *Die Arbeiterin im Kampf ums Dasein* (The woman worker

---

39. Adelheid Popp, *Erinnerungen aus meinen Kindheits- und Mädchenjahren: Aus der Agitation und anderes* (Stuttgart: Dietz, 1915).

40. Adelheid Popp, ed., *Gedenkbuch: 20 Jahre österreichische Arbeiterinnenbewegung* (Vienna: Kommissionsverlag der Wiener Volksbuchhandlung, 1912).

41. Adelheid Popp, *Der Weg zur Höhe: Die sozialdemokratische Frauenbewegung Österreichs. Ihr Aufbau, ihre Entwicklung und ihr Aufstieg* (Vienna: Frauenzentralkomitee der Sozialdemokratischen Arbeiterpartei Deutschösterreichs, 1929).

in the struggle for existence), *Mädchenbuch* (Book for girls), *Haussklavin-nen* (Female house slaves), and *Frauenarbeit in der kapitalistischen Gesellschaft* (Women's work in capitalist society), a thirty-page brochure on issues such as prostitution and abortion.[42] In 1895 she served a four-teen-day jail term for her criticism of the institution of marriage in an arti-cle that appeared in the *Women Workers* newspaper. Popp's nonautobio-graphical works illustrate strong commitment to gender-specific aspects of economic exploitation.[43]

Scholars of working-class autobiographies insist that workers' auto-biographies differ fundamentally from bourgeois autobiographies in the self-identities these texts promote.[44] Unlike the individual identity of the bourgeois writer, the argument goes, the identity of the worker is based in the class collective. The topos that one's own story is just another version of the "lot of hundreds of thousands," as Popp writes in the introduction to the fourth edition of *Working Woman,* can be found in almost all work-ing-class texts, often in conjunction with the mention of a mentor to whose encouragement the particular life story owes its existence. In the following section I look at the context and the reception that produced working-class autobiographies as political documents of suffering and salvation. The struggle to claim these texts for one's own side, which accompanies the working-class autobiography from its beginnings, suggests that the life stories of workers with their emotional appeal lend themselves to various readings from a number of ideological and class positions.

The title of Popp's autobiography, which merely identifies the author's class and gender, resembles the title of most other working-class autobi-ographies in its descriptive and deliberately unpoetic language.[45] In her preface to the third edition of *Working Woman,* the first one with her name on the cover, Popp explains why she withheld her proper name on the pre-vious two, despite her friends' pleas to give up her anonymity.

---

42. *Die Arbeiterin im Kampf ums Dasein* (Vienna: Brand & Co., 1911); *Mädchenbuch* (Vienna: Wiener Volksbuchhandlung, 1911); *Haussklavinnen: Ein Beitrag zur Lage der Dienstmädchen* (Vienna: Wiener Volksbuchhandlung, 1912); *Frauenarbeit in der kapitalisti-schen Gesellschaft* (Vienna: Verlag des Frauenzentralkomitees, 1922).

43. For a complete bibliography see Sigrid Schmid-Bortenschlager and Hanna Schnedl-Bubeniček, *Österreichische Schriftstellerinnen, 1880–1938: Eine Bio-Bibliographie* (Stuttgart: Heinz, 1982), 139.

44. For instance, Emmerich, *Proletarische Lebensläufe;* and Klucsarits and Kürbisch, *Arbeiterinnen.*

45. For instance, Fischer, *Denkwürdigkeiten und Erinnerungen;* or Bromme, *Lebens-geschichte eines modernen Fabrikarbeiters.* Most autobiographers include their class back-ground or occupation in their titles.

I did not write the narrative because I esteemed it of some individual importance, but, on the contrary, because I recognised in my lot that of hundreds of thousands of the women and girls of the working class, because I saw great social phenomena at work in what surrounded me and brought me into difficult situations. (13)[46]

The explicitly stated goal of the autobiography lies not in the individual's development but, on the contrary, in the representative validity of her own fate for the collective of women workers. Only after she has come to understand herself as a site upon which "great social phenomena" act does she feel empowered to tell her story. In the opening and closing lines of her preface Popp evokes the name of August Bebel as the "biggest German pioneer of woman's liberation," who had accepted the "responsibility of publishing the story of my youth" (13). Effacing her name and conspicuously elevating Bebel's as the authority on her narrative, Popp inadvertently illustrates the relationship between the workers' and the women's questions. It takes Bebel's individual male identity to legitimize Popp's entry into the public sphere—not as an individual, but as the anonymous representative of an oppressed female collective. In the preface to his own autobiography, *Aus meinem Leben* (My life), by comparison, Bebel constructs the relationship between himself as the writing subject and the public in the opposite way.[47] Where Popp felt it necessary to assert the legitimacy of her project by stressing its collective validity, Bebel can point to his prominent position in the public sphere and conclude that the public has a legitimate right to demand the truth about his life. "If, due to favorable circumstances, one obtained, as I did, an influential position, then the public has a right to learn about the conditions that led to it."[48] Whereas Bebel offers the story of his childhood and youth as the background to his public life, Popp's entire autobiography focuses on the first twenty-two years of her life, before she reaches a position of public visibility. Kay Goodman has rightfully remarked on the "relative lack of external perspective" in *Working Woman* and Popp's unwillingness to elaborate on her own considerable accomplishments as one of the first women leaders of Social Democracy.[49] Popp does not mention her involvement in the founding of the *Arbeiterinnen-Bildungsverein* in 1890 and the women's

---

46. This statement is reproduced on the cover of Emmerich, *Proletarische Lebensläufe*, underneath a photograph of an assembly of workers in a narrow street.

47. August Bebel, *Aus meinem Leben* (Stuttgart: Dietz, 1910–14), trans. as *My Life* (London: Unwin, 1912). Bebel's title evokes Goethe's *Aus meinem Leben. Dichtung und Wahrheit;* see Goodman, *Dis/Closures,* 199.

48. Bebel, *Aus meinem Leben,* 7.

49. Goodman, *Dis/Closures,* 199.

reading club Libertas in 1893, and she downplays her work as editor-in-chief for the *Arbeiterinnen-Zeitung* from 1892 on. Popp's readers praised the revolutionary enthusiasm of their comrade. The autobiographer herself chose to emphasize the story of her suffering and contented herself with merely hinting at her achievements. While August Bebel's story as the father of the socialist women's movement has been told many times, Adelheid Popp's biography has yet to be written.[50]

In the introduction to the fourth edition (1922) Popp reiterates the collective nature of her experience, attributing the incentive to write her life story to Adolf Braun, a prominent Socialist and, together with Victor Adler, founder of the Sozialdemokratische Partei Österrreichs and journalist for the *Arbeiter-Zeitung*. Without Braun's encouragement, she recalls, she would never have dared

to bother the public with my memoirs because I know that around the time when the "story of my youth" took place the fate of the proletarian woman was almost universal. Thousands could tell the same story that I have told as far as suffering and enduring are concerned. I only allowed myself to be convinced that committing my experiences to writing could be helpful because, even though countless women had to suffer like me, only very few found the path to the ascent from a downtrodden and enslaved youth. To show this path and the struggles it commands but also the possibility of victorious success, in my mind, justified the step of talking about myself.[51]

In the 1910 preface Popp had justified the publication of her autobiography with her insight that working-class suffering has its explanation in the "great social phenomena" that cause it. By 1922 she differentiates between herself and the "thousands" of proletarian women who shared her fate, using her own unique "ascent" as a legitimization for bothering the public. Bebel in his introduction and Popp in her prefaces characterize the masses of women workers as a collective bound together by common suffering. Popp acknowledges the support of individual men and addresses a collective of nameless women. What distinguishes Popp from the collective of victims and makes her story singular is the fact that she turned the experience of victimization into a "victorious success." Popp's introductions differ from the body of her autobiographical narrative in

50. For instance, Hermann Wendel, *August Bebel: Eine Lebensskizze* (Berlin: Verlag für Sozialwissenschaft, 1923); Horst Bartel, *August Bebel: Eine Biographie* (Berlin: Dietz, 1962); and Brigitte Seebacher-Brandt, *Bebel: Künder und Kärrner im Kaiserreich* (Berlin: Dietz, 1990).

51. Popp, *Jugend einer Arbeiterin,* 23; my translation.

their intellectual style and a more faithful adherence to the Marxist position on the class collective. *Working Woman* focuses on the suffering individual. In this, Popp follows the model of the sensational novel with its intimate connection between suffering and femininity.

August Bebel's *Women under Socialism* enjoys canonical status in the literature of the proletarian women's movement and therefore deserves a closer look here as the voluminous story of women's oppression that informed Popp's narrative (84).[52] Bebel's book juxtaposes women's suffering in a capitalist society with their potential liberation under socialism. It offers a three-part analysis of the status of women in the past, present, and future, following Marx and Engels's basic premise that the solution to the women's question will follow from the solution to the social question. Bebel's demands include political equality for women, specifically the right to vote; access to education; free choice of marriage partner; and the right to divorce. Like most of his contemporaries, he never questions the family as the basic unit of society and the primary role of women as mothers. With the support of copious statistics and scientific quotations from European and American sources, Bebel voices his demand for women's equality through the contemporary discourses of sexual difference and sexology. Indeed, large sections of *Women under Socialism* read like a history of female sexuality from the past to the present, from classical Greece to India and the North American Indians. For Bebel, all sexual relations outside of egalitarian marriage, and the range of his examples includes the feudal *ius primae noctis,* tribal bride bartering, and prostitution, are weighty indications of women's oppression through the ages and around the world.

Sexual dysfunction, then, is one of the principal manifestations of women's suffering, and Bebel dedicates several chapters to venereal disease, prostitution, abortion, and infanticide. Capitalism, for Bebel, sexualizes the relationship between women's bodies and work regardless of their class status. Denying women the right to regular occupation is as hazardous to the female body as overwork:

> The idle, voluptuous life of many women in the property classes; their refined measures of nervous stimulants . . . incites still more the sexual senses, and naturally leads to excesses.
>
> Among the poor, it is certain exhausting occupations, especially of a sedentary nature, that promotes congestion of blood in the abdominal organs, and promotes sexual excitation. One of the most danger-

---

52. Bebel's *Die Frau und der Sozialismus,* one of the most widely read socialist texts, came out in 1881 and circulated illegally in Germany until the anti-Socialist laws were repealed in 1890.

ous occupations in this direction is connected with the, at present, widely spread sewing machine. . . . Excessive sexual excitement is also promoted by long hours of work in a steady high temperature . . . especially when both sexes work together.[53]

In this passage, Bebel constructs a causal connection between capitalist modes of production and female sexual pathology. Capitalism turns the female body into a sensational site of sexual overstimulation. Female sexual pathology, therefore, yields an effective and sensationalist critique of capitalism. Healthy female sexuality has its place in marriage, Bebel argues, drawing on the work of sexologists like Richard von Krafft-Ebing and Paolo Mantegazza. Quoting the cultural anthropologist Heinrich Ploß, Bebel maintains that women's physical and mental health depends on regular—but regulated—intercourse.[54] His arguments mirror the state's increased efforts in the late nineteenth century to control sexual behavior through family politics and health care systems.[55] Among married couples bound together by the shared responsibility for children, the wife exerted a stabilizing influence on her husband's sexuality; put in its proper place, female sexuality served a controlling function.[56] Women thus appear in multiple and contradictory roles. As victims of individual males and a male-dominated society, they need the protection of a socialist community. As wives and mothers, it is their function to keep male sexuality in check. As sexual beings, they present a potential threat to social discipline if their sexuality remains uncontrolled.

Bebel's progressive social politics and conservative gender politics resurface in Popp's construction of self as a socialist and woman as well as in her descriptions of other women workers. Popp's narrative validates Bebel's assessment that society has a profound impact on female sexuality. Growing up poor in capitalist society, she experiences sexuality as another form of victimization. Female sexuality, however, is a potentially disruptive force that governs the relationship between Popp and her fellow women workers, whose sexual licentiousness prevents her from associating with them. Popp had to become a socialist agitator in order to speak to women workers. In *Working Woman,* Popp situates sexuality at the fault lines between class solidarity and gender identity.

---

53. Bebel, *Woman under Socialism,* 139–40.

54. Ibid., 85.

55. See George Mosse, *Nationalism: Middle-Class Morality and Sexual Norms in Modern Europe* (Madison: University of Wisconsin Press, 1985), 9.

56. Hull, "Bourgeoisie and Its Discontent," 254.

When *Working Woman* first came out, Adelheid Popp was forty years old, a widowed mother of two sons and a full-time editor of *Arbeiterinnen-Zeitung,* which by then had achieved a circulation of 13,400 copies.[57] By 1910 the Austrian Social Democratic Party had more than one hundred thousand members, about 10 percent of them women.[58] Since Popp had become a member of the party in the late 1880s, the economic conditions of the working class had improved dramatically. Child labor had largely disappeared, an international law protected women from night work, and workers' accident insurance had been made mandatory.[59] While women had not yet gained the right to vote, Popp, as an individual and as a party functionary, could look back at the past twenty years as a history of outstanding achievement.

In *Working Woman* Popp foregrounds the story of her destitute childhood and youth rather than an account of her professional success. To reach her declared goal of encouraging women workers to join the working-class movement, she chose to appeal to the emotions of the reader with what Mary Jo Maynes has termed the "wrong sort of childhood."[60] Popp begins her narrative by contrasting an assumed normality of family life with her own, very different, past realities:

> Most persons, if they have grown up under normal conditions, look back in times of heavy distress, with gratitude and emotion to their happy, beautiful, careless youth, and sigh, perhaps wishing: "If it could only come again!"
> I face the recollections of my childhood with other feelings. I knew no point of brightness, no ray of sunshine, nothing of a comfortable home in which motherly love and care guided my childhood. (15)

The melodramatic language of the opening lines draws the reader into a sensational story of suffering.[61] The child's pain serves as point of departure for the narrative journey that will lead the narrator, and with her the reader, to uncover the economic and social violence responsible for this suffering. "Sensationalism," Cvetkovich asserts in the concluding section

---

57. Klucsarits and Kürbisch, *Arbeiterinnen,* 364.

58. Ibid.

59. Health and accident insurance had become mandatory in Austria in 1889; however, in 1906 half of all industrial workers still worked more than ten hours a day; see Vincent J. Knapp, *Austrian Social Democracy, 1889–1914* (Washington, D.C.: University Press of America, 1980), 108–9.

60. Maynes, *Taking the Hard Road,* 63.

61. On negated metaphors of light and paradise in working-class autobiographies see Maynes, "Childhood Memories," 144–45.

of *Mixed Feelings,* "is the strategy of a culture in which it is increasingly difficult to grasp the social structure from the experience provided by any one location or perspective."[62] Popp invites the reader to join her in reliving her past through the eyes of a child who is by definition unable to understand the structures underlying her experience. "I only attained this knowledge much later," she comments repeatedly on the gap between her mature insights into the mechanisms of suffering and exploitation and her childish ignorance (18). The blind suffering of the presocialist self supports the validity of the analytical insights of the socialist individual, while socialist theory of capitalist power relationships retroactively endows this suffering with meaning.

The autobiographer's abnormal childhood presents an effective narrative foil for the development of a "correct" class consciousness. Most of the autobiographical sketches that Popp collected in her *Memorial Book,* for instance, begin with reports of poverty and domestic violence, experience of child labor at an early age, and the deprivation of formal education despite the authors' desire to attend school. The wrong sort of childhood, in other words, makes for a good story. Its emotional content is a powerful tool of political agitation.

Although Popp's *Working Woman* proceeds in roughly chronological order, she omits specific dates or names of places and individuals. The text weaves episodes of family violence, poverty, and illness into a tapestry of a working-class childhood that is both singular and universal. While Popp experiences her childhood in singular isolation, she gives her story universal validity by leaving out individualizing details. Yet Popp's abnormal childhood contains a crucial element of normalcy. "In spite of this," she asserts after describing her impoverished background, "I had a good, self-sacrificing mother, who allowed herself no time for rest and quiet, always driven by necessity and her own desire to bring up her children honestly and to guard them from hunger" (15). Her mother, Popp insists, fulfilled the maternal ideal even though she could not provide the young narrator with the model childhood that serves as her point of reference. The opening constellation with the maternal mother and the suffering child powerfully illustrates the failure of society.

Popp's depiction of family violence is common in working-class autobiographies in which fathers and husbands appear as the victimizers of women and children.[63] Popp underscores the positive representation of

62. Cvetkovich, *Mixed Feelings,* 203.

63. Maynes, *Taking the Hard Road,* 78, and "Childhood Memories." Maynes points to the differences between German and French accounts of childhood. The German autobiographers adopt the role of the child martyr, while French working-class autobiographers tend to report positively on family relationships and experiences in school.

her mother with the description of her abusive father, whose early death leaves her mother responsible for five children. Popp continues her introductory vignette of violence and poverty with descriptions of Christmas celebrations. Even though she denigrates the Christian religion as a tool of domination in the hands of the ruling class, Popp repeatedly uses Christmas as an example of intimacy and consumerism within the family to illustrate the emotional and material deprivation of her childhood. The image of the child's bodily and psychic pain serves as an effective point of departure for a narrative that wants to mobilize the reader's potential for political action and thus ensure a future of better childhoods. The experience of this suffering, however, is grounded in the family with its two poles of a father with a "hasty temper" and a "self-sacrificing mother" (16, 15). While all members of the family are victims of poverty, women and children are also victims of male violence.

The ties that bind Popp's family together are both emotional and economic. Economic necessity forces all family members, including young children, to contribute to the family income. Popp's family thus deviates from the idealized private institution that is held together by affections outside the realm of economics. Instead, in her family the experience of work permeates all aspects of the domestic sphere. While emotional relationships are "invisible," the unnatural economic relationships in Popp's narrative become visible through and on the worker's body. Young Adelheid experiences her father's death, which left the family in even deeper poverty, as an expensive rather than an emotional event. Her "inappropriate" delight in being able to wear nice clothes at his funeral illustrates her childish incomprehension and the falseness of a world in which economics take precedence over emotions.

Popp characterizes family members according to their occupational status and their contribution to the family income. She learns to operate a sewing machine, she states, to "repay my mother for all she had done for me" (51). Popp reads the relationship with her mother through the obligation to provide mutual economic support. The ability to work, not age, determines the end of childhood. At the age of ten, upon having to register the family with the police, Popp fails to enter her name under the appropriate category. "[B]ut as I did not consider myself a child—I was a working woman," she remains unregistered (31). Regenia Gagnier has noted that the concept of childhood cannot be easily applied to working-class life narratives, because their authors were forced to start to work at very young ages.[64] Nevertheless, Popp's narrative of her nonchildhood is

---

64. Regenia Gagnier, "Social Atoms: Working-Class Autobiography, Subjectivity, and Gender," *Victorian Studies* 30 (1987): 344.

informed by her notions of a normal childhood. In the retrospective evaluation of her youth, she emphasizes the regret of having been deprived of
her childhood by the need to work. Defining herself as a victim of hardship, Popp also hints at her positive sense of independent agency gained
through work.

Work leaves its mark on the body most dramatically in the form of illness that is experienced as physical, emotional, and economic. The fatal
bone cancer of one of Popp's brothers has an immediate economic impact
on the young narrator, forcing her to begin work at the age of ten to make
up for her brother's lost income. "[H]is wounds did not heal. Then I was
obliged to begin to help earn," Popp reports matter-of-factly (22). Later,
another brother, returning from his military service, is unable to find
employment. The "strong, healthy man" had to rely on his younger sister
and mother for support (52). The healthy unemployed body is as much of
a liability as the ill body. Work governs all relationships between the
worker and the world.

As a young adolescent Popp suffers several episodes of a severe but
unspecified illness among whose symptoms are anxiety attacks and recurring fainting spells. The doctors, in accordance with nineteenth-century
notions of hereditary alcoholism, trace Popp's "nervous illness" to her
father's alcohol abuse (42). With rest and improved nutrition in hospitals
and a mental institution she recovers, but the experience leaves her with an
acute sense of vulnerability and a "fright" that she overcomes only after
she has left the factory for the editorial office (77). The hardships of her
daily life as a young worker necessitate repeated hospital admissions; in
the end, she narrowly escapes permanent institutionalization in a poorhouse in her parents' native Bohemia. The structure and significance of the
mental institution and the poorhouse are beyond the young narrator's
grasp. The absence of a framework that helps her to understand the social
relationships responsible for her suffering makes her doubly vulnerable,
and it renders the need for an interpretation even more pressing.

The body functions solely as the—unreliable—means of survival. It
provides neither pleasure nor self-definition. As if to compensate for these
negative connotations of the body, Popp repeatedly describes the clothes
she buys and wears as a source of a positive self-image (28, 43, 65). As a
young girl she fantasizes about moving up to the better social position of a
lady-in-waiting or a teacher, because she finds these women's dresses
appealing (29). While she emulates the bourgeois dress code and interprets
her desire to dress in style as inherently feminine, Popp nevertheless maintains a critical position toward upper-class women, contrasting the comfortable idleness of the wives of government officials with the unrelenting
labor of working-class girls (34). As an autobiographer, especially in her

descriptions of childhood, Popp's analysis of class exceeds her critique of female gender roles; as a journalist and political agitator, by contrast, she foregrounded the critical investigation of gender arrangements. Some of the most disturbing experiences Popp relates in *Working Woman,* however, bare the link between poverty and gender and its impact on the female body and psyche.

The first sixty or so pages of *Working Woman* introduce an autobiographical subject who is constituted through work, suffering, and family relationships that are a source of support as well as oppression. The young self cannot, as yet, translate her firsthand knowledge of suffering into an analysis of its causes. While malnutrition, sleep deprivation, and economic insecurity might explain the young narrator's anxieties, Popp offers yet another interpretation. Her first fainting spell, she reports, occurred a few weeks after a male tenant who shared the family's bedroom attempted to rape her (42). Sexuality, like poverty, is a force whose expression the young Adelheid endures as suffering without understanding its implications. Work and its physical consequences, family pressures, and sexuality merge into an overwhelming experience of oppression. Popp reports a Christmas when she contemplated suicide because she found herself trapped in a cycle of sexual assault, family pressure, and economic need. After a sexual advance by a superior she refused to return to the factory despite her mother's order to do so and the ever-present shortfall in the family budget. An attempt to prompt a well-to-do aunt to come to her financial rescue fails. While she is "hastening through the better streets to my new goal—the water" (64), a well-dressed gentleman approaches her and attempts to lure her into his apartment for "ten florins" (64). Overcome by an "inexpressible fear," she rushes home, only to be scolded by her mother (65).

Popp's wrong childhood almost ends in suicide. Caught in a cycle of poverty, sexual harassment in the factory, the lure of prostitution on the street, and lack of compassion at home, the young Adelheid reaches a point of utmost despair. "The burden of this childhood influenced my disposition for a long time, and made me a creature disliking mirth from my earliest years. Much had to happen, something great had to step into my life to help me to conquer," she sums up this section of her narrative (66), preparing the reader for a dramatic revelation. The solution to her problems, the first section of Popp's *Working Woman* starkly conveys, must encompass economics, sexuality, and family.

Reading and the often wearisome acquisition of an education represent a recurring theme in working-class autobiographies.[65] Reading sets the sub-

---

65. Maynes, *Taking the Hard Road,* 91.

ject apart from family members and peers and provides the autobiographer access to alternative—and better—worlds. Following her desire to read whatever books she could get hold of, Popp becomes engrossed in the full range of popular literature from "stories of Indians, romances hawked about the streets, newspaper stories" to the "stories of unhappy queens" and the "novels of the Jesuits" (36). She acquires her reading material from secondhand bookstores or borrows pulp novels from friends and libraries. Popp's reading is limited by exactly the economic constraints that Franz Mehring, in his review of Holek's autobiography, had in mind when he demanded a proletarian literature: Her tight budget forces Popp to take the lending charge out of her lunch money; long working hours and limited funds for light restrict her reading to weekends and daytime (38). Reading, she emphasizes, was "the only pleasure I had," yet, she adds from the position of mature socialist insight, it served a compensatory function (35).

> I was withdrawn from real life, and identified myself with the heroines of my books. . . . I was continually with my thoughts in quite another world, and neither saw nor felt anything of the misery around me, nor felt my own. (36–37)

The mature narrator's acknowledgment that she was devouring the "wrong" books does not dim her memories of the pleasures of reading. Popp's early reading materials included titles like *Isabella of Spain* and the *White Lady in the Imperial Palace,* which belong to the genre of sensational literature (36). "Melodramas," Cvetkovitch suggests, "are pleasurable because they provide readers with the satisfaction of locating the source of women's pain" in the "circumstances" surrounding her rather than in her "social position as a woman."[66] Popp's trivial literature is for the most part women's literature that invites the reader to identify with female suffering and weep cathartic tears. Popp bears witness to the power of sensationalism when she confesses that her heroines' predicaments blinded her to her own suffering; at the same time, the mature narrator asserts her intellectual capability when she rejects sensational literature and the "false" emotional responses it elicited.

With *Working Woman* Popp offers a counternarrative to the sensational stories with which she and her female readership grew up. Yet her story retains the most important element of the sensational genre—the reader's identification with the suffering subject. The story of Popp's wrong sort of childhood is, in part, such an effective narrative because

---

66. Cvetkovitch, *Mixed Feelings,* 104.

both the writer and her audience are intimately familiar with the pleasures of passionate reading. Unlike the popular books of her past, Popp guides her readers to the social causes of her pain and suggests active membership in the Social Democratic Party as the solution. Yet her narrative gives sufficient emphasis to the protagonist's dramatic suffering, allowing the reader to empathize with her pain.

Popp's critical analysis of her presocialist reading habits echoes socialist literary theory. In his 1872 speech "Wissen ist Macht—Macht ist Wissen" (Knowledge is power—power is knowledge), one of the socialist texts that helped shape her position on proletarian culture, Wilhelm Liebknecht addresses this question:

> The cheapest tabloids, which mainly circulate among the common people—I include so-called serialized novels in this count—are almost exclusively—I believe one can say: exclusively—miserable trash in terms of form; in terms of content, they are opium for the mind and poison for the morality.[67]

Liebknecht condemns *Schundliteratur* both for its inferior aesthetic qualities and its undesirable influence on the reader's intellectual and moral constitution; with his phrase "opium for the mind," he equates popular literature with Marx's condemnation of religion, suggesting that both obscure material reality. Instead, he promotes an ideal of education that evokes Johann Wolfgang von Goethe's *Wilhelm Meister* and the bourgeois tradition of the bildungsroman. The German classics, he suggests, further the "harmonious development of all faculties that rest dormant in the individual."[68] Liebknecht's Goethean formulation aligns the project of proletarian education with the canon of German high culture and its promotion of the subject as individual. In the absence of a fully developed "second culture," the theorists of Social Democracy ultimately failed to reconcile the contradiction between the individualism of bourgeois high culture and the collectivism they envisioned as the basis of proletarian culture. The proletarian autobiographer Adelheid Popp solved this problem by putting the sensationalism of mass culture into the service of political progress.

Longing to educate herself according to the dictates of Social Democratic leaders, Popp gradually abandons popular literature and sets out to expand her knowledge by attempting to read multivolume standard histories and encyclopedias cover to cover (79). Accepting Franz Mehring's

---

67. Wilhelm Liebknecht, *Wissen ist Macht—Macht ist Wissen, und andere bildungspolitisch-pädagogische Äußerungen,* ed. Hans Brumme. (Berlin: Volk und Wissen, 1968), 73.
68. Ibid., 88.

argument that bourgeois humanism is a precursor to socialism, Popp devours the classics before she graduates to the key texts of socialism. She works her way through the staples of the bourgeois canon with works by Friedrich Schiller and Alphonse Daudet, and later she reads Nikolaus Lenau, Christoph Martin Wieland, and Adelbert von Chamisso. Popp's list of "better books" include texts with female title figures such as Schiller's *Braut von Messina* or Lenau's *Anna* (76). She initially rejects Goethe, considering him to be immoral, but she learns to appreciate *Wahlverwandtschaften* and *Iphigenie* with their female protagonists (66).

With her adoption of the classical bourgeois canon Popp also accepts the split between high and popular literature. The end of her wrong childhood coincides with her renunciation of the wrong sort of reading. Chronologically, her canon ends with *Vormärz*-poets Lenau and Georg Herwegh, member of the Young Germany and participant in the 1848 revolution. In accordance with Kautsky's rejection of naturalism as a product of bourgeois aestheticism, this historical dividing line excludes the works of bourgeois realism and naturalism. Popp ends her autobiography with a poem by Herwegh that she quotes to herself while serving a prison term because of an article that criticized the institution of marriage. With its vision of a better future, the poem demonstrates the revolutionary optimism Mehring had demanded. At the same time, the prison scene indicates that Popp accepts the bourgeois tradition of poetry recitation for its elevating effect on the reader's emotions. Good literature arouses good emotions. For Popp and many other working-class autobiographers, reading educates and elevates the self in the service of the class collective. Using herself as an example for others, Popp puts into practice and promotes the paradigm of socialist cultural politics according to which high literature furthers the emancipation of the working class. The right kind of reading is instrumental in the autobiographer's development toward class consciousness.

In an environment in which reading as a leisure-time activity remained the exception either because people were illiterate, like Popp's mother, or because they did not have the time to read, reading retained its ties to an oral tradition. The young Popp was a gifted storyteller. She very often entertained family, colleagues, and even employers by retelling the stories she had read, transforming reading from a solitary activity into a collective event and establishing a relationship with her environment that prefigures her activities as a public speaker.

Popp's criticism of mass literature was twofold. Not only did trivial novels prevent the working-class subject from identifying the sources of her own suffering, it was also suffused with sexuality. Much of Popp's early reading material, she reports, contained sexually "explicit" scenes, which, she insists, she did not understand at the time. "As my mother could not read, no one exercised any supervision over my reading," she explains, and thus her lack of discrimination (37). Reading—she confirms a late-eighteenth-century conviction—requires surveillance. To demonstrate the seductive nature of trivial literature, Popp points to the sexual content of her reading material; at the same time, she illustrates her younger self's immunity to this type of temptation by quoting at some length a sexually explicit passage from a collection of French erotic stories that she claims not to have understood at the time (41). In light of the dangers to morality that Liebknecht and others had diagnosed, the narrator's immunity enables her to leave behind the sexualized sphere of mass culture.

Popp's recollections of her responses to her reading material double as a discussion of her conflicted attitude toward sexuality. With its appeal to the imagination, the act of reading itself becomes sexualized. The sexual content of many of the young Adelheid's books only accentuates the seductive nature of mass literature. Referring to Popp's reactions to having been sexually molested by a lodger and the nightmares that ended only when she becomes a socialist, Popp's mother argues that reading leads to false interpretations of reality (44). Similarly, when Popp refuses to return to her workplace after an incident of sexual harassment, her mother accuses her of being "over excited" and attributes her unwillingness to grant sexual favors in return for better pay to her daughter's excessive reading (59). In this case, however, Popp relies on her books for a counterargument: "I had read in books so much about seduction and fallen virtue that I had created the most horrible fancies for myself. So I did not go in" (61). Despite the self-mocking tone and her imitation of melodramatic language, Popp credits to popular literature her ability to resist sexual exploitation despite social and economic pressures. While her reading might have been of the wrong sort, at least in this instance it led to the right results. Perhaps unwittingly, Popp acknowledges that mass literature can empower its female readership to resist oppression.

The story of Popp's reading habits continues in her condemnation of her fellow women workers. She denounces the sexualized behavior of female workers with arguments and vocabulary similar to her rejection of pulp fiction. She sees the factory, with its concentration of married and unmarried women, as a space that escapes the controlling discipline of social rules of female conduct. Popp repeats the charges commonly directed against working-class women from a position of bourgeois respectability,[69] accusing them of having love affairs, attending the theater

---

69. Mosse, *Nationalism and Sexuality,* 90.

(62), and generally being sexually unrestrained (43). Popp mentions repeatedly that she herself did not participate in her colleagues' enjoyments (43), kept a distance from her fellow workers (74), and refused to frequent public places because of the pervasive presence of sexuality (73, 81). She characterizes women workers with their propensity for engaging in sexual behavior as the less-educated sex, susceptible to the intertwined seductive forces of mass culture and sexuality (85).

George Mosse has shown that the Wilhelminian state saw its stability threatened by so-called female revolutionaries, including women who refused to accept the dress code or sexual conduct established by standards of bourgeois respectability.[70] Analogous to the feminization of mass culture, turn-of-the-century discourse feminized the masses as a threat to its social and cultural institutions. In linking the success of the socialist movement to the respectable conduct of its female members, Popp denigrates female sexuality as a threatening force, illustrating that socialist attitudes on respectability closely mirrored those of the dominant bourgeois society.

Popp's complicity in replicating misogynist patterns of thinking can be attributed to internalized negative representations of women that prevailed in her culture. They also attest to her desire to claim difference within difference, that is, from other women workers. Popp dissociates herself from the attraction of mass literature and sexualized activities such as theater and dancing and replaces them with a disciplining program of education and desexualization. If women's reading and female sexuality are indicative of the quality of the present and future society, as August Bebel's *Women under Socialism* suggests, Popp's *Working Woman* shows how women can attain this goal.

Sexuality, in particular female sexuality, runs through Popp's *Working Woman* like an elusive leitmotif that escapes its "proper" place. The young narrator experienced sexuality as an incomprehensible force imbued with a negative, even threatening, connotation. As she becomes a socialist, her desire to associate with like-minded people is thwarted by her fear of sexuality, the two themes often intertwined in one paragraph. Torn between her reluctance to go to public places—including the factory—because of possible sexual implications, and her wish to communicate with other socialists, Popp finds herself in the private sphere of the home longing for a public community. "So I always sat at home busy with a book or needlework, whilst half unconsciously I developed a powerful longing for intercourse with companions who would share my thoughts and feelings" (88). The community she longs for is one in which sexuality has its proper place.

---

70. Ibid., 90ff.

The "true" working-class autobiography, according to Karl Kautsky and Franz Mehring, follows its subject from suffering to socialism. The worker's progress from blindness to class-consciousness mirrors the religious conversion narrative and its depiction of the convert's path from sin to salvation. Both the religious conversion narrative and the worker's autobiography engage the reader's emotions with the aim of transforming the reader into a future convert. In her study on women's religious conversion narratives, Virginia Lieson Brereton observes that the "assumption behind the narrative was that readers or hearers, deeply stirred by the conversion account, would go from vicarious participation to experiences of their own."[71] *Working Woman* devotes considerable narrative space to Popp's life before she encountered socialism to accomplish this goal.

The exchange of false beliefs, including the wrong sort of reading, for correct socialist analysis is the most important organizing principle of Popp's narrative and the pivotal point around which her autobiography revolves. According to *Working Woman,* Popp's interest in politics began to develop in the mid-1880s, when she was about fifteen years of age. She mentions the state of emergency of 1884 declared by the Taaffe government, during the course of which Social Democrats were arrested, workers' associations prohibited, and some of their leaders deported from Austria. Her understanding of these events was clearly limited; she recalls reading the public announcement: "As I remember, it forbade the assembling of several persons" (82). Instinctively grasping the magnitude of the event, she proceeded to inform her fellow workers by getting up on a table to deliver a speech about what she had read. By 1890 she welcomes the repeal of the anti-Socialist laws in Germany, "although I was outside the party and known by no one" (88). She must have officially joined the party shortly thereafter.

Popp became aware of the socialist movement during a time of mass strikes in Vienna and the harsh political repression of workers that accompanied them. From the newspaper reports about the 1888–89 congress at Hainfeld, in which Austrian Social Democrats confirmed their unity, Popp recalls, she learned about the party's resolve to treat women as equals. Finally, she mentions the 1889 Second International in Paris, which proclaimed May 1 as an international workers' holiday and demanded an eight-hour workday. These historical references provide a chronology of events, which, however, is of minor importance to Popp. The events of the years 1888–92, her years as a factory worker before she joined the *Arbeiterinnen-Zeitung,* serve as a background for Popp's personal responses to these developments and allow her to illustrate her changing views.

---

71. See Brereton, *From Sin to Salvation,* 27.

Popp traces her "conversion" to empathetic reading. She follows with great interest the newspaper reports about the tribulations of the European aristocracy, stories of mysterious murders blamed on the anarchists, and the political trials involving socialists, most likely the prosecutions in the aftermath of the large strikes of 1889 in Vienna. "None of those details for the sake of which people say women read the papers appealed to me," remarks Popp, distancing herself from what she presumes to be the consensus about women's reading habits (85). Popp links her initial interest in Social Democracy to the victimization of Social Democrats by state oppression. The persecuted Social Democrats, she states, became her heroes, and she identified with them as she had previously sympathized with the protagonists of popular literature. "The theoretical parts I could not at first understand, but I understood, and took hold of, all that was written of the sufferings of the working classes, and I first learnt from it to understand and judge my own lot" (87). The insight that suffering is a common experience rather than an isolated fate is the decisive turning point in Popp's life. Having come to understand that she is part of a community created by suffering holds the key to Popp's salvation. Empathy for the wrong people, real or fictitious, had prevented her from gaining this insight. Her failed attempts to win the sympathies of members of the upper classes taught her that the end to her suffering could only be brought about through the solidarity among members of her own class.

Her rejection of religion, like the wrong sort of reading, separates the mature narrator from her younger self. "I learnt to see that all that I had suffered was the result not of a divine ordinance, but of an unjust organisation of society," says Popp, describing her lapse from Catholicism (87). While she replaces religious explanations with secular materialist analysis, the choice of a word like "suffered" *(erduldet)* evokes a Christian worldview and the Passion of Jesus Christ. In her narrative Popp precedes her interest in Social Democracy with the description of a phase of intense religious identification, which culminates in her communion and several pilgrimages. Socialism replaces Catholicism and monarchism as a worldview, but in many respects Popp continues to use the language of Christianity. Dressed in her Sunday clothes, she enters the room in which the Social Democratic newspaper is sold, feeling herself to be setting foot in a "sanctuary" (90). Mocking the contradictions she cannot yet resolve, she admits to praying at night to the Virgin Mary after a day of rallying against the Christian religion, thinking to herself, "Still, it may perhaps be true" (91). Unlike the religious sinner, Popp does not castigate herself for her prior beliefs, showing sympathy rather than censure for her younger self. Social Democracy gives meaning to everything that happened "before." In the religious conversion narrative, the sinner overcomes her vileness. In Popp's prototypical working-class autobiography, she comes to understand the evils of society and can now work toward their eradication. In both cases, however, the autobiographical subject declares herself to be a person different from before.

For Popp, as for the majority of her contemporaries of all classes, the political domain is male. She observes, for example, that the Social Democratic newspaper, which by now has become her exclusive source of political information, never addresses the "Woman Question" (93). Her gender seems an impassable barrier to political activity, leading her to fantasize being a man rather than promoting a change of attitude.

> I was held to be an exception, and I looked upon myself as such. I considered the social question, as far as I then understood it, as a man's question just like politics. Only I would have liked to be a man, to have a right to busy myself with politics. (93)

Her conflicted interest in politics, which marks her as an exception to herself and to others, illustrates the dilemma posed by universalized gender roles and the particularities of class. Only after Popp has learned that the Social Democrats did in fact support women's issues does she feel empowered to become actively involved in the socialist women's movement. She begins to attend public meetings despite the legal ban on women's attending political gatherings. As a worker she experiences no qualms about breaking the laws of a society she had come to understand as oppressive. By contrast, she can only overcome her "sexual" inhibitions as a woman within the framework of party politics. Thinking back on her first political meetings, Popp poignantly describes the immobilizing effects of internalized gender roles and external mechanisms of women's exclusion from politics:

> But I did not yet venture on a word, I had not even the courage to applaud. I considered it unwomanly and only right for men. Besides, they only talked of men at the meetings. None of the speakers addressed the women, who certainly were only present in very small numbers. It all appeared to be about the suffering and misery of men. I perceived with sorrow that no one spoke about the working women, that no one turned to summon them to fight. (93)

Her assumptions about gender, Popp admits, prevented her from even minor participation, such as applauding a speaker. Her depiction of the working-class public sphere as male dominated—not only in terms of its demographics but also in terms of a rhetoric that disregards the realities of female suffering—makes her hesitancy to enter into it quite understandable. In these passages, however, Popp also succeeds in laying open the contradictions between the party's official position on the woman question and women's exclusion from the political process. Popp's impending entry into the public sphere of Social Democracy is mired in her own conflicting feelings about femininity as much as in the inconsistencies of the party's politics.

Popp delivers her first public speech in front of an almost exclusively male audience at a branch meeting of an unspecified industry (105). Embarrassed by the women workers' lack of interest in politics—only nine attended the meeting—Popp rises to defend her sex, arguing that women workers have suffered "mental neglect" (107; translation modified) and appealing to the men to provide them with access to education. Popp's disapproval of her colleagues' sexual morals reappears in the idea that they do not understand the need of becoming organized because of their lower level of education. *Working Woman* quotes in its entirety Popp's first article, which reflects her zeal in "improving" women workers. "Working Women! Show that you are not quite depraved and mentally stunted," she urges her colleagues (109). Drawing on Enlightenment concepts of the mechanisms of emancipation, Popp proposes that the moral and intellectual status of women is lower than that of men, and therefore must be raised to "higher human existence" through education and organization.[72] Emphasizing that the double burden of women as mothers and workers makes them even more vulnerable to socioeconomic exploitation than their male counterparts, she encourages women to join the ranks of Social Democracy (108). Popp's enthusiasm empowers her to sacrifice time, money, and even health to her political work. The condition of women workers becomes her preferred topic as an agitator because, she notes, her own suffering lent her speeches authenticity and persuasiveness (116). "I had become an object of general attention," she comments about the public reaction to her work as a woman agitator (115). The hard-won understanding of the collective nature of her fate allows Popp to hint at her position as an outstanding individual.

More than an internal change of a private worldview, Popp's path to socialism is her passage into the public sphere of political agitation. The most difficult hurdles are her reservations against female presence and participation in the public sphere, on the one hand, and her belief that the company of female factory workers is as infused with sexuality as the pages of popular literature, on the other. Popp has to desexualize the meet-

---

72. Popp, *Jugend einer Arbeiterin,* 174. On the Enlightenment idea of improvement through education see, for instance, Theodor von Hippel, *Bürgerliche Verbesserung der Weiber* (1792); and Christian Wilhelm Dohm, *Bürgerliche Verbesserung der Juden* (1783).

ing hall and the factory before she can enter it. "I had formerly held myself aloof so that too much intimacy might not arise between my fellow workers and myself," she points out, describing her presocialist position. "Now that I had an object before me . . . I gave up my reticence, and told my comrades all that I had read of the workers' movement" (88–89). Socialism born out of enlightenment enables Popp to conquer her fear of intimacy with her female colleagues in the sexualized atmosphere of the factory.

In her interaction with male workers, the common cause diffuses any sexual implications.

> Then came the propaganda for the labour holiday on the 1st of May. . . . I wanted to work for it, and sought for companions who thought as I did. I had noticed among the workers one who wore a broad hat. I hoped from it that he might be a Social Democrat. I watched for an opportunity to speak to him, and did things I had never done before. The workmen washed their hands at the end of the day's work in the courtyard. Many girls also went in. I had never done so to avoid being obliged to hear the talk which was so distasteful to me. But now I mixed with them and succeeded in speaking to the owner of the broad hat. I was not deceived. He was an earnest, intelligent workman, and a member of the trade union. (102–3)

The sexualized banter around the water faucet creates the wrong kind of community between male and female workers. Only the hope for a conversation about socialism makes it possible for Popp to tolerate the company she perceives as immoral. If insight into the collective nature of workers' suffering constitutes Popp's primary conversion experience, mastery of her dread of sexuality is the second step she must take before she can assert an identity as a socialist agitator. Popp interprets the sexual content of her reading materials, the licentiousness of the factory, the dance halls, and the taverns, as expressions of lower-class life, which she, importantly, does not condone. She concurs not only with Bebel and his vision of a future society, and Liebknecht, who condemned trivial literature for its indecent content and effect, but with the sexologists and the government officials of her time. Socialism also means severing the ties that link the lower classes, particularly women, with unrestrained sexuality.[73]

The mother-daughter relationship emerges as Popp's most important personal relationship and as the one fraught with the most problems. "When

---

73. Male workers and union leaders often shared this view and used it as an argument against female presence in the workplace (Canning, "Gender and Politics," 122).

I urged others to overcome all difficulties, I used no empty phrases, because I myself was constantly struggling against just such great obstacles, against material poverty, and against the mental pain I had to endure through my mother" (117). In the conflict between mother and daughter, definitions of female gender identity and the place of sexuality in the life of the woman worker find their most acute and contested expression. Popp's mother represents the utterly exploited, uneducated working-class woman, who never learned to read or write because she was forced to begin contributing to the family income at the age of six. Throughout *Working Woman,* Popp's mother remains nameless, emphasizing that her fate, too, is the anonymous story of hundreds of thousands. Mother and daughter experienced similarly "abnormal" childhood fates, yet Popp's mother vehemently rejects her daughter's dedication to the betterment of the living conditions of workers and their children. To join the Social Democrats, Popp not only had to overcome her own "false" beliefs but also to contend with her mother's fierce opposition to her involvement in class struggle. In the end, her mother's unyielding "false" consciousness remains a thorny reminder that the material conditions of someone's life do not always result in the appropriate consciousness.

The psychic pain caused by the conflict with her mother dominates the last part of Popp's autobiography, just as the description of her childhood suffering had dominated the first half. As a child and adolescent, Popp was too young to understand the causes of her suffering; her mother, she states, is too old to understand the content and necessity of her political work. Popp's intimate account of her relationship with her aging mother suggests that conflicting notions of women's proper conduct were not only a public issue Popp had to negotiate in her association with women workers, but a problem that pervaded the private sphere of her home.

When Popp leaves the factory in 1892 to become the first editor of the newly founded *Arbeiterinnen-Zeitung,* friction with her mother intensifies. Insisting on a woman's role as wife and mother, Popp's mother disapproves of her daughter's occupation as an editor, journalist, and public speaker.[74]

> My mother had no pleasure in my altered way of life. She would have preferred me to have remained in the factory, and then to have mar-

---

74. Parental opposition to their children's involvement with Social Democracy is a recurring element in worker's autobiographies. According to Jochen Loreck's empirical study *Wie man früher Sozialdemokrat wurde,* the parents of most socialists were opposed to their children's political views. Of the thirty-three autobiographers whose texts Loreck evaluated, few had fathers in favor of socialism, but none of the mothers approved of their children's political opinions (238).

ried. The old woman, who looked back on a long series of sufferings and deprivations, who under the most terrible of conditions had borne a child every two years and had then fed it the breast for sixteen to eighteen months to be saved longer from another confinement, this woman, crippled and prematurely bent from hard work, could picture no other lot for her daughter than a good marriage. To marry her daughter well was her thought and aspiration, and I had much to go through when I refused a marriage, the only object of which was to lighten my lot and free me from the factory. She looked on marriage and children as the destiny of a woman. However much at first she was flattered by the praise of me that she heard, just the same degree later she was displeased when she perceived that I wanted to devote myself to public work. The more busy I was as a speaker, the more unhappy she became. (120–21)

Popp describes the disagreement with her mother about gender roles as a controversy over the interpretation of experience. Her emotional account of her mother's "reproductive suffering" epitomizes a woman's lack of control over her body and the debilitating consequences of numerous unwanted pregnancies.[75] Her mother's life story is a powerful argument in favor of women's involvement in politics and against the myth that motherhood is always joyful. The old woman's stubborn opposition confirms what Popp already knows: women are reluctant socialists. While Popp ascribes her fellow women workers' lack of political commitment to their sexual licentiousness, her mother, by contrast, cites traditional notions of femininity against her daughter's involvement in politics. The mother-daughter conflict, then, is not about the content of socialism and class struggle but about definitions of gender and sexuality, and, if we recall her mother's response to the incident of sexual harassment in the factory, it precedes Popp's involvement with Social Democracy. For Popp's mother, gender definitions dictate that a woman's place be in the home; her sexuality serves to attain and secure this position. Popp, by contrast, begins to question conventional gender roles and expands her activities beyond the home by desexualizing the public sphere.

Since Popp's mother was in no position to interfere with her daughter's activities, her voice in the text functions as a catalyst for Popp's formulating and pursuing her program of self-education and political activism.[76] Women like her mother, who cannot speak for themselves in

---

75. Regenia Gagnier, *Subjectivities: The Pragmatics of Self-Representation* (New York: Oxford University Press, 1991), 60.

76. Goodman, *Dis/Closures,* 198.

public, need women like Popp to speak for them. In a frequently quoted episode from Popp's autobiography Friedrich Engels and August Bebel visit Popp's home to persuade her mother that her daughter's work is important. Her mother sees the two leaders of the socialist movement merely as potential husbands and rejects them because of their age (97). In *Working Woman,* the tensions between traditional gender roles and class politics reach their highest intensity in the relationships between women.

Popp begins her narrative by portraying her mother as an ideal maternal figure and closes it with a distressing assessment of the mother-daughter relationship and the maternal role. Marianne Hirsch identifies mothers as "primary negative models for the daughter."[77] "The maternal role," Hirsch argues in reference to nineteenth-century novels,

> was figured in ways that was ultimately debilitating to women— equally so to those women who could afford to try to live up to the social ideal of maternity and to those women who because of economic necessity could not. The mother became either the object of idealization and nostalgia or that which had to be rejected and surpassed in favor of allegiance to a morally and intellectually superior male world.[78]

While Popp casts her political allegiance with the predominantly male world of Social Democracy, she accords to her contentious relationship with her mother far more depth and space in the narrative than to her relationships with socialist comrades. In the end, the shared misery of mother and daughter transcends their profound disagreement over gender roles. Popp and her mother are the central nuclear unit; all other family relationships, including her brothers and their wives and even Popp's two sons, remain secondary. A history of common suffering and the language of filial love bind mother and daughter in a discordant but indivisible union.

> It has always grieved me that I have found no understanding sympathy in the mother I loved so much. . . . But the thought of leaving her never occurred to me. We had borne so much sorrow together, how should she not be with me now that many dark shadows had vanished from me? (119, 122)

---

77. Marianne Hirsch, *The Mother/Daughter Plot: Narrative, Psychoanalysis, Feminism* (Bloomington: Indiana University Press, 1989), 11.
    78. Ibid., 14.

Her distrust of female sexuality, Popp had explained earlier, almost kept her from forming alliances with other women; the nonsexual bond between mother and daughter, by contrast, outlasts all other relationships.

In the preface to the third edition of *Jugendgeschichte einer Arbeiterin,* Popp explains her decision to add a section on her marriage to Julius Popp, "not in order to speak about myself, but to show by my individual experience that the public activity of a woman is not inevitably hampered by her marriage and duties as wife and mother" (14). The story of her marriage serves an exemplary rather than a personal purpose and assures potential critics that Popp rejects neither matrimony nor motherhood. But the foundation of her union with party functionary Julius Popp is shared political convictions. While she does not provide the reader with details of her marriage, she insists that "I have never repented entering into this marriage. It changed me from a precociously serious young girl into a joyous woman" (132). Marriage with a socialist, then, provides a space for male-female relationships untainted by sexual exploitation and victimization. Motherhood is a burden for Popp and a distraction from her political work rather than a source of positive self-definition or an emotionally rewarding experience, and she does not identify her two children by gender or name. Popp speaks as the daughter of a victimized mother, not as the mother of children who will have a better future because of her political work.

Could Adelheid Popp have written a different autobiography? Could she have done what August Bebel did in *Aus meinem Leben,* that is, use his life story to tell the history of Social Democracy? Adelheid Popp elected to tell this history in other kinds of publications. In 1912, she edited a collection of twenty short autobiographical texts written by members of the Austrian socialist women's movement—aptly titled *Memorial Book.* Popp aimed to encourage communication between different generations of working-class women and to confirm the existence of an organized collective. In her brief introduction, Popp writes about the founding of the Women Workers' Educational Association in June 1890, an occurrence she omitted from *Working Woman,* and the inauguration of the *Arbeiterinnen-Zeitung* in 1892 as decisive events that mark the beginnings of the Austrian women's movement. In her own contribution to *Memorial Book,* she commemorates these events with precise dates and the names of the many women who were instrumental in the early years of Austria's women workers' movement. Unlike *Working Woman,* which she had published only three years earlier, *Memorial Book* offers a historical perspective on the events Popp helped to bring about. It is in this context that she makes known her own achievements.

In the introduction to her 1929 publication *The Upward Path,* Popp refers to the political purpose of her *Memorial Book* from an historically still more advanced position.

> *Memorial Book* was meant to be a medium to promote and publicize the political organization of women, and it did serve this purpose. It contained personal experiences and reminiscences of the first female pioneers. It was not possible to report with the objectivity of hindsight about a movement that was still searching for means that might best suit this objectivity. All bitterness and disappointments of the young women's movement were still too fresh to guarantee a dispassionate overall view. This shaped the character of *Memorial Book:* It presented a collection of personal memories of the early years.[79]

After almost forty years of women's movement in Austria, "sober historicity" replaces the personal and subjective accounts of the early years. As the organizational structure of the movement solidifies and becomes history, personal stories can be historicized. Striving for more objectivity, Popp also reassesses the independent importance of the movement by putting women into *The Upward Path*'s subtitle: *Die sozialdemokatische Frauenbewegung Österreichs.* With *The Upward Path,* Popp inserts the story of the Austrian women's movement into a broad, international historical context that included bourgeois as well as presocialist feminists. The personal has given way to the political.

Working Woman is one of many turn-of-the-century lower-class life stories. Comprising authentic and fictitious texts, written by factory workers, waitresses, prostitutes, and middle-class reformers, these texts addressed not only class but also morality, sexuality, family, and gender. They were motivated by the social transformations that accompanied modernization and the consensus that autobiography was uniquely suited to exploring these issues and to inspiring reform. As a lower-class woman Popp lacked the cultural and the literary models available to her contemporary fellow autobiographers like Marie von Ebner-Eschenbach or August Bebel. Marxism provided her with a theory of class that could not account for her experiences of sexuality and gender. The language and imagery of sensationalism allowed Popp to tell the story of a lower-class girl who knew that her subjectivity was shaped by her gender as much as by her class.

Adelheid Popp's *Working Woman* has gained more fame as a representative "working-class autobiography" than as the life story of an indi-

---

79. Popp, *Der Weg zur Höhe,* 5.

vidual autobiographer. The cover of the 1983 reprint, for instance, shows a photomontage featuring an exhausted child of indiscernible gender resting on its arms between gigantic cogwheels. The volume contains a number of photographs of exemplary working-class misery around 1900 without claiming any direct relationship to Popp's narrative. Adelheid Popp herself is better known as an autobiographer than for her contributions to the Austrian Social Democratic Party and the socialist women's movement. Historians of Austrian Social Democracy tend to refer her name to the margins of male history, and her many journalistic and agitational texts have received only minimal scholarly recognition. *Working Woman* has found its place in the canon of working-class history as a historical document rather than as a literary text. As a political leader, Adelheid Popp has yet to enter the history books.

*sensational novel stuff not convincing – mundely –
but very careful, reading of Popp
and CLOSE*

*again, though: autobiography as history?
(although less than in previous chap)*

this is all too pat, somehow

"But I Wanted to Write an Honest Book": *The Confessions of Wanda von Sacher-Masoch*

One day in 1905 a tiny woman in a tight-fitting, mangy fur coat marched into the offices of the Parisian publishing house Mercure de France, walked past the stunned and frightened "men of letters" gathered there, and presented a manuscript to Rachilde, the chief editor.[1] "Madame Wanda de Sacher-Masoch," recalls the French writer André Salmon in his memoirs, "Madame de Sach . . . Venus in Furs . . . In person! Herself."[2] The appearance of the startling guest, scandalous in her deteriorating fur coat, conjured up an erotic scenario. "Wanda naked underneath her magnificent furs . . . the whip hissing in the bedroom . . . a new vice . . . a supreme vice . . . somber and conjugal . . . Venus at last."[3]

Wanda von Sacher-Masoch, a fiction writer and autobiographer, was the widow of the Austrian writer Leopold von Sacher-Masoch (1836–1895). For Salmon and the other gentlemen gathered in Rachilde's office, she was "Venus in Furs," the female protagonist of Leopold von Sacher-Masoch's transgressive literary fantasy of the whip-wielding dominatrix and her submissive male slave. Salmon's breathless celebration of Wanda as Venus, his vision of the fifty-seven-year-old woman naked again under her once magnificent furs, and his imaginary return to the inception of the "vice" that we have come to know as "masochism," show how inex-

---

1. André Salmon, "Une Heure avec Wanda de Sacher-Masoch," in *Souvenirs sans fin: Premiere Epoque (1903–1908)* (Paris: Gallimard, 1955), 259. Rachilde (1860–1953), born Marguerite Eymery Vallette, is the author of several novels about the effacement of sexual difference; titles include *Monsieur Vénus* (1884); *La marquise de Sade* (1887); and *La jongleuse* (1900).
2. Salmon, "Une Heure avec Wanda," 258.
3. Ibid.

tricably intertwined Wanda von Sacher-Masoch's life had become with the literature of sexual scandal.[4] More than thirty-five years after Leopold von Sacher-Masoch published his masochist novella, *Venus in Furs,* he and the woman associated with him had become the material of a collective fantasy. And now Wanda proposed to tell this story one more time, publicly and in her own words. The title of her manuscript: *Les Mémoires de Wanda de Sacher-Masoch.*

Meine Lebensbeichte: Memoiren (translated as *The Confessions of Wanda von Sacher-Masoch*) cannot be understood without the autobiographer's relationship to the person and the work of Leopold von Sacher-Masoch, her husband of ten years.[5] It was, of course, Leopold's work, most importantly his 1870 novella *Venus in Furs,* that inspired sexologist Richard von Krafft-Ebing to borrow the Slavic and, as it were, the maternal component of Sacher-Masoch's name to denote the sexual practice we know as "masochism."[6] *Venus in Furs* and the enactment of the masochist ritual between the cruel woman and her male slave is the plot that defined Leopold and Wanda von Sacher-Masoch for their contemporaries and continues to do so for present-day readers as well.[7]

---

4. By the 1880s flagellation novels enjoyed such popularity that Albrecht Koschorke, *Leopold von Sacher-Masoch: Die Inszenierung einer Perversion* (Munich: Piper, 1988), describes masochism as a "epochenspezifisches Sozialprodukt" (111).

5. The autobiography was first published in Germany as *Meine Lebensbeichte: Memoiren* (Berlin: Schuster & Loeffler, 1906). The French translation came out a year later: Wanda de Sacher-Masoch, *Confession de ma vie* (Paris: Mercure de France, 1907). The autobiography was republished in France in 1967 (Paris: Claude Tchou). The English translation is a somewhat shortened version of the German original: *The Confessions of Wanda von Sacher-Masoch, by the Wife of Leopold von Sacher-Masoch, the Author of "Venus in Furs,"* trans. Marian Philipps, Caroline Hébert, and V. Vale (San Francisco: Re/Search, 1990); the blurb on the back states incorrectly that the autobiography was "originally published in French in 1907." Michael Farin's 1986 German reedition, *Die Beichte der Dame im Pelz* (Rastatt: Moewig, 1986), is unfortunately out of print. Unless otherwise noted, all references are to the English edition; page numbers are given in the text.

6. In *Psychopathia Sexualis* Krafft-Ebing defines masochism as follows: "By masochism I understand a peculiar perversion of the psychical *vita sexualis* in which the individual affected, in sexual feeling and thought, is controlled by the idea of being completely and unconditionally subject to the will of a person of the opposite sex; of being treated by this person as by a master, humiliated and abused" (131). Despite the gender-neutral language of this definition, only two out of thirty-three of Krafft-Ebing's case studies refer to female masochists. *Psychopathia Sexualis* was first published in 1886, but the term *masochism* does not appear until the 1890 edition. Leopold von Sacher-Masoch resented the association of his name with sexual pathology.

7. Barbara Hyams, "The Whip and the Lamp: Leopold von Sacher-Masoch, the Woman Question, and the Jewish Question," *Women in German Yearbook* 13 (1997): 67–79, has suggested a new look at Sacher-Masoch's work without the masochist component.

Fig. 4. Wanda von Sacher-Masoch. (Courtesy of Bildarchiv der Österreichischen Nationalbibliothek, Vienna.)

André Salmon's recollections of his "Hour with Wanda von Sacher-Masoch" hint, perhaps unwittingly, at the predicaments facing an autobiographer whose story has entered into the public imagination. How can she write her life if it has already been told? Will the "real" story command credibility against the evidence of the fictional versions preceding it? All autobiographers rely on plots that have been narrated before. Yet Wanda von Sacher-Masoch set out to tell a story with which her contemporaries not only were familiar but whose central theme was fixed in the collective erotic imagination: The legend of a celebrated writer and his muse, and their story of sexual perversion. She had donned her fur coat once again and became Venus one more time to secure a publisher for the autobiography she hoped would liberate her from the fiction that was her life. Wanda von Sacher-Masoch's autobiography is a counternarrative aimed at setting the record straight. Her theatrical appearance at the Mercure de France suggests that her life story had no reality without its fictions. Offering the manuscript to Rachilde, whose works equal Leopold von Sacher-Masoch's in their depiction of female cruelty, she perhaps hoped to find a woman who would receive her memoirs with sympathetic understanding. And Rachilde, Salmon assures us, greeted her with kindness and agreed to publish Wanda von Sacher-Masoch's version of "Venus in Furs."

Of the autobiographies discussed in this book, *Confessions* was the most controversial because for many critics it was a direct reflection of the modern age and its culture. "The story of Sacher-Masoch's marriage, an exquisite case for psychological brooders, in the superbly typical traits of its progression, deserves to be permanently remembered as one of the most peculiar outgrowths of modern decadence," one reviewer commented, welcoming the shock effect of *Confessions* and the debates it triggered.[8] Others read Wanda von Sacher-Masoch's autobiography as a sign of cultural decline. "The scandalous memoirs," Felicity Nussbaum argues in her book on eighteenth-century women's autobiographies, "relegated unlicensed sexuality to the lower classes."[9] By the late nineteenth century, middle-class women also wrote confessional autobiographies, reminding contemporaries that the sexual crisis was an all-pervasive phenomenon of which confessional memoirs were documentation and symptom. In addition to sexual norms, Wanda von Sacher-Masoch and her work violated the boundaries of class and race. A woman with little formal education,

---

8. S. K. Wohlfeld, "Sacher-Masochs Ehegeschichte," *Die Wage* 9, no. 40 (1906): 972–74, reprinted in *Leopold von Sacher-Masoch: Materialien zu Leben und Werk,* ed. Michael Farin (Bonn: Bouvier, 1987), 225.

9. Felicity A. Nussbaum, *The Autobiographical Subject: Gender and Ideology in Eighteenth-Century England* (Baltimore: Johns Hopkins University Press, 1989), 179.

she transformed herself into a published writer and autobiographer. Born into the lower middle class, she married an aristocrat from a respected family. The wife of a sexual deviant, she not only crossed into the territory of heterosexual perversion but also recounted experiences of lesbian love in her memoir and adulterous affairs with Jewish men. While autobiographers such as Lazarus or Popp earned praise for the solutions they offered to social questions, the story of Wanda von Sacher-Masoch's life in the minds of many epitomized the ills of the modern age.

Wanda von Sacher-Masoch's contemporaries were both alarmed and fascinated by the "sexual anarchy" of their time.[10] As scholars of sexuality undertook to produce scientific knowledge about sex, confessional memoirs flooded the turn-of-the-century book market, offering readers their uncensored truths about the secrets of deviant sexuality. Wanda von Sacher-Masoch thus could count on an audience that was familiar with the genre of the confessional memoir as well as curious about her association with Leopold. In writing her autobiography, she submitted her truth against several competing versions. Leopold von Sacher-Masoch's masochist fantasy *Venus in Furs* is the principal text against which the autobiography demands to be read. Richard von Krafft-Ebing's interpretations of masochism represent another context. As products of high literature and science, *Venus in Furs* and Krafft-Ebing's scientific case studies are male forms of writing. Wanda von Sacher-Masoch's story of sexual perversion, by contrast, insists on a female perspective in both content and form. Unlike the case studies of a Krafft-Ebing or a Freud, confessional memoirs do not owe their existence to the narrative and interpretative authority of scholars of sexuality. Instead, they are inspired by the writer's desire to tell a sensational story and the public's interest in "this sort of reading." Wanda von Sacher-Masoch's autobiography is no more "literary" than those of Adelheid Popp or Margarethe von Eckenbrecher. Her life with Leopold, however, taught her about the power of master texts. *Confessions* is as much about sex as it is about writing.

Wanda von Sacher-Masoch's *Confessions* caused a vicious if short-

---

10. The term "sexual anarchy" was introduced by Grete Meisel-Hess in *Die sexuelle Krise: Eine sozial-psychologische Untersuchung* (Jena: Biederich, 1909), translated as *The Sexual Crisis: A Critique of Our Sex Life* (New York: Critic and Guide, 1917), to describe the effects of double moral standards on men: "The sexual anarchy created and permitted by the masculine code of sexual morals has set its mark upon them [men]" (92). Recent works on turn-of-the-century culture and sexuality include Showalter, *Sexual Anarchy;* Apter, *Feminizing the Fetish;* Dijkstra, *Idols of Perversity;* Gail Finney, *Women in Modern Drama: Freud, Feminism, and European Theater of the Turn of the Century* (Ithaca: Cornell University Press, 1989); and Felski's *Gender of Modernity* with a discussion of Leopold von Sacher-Masoch's works.

lived "crisis" before both the author and her work fell into oblivion.[11] While it comes as no surprise that *Confessions* met with a hostile reception, an analysis of what exactly troubled the reviewers reveals the contested position of an autobiographer like Wanda von Sacher-Masoch. In his review article titled *"Meine Lebensbeichte:* Eine Ehrenrettung" (*Confessions:* A vindication) cultural philosopher and literary critic Theodor Lessing denounced *Confessions* as a "poisoning book"[12] and accused the autobiographer of having created a "fabric of dangerous pathological lies."[13] Drawing on the century-old tradition of pathologizing women's words as well as female sexuality, Lessing condemned Sacher-Masoch's book as a particularly unsavory example of the artistic cult of decadence and the countless memoirs of "lost" and "fallen" women it inspired.[14] Lessing, however, was not offended by the description of female sexuality or male masochistic sexual practice. Applying the all too familiar double standard, the critic admonished that *Confessions* reveals both too little and too much, concealing certain facts about the autobiographer's sexual history and disclosing too many aspects about her husband's sexual conduct. Lessing urges his readers, in particular the sexologists of his day and the executives of the publishing industry, to "forget" Leopold von Sacher-Masoch's "sexual tragedy" and instead to honor his work.[15] Wanda von Sacher-Masoch challenged the hierarchy that privileged the male literary

---

11. The only edition currently in print is Christa Gürtler's edition of the short prose, *Damen mit Pelz und Peitsche* (Frankfurt am Main: Ullstein, 1995). For critical literature that focuses substantially on Wanda von Sacher-Masoch, see Christa Gürtler, "Damen mit Pelz und Peitsche. Zu Texten von Wanda von Sacher-Masoch," in *Schwierige Verhältnisse: Liebe und Sexualität in der Frauenliteratur um 1900,* ed. Theresia Klugsberger, Stuttgarter Arbeiten zur Germanistik, 262 (Stuttgart: Heinz, 1992), 71–82; Isolde Schackmann, "Das Bild der 'Emanzipierten': Herrin und/oder Gefährtin. Zu zwei Novellen von Wanda von Sacher-Masoch und Irma Troll-Borostyáni," in Klugsberger, *Schwierige Verhältnisse,* 83–102; and Sigrid Schmidt-Bortenschlager, "Frauenliteratur im 19. Jahrhundert—Ideologie, Fiktion, Realität. Dargestellt am Beispiel der Thematik 'Versorgungsehe,'" in *Begegnung mit dem "Fremden": Grenzen-Traditionen-Vergleiche,* Akten des 8. Internationalen Germanisten-Kongresses, Tokyo, 1990, ed. Eijiro Iwasaki (Munich: Iudicium, 1991), 246–50.

12. Theodor Lessing, *"Meine Lebensbeichte:* Eine Ehrenrettung," *Die Gegenwart* 35 (1906), no. 32, 85–88, and no. 33, 104–7, reprinted in Farin, *Leopold von Sacher-Masoch,* 219.

13. Ibid., 205.

14. Ibid. Lessing had in mind publications such as *Tagebuch einer Verlorenen* and Felix Salten's anonymously published "diary" of *Josefine Mutzenbacher: Die Lebensgeschichte einer wienerischen Dirne, von ihr selbst erzählt* (1906; Munich: Rogner & Bernard, 1996).

15. Farin, *Leopold von Sacher-Masoch,* 219. Theodor Lessing had personal ties to Sacher-Masoch's family. After the writer's death, he was the private teacher of Sacher-Masoch's children from his marriage to his second wife, Hulda Meister. Ludwig Jacobowski, editor-in-chief of *Die Gesellschaft,* collected money for these children; see "Für die Kinder von Sacher-Masoch," *Die Gesellschaft* 16, no. 3 (1900): 132.

work as a unique artistic achievement over the female autobiography as a secondary product of a minor subject. In Lessing's eyes, *Confessions* presented yet another version of the emerging genre of sensationalist female confessions that corrupted the standards of literary high culture perhaps even more than the norms of respectable sexual conduct.

Lessing's fervent rebuff of *Confessions* is of interest because both his review and the autobiography itself identify the relationship between the female- and the male-authored text as a space in which the struggle over gender and genre hierarchies is carried out. To this day, critics label *Confessions* as at least partially "untrue" and dismiss it as Wanda von Sacher-Masoch's attempt to exonerate herself from the accusation of promiscuity and participation in sexual perversion. Holger Rudloff, for instance, rejects her autobiography as a willfully deceptive documentation of an unusual marriage,[16] and Michael O'Pecko goes so far as to claim that Leopold's work was "almost obliterated after his death by the invective of *Meine Lebensbeichte.*"[17]

Fearing for Leopold's credibility within the tradition of high culture, turn-of-the-century as well as contemporary critics apply a gendered definition of autobiographical truth to discredit Wanda von Sacher-Masoch's narrative. Critics draw on her lower-class background to dispute her ability to write, while considering her book dangerous at the same time. Female autobiography, especially an autobiography that does not adhere to the conventions of high literature as Georg Misch had begun to spell them out, thus poses a threat to the male literary work because it obscures the truth about female sexuality while putting into words aspects of male sexuality better left unspoken. The history of reception and the critical skirmish over Sacher-Masoch's female autobiographical truth suggests that *Confessions* provokes anxieties that reach well beyond the "instabilities of the late nineteenth and early twentieth centuries" and the scope of this particular autobiography.[18] At stake are the line of demarcation between truth and lie, the difference between masculinity and femininity, and the protection of male-defined high culture from a feminized culture of decadence.[19] The desire for discernible distinctions is propelled by the fear that these differences might not be enforceable.

---

16. Holger Rudloff, *Pelzdamen: Weiblichkeitsbilder bei Thomas Mann und Leopold von Sacher-Masoch* (Frankfurt am Main: Fischer, 1994), 21.

17. Michael T. O'Pecko, "Comedy and Didactic in Leopold von Sacher-Masoch's *Venus im Pelz," Modern Austrian Literature* 25, no. 2 (1992): 2.

18. Sidonie Smith, *Subjectivity, Identity, and the Body: Women's Autobiographical Practices in the Twentieth Century* (Bloomington: Indiana University Press, 1993), 54.

19. Lessing explicitly takes offense with the motto on the front page of *Confessions,* for which Wanda von Sacher-Masoch had chosen two lines from Goethe's *Faust:* "Mich faßt ein längst entwohnter Schauer / Der Menschheit ganzer Jammer faßt mich an" (*"Meine Lebensbeichte:* Eine Ehrenrettung," 205).

Feminist scholars have argued that women's autobiographies traditionally have met with critical disbelief because their writers were not trusted to speak the truth upon which the autobiographical contract is based. Leigh Gilmore, in her study *Autobiographics,* emphasizes that concepts such as subject and identity, both of which are fundamental to the writing and reading of autobiographies, depend on specific cultural practices rather than universal standards: "Whether and when autobiography emerges as an authoritative discourse of reality and identity, and any particular text appears to tell the truth, have less to do with that text's presumed accuracy about what really happened than with its apprehended fit into culturally prevalent discourses of truth and identity."[20] While none of Wanda von Sacher-Masoch's critics doubted Leopold von Sacher-Masoch's masochistic disposition, they deemed it necessary to separate the "truth" about his sexuality from his identity as a serious writer. What is also at stake is the knowledge about sexuality and who gets to produce it. *Confessions* has thus variously been accused of telling too much and too little, of lying and being overly explicit. The discursive links between writing and sexuality, the gender of the author and the power to speak, circumscribe the contested position of the female autobiographer in turn-of-the-century Germany. Wanda von Sacher-Masoch most likely did not tell the truth on every page of her autobiography. As she embarked on what Michel Foucault has described as this "strange endeavor" of telling the truth about sex, she found herself, if briefly, in the center of the modernity debates.[21] Both she and her reviewers knew that her autobiographical truth documented the feminization of sexual and literary culture and a loss of masculinity.

Not everyone condemned Wanda von Sacher-Masoch and her *Confessions.* André Salmon was obviously fascinated by his chance encounter with her. Journalist and critic Alfred Gold acknowledged the emotional effect of confessional memoirs. "Lined up in a section of my bookshelf I see books of a genre that has an impact now, Oscar Wilde, Wanda v. Sacher-Masoch, Linda Murri—confessing books. The genre is not without an inherent, shared appeal; the tear wells, the earth has us back, the linguistic art of naive and unmediated observation comes into wonderful might, life appears as a poet."[22] Gold attributes a cathartic function to confessional literature, allowing both reader and writer to undergo a

---

20. Gilmore, *Autobiographics,* ix.

21. Michel Foucault, *The History of Sexuality,* vol. 1: *An Introduction,* trans. Robert Hurley (New York: Vintage Books), 57.

22. Alfred Gold, "Beichtende Bücher," *Die neue Rundschau* (1906): 1278. All three of the confessional memoirs reviewed by Gold were written by sexual outsiders. Gold focuses mainly on the Italian Linda Murri's divorce story, which he likens to Gabriele Reuter's 1895 novel *Aus guter Familie.*

Faustian rebirth. Moreover, the genre permitted a degree of honesty absent from conventional autobiography. "Confessing books! The adulteress disarms the silly catchword and writes about her fate. Perhaps she is situated at the beginning of a better era. Sacher-Masoch's widow does this as well, and I cannot really deny respect to her diary of spicy indiscretion either."[23] Confessional memoirs challenge bourgeois conventions. For Alfred Gold, this was a positive quality.

Paradoxically, Sacher-Masoch's autobiography has contributed to obscuring her biography. Her own narrative breaks off in 1898 with the death of Jakob Rosenthal, a journalist and publisher for whom she had left Leopold von Sacher-Masoch. To this day, most literary encyclopedias do not offer any biographical data beyond 1906, the year that *Confessions* was published. Declaring the autobiography to be the death of its author, some encyclopedists conjecture that Wanda von Sacher-Masoch died "after 1906."[24] Her "untruthful" autobiography must have made biographical facts irrelevant to those who shaped the literary canon for the turn of the century and beyond.

Wanda von Sacher-Masoch was born on March 14, 1845, in Graz, Austria, as Angelica Aurora Rümelin. Her father, a military administrator and later a clerk for a railway company, left the family around 1860. Trained as a seamstress, Angelica Aurora supported herself and her mother by taking in piecework. In 1871, she met Leopold von Sacher-Masoch, a historian and writer with an international reputation. A child born to the couple in 1872 died a few days after his birth. On October 12, 1873, Angelica Rümelin married Leopold and changed her name to Wanda von Sacher-Masoch. The first years of marriage were ones of financial difficulties, necessitating repeated changes of residency. After a brief period in Vienna, the couple moved to Bruck an der Mur, a provincial center in Styria. In 1874 and 1875, two sons, Alexander and Demetrius, were born, and Leopold's daughter from a previous relationship, Karoline, joined the family. The marriage began to dissolve in 1882 while the family was residing in Leipzig, and, after several years of separation, ended in divorce in 1886. From 1883 Wanda lived in Paris with her son Demetrius and the journalist Jakob Rosenthal, until Rosenthal left her in 1888.[25] Little is known about her life after the publication of *Con-*

---

23. Ibid.

24. Wilhelm Kosch, *Deutsches Literatur-Lexikon. Biographisches und bibliographisches Handbuch,* 2d ed., vol. 3 (Bern: Francke, 1956), 2357.

25. Jakob Rosenthal was a German-born journalist and coeditor of Leopold von Sacher-Masoch's Leipzig-based journal *Auf der Höhe.* Rosenthal, who later worked for the *Figaro,* made a name for himself under the pseudonyms "Armand" and "Jacques St.-Cère." He died in Paris in 1898.

fessions in 1906 and a second autobiographical text, *Masochismus und Masochisten* (Masochism and masochists) in 1908.[26] She continued her literary activities as translator and writer into the 1920s, publishing her stories in journals.[27] Leopold's biographer Bernard Michel reports that Wanda von Sacher-Masoch died in France in 1933.[28]

For the present-day reader, *Confessions* might not be as scandalous as it certainly was for Wanda von Sacher-Masoch's contemporaries. Just like many of Leopold's stories and novels, Wanda's autobiography tells the story of a sexual perversion by omission of the sexual act rather than through its exposure. Subdivided into short segments of one to four pages each, *Confessions* presents itself as a conventional chronological narrative, beginning with the narrator's family background and her early childhood. The style is descriptive rather than reflective, following external organizing principles such as the appearance of new characters or a change of residency. Sacher-Masoch did not indulge in the stylistic experiments of modernism. Her five-hundred-page autobiography does, however, include characters and events representing the abnormal sexual practices that occupied the collective fantasy at the turn of the century. The most important protagonist of these sexual plots is, of course, Leopold von Sacher-Masoch, the feminized man of masochism who relinquishes his sociosexual dominance to a cruel woman. Opposite Leopold the autobiographer introduces his typological counterpart, a mannish woman who is also a lesbian and a prostitute. Taking up a sexual subject position in contrast to both of these figures, the narrator writes herself into the culturally sanctioned female role of wife and mother. *Confessions* thus organizes the subject positions of its characters along the binary opposition of conventional and perverse sexualities. The narrator's participation in Leopold's sexual aberrations as well as her role as an object of lesbian desire, however, complicates the picture by placing the female subject of this autobiography on both sides of the divide. In *Confessions,* Wanda von Sacher-Masoch plays off conventional femininity against transgressive female sexuality and feminized male sexuality. The autobiographical subject that emerges through these constellations refuses to take up an unambiguous position within the sociosexual system of her time. Instead, Wanda von Sacher-Masoch's narrative probes the limits of the culturally sanctioned categories of identity.

---

26. Wanda von Sacher-Masoch, *Masochismus und Masochisten. Nachtrag zur Lebensbeichte* (Berlin: Schuster & Loeffler, [1908]).

27. *Wanda und Leopold von Sacher-Masoch: Szenen einer Ehe. Eine kontroversielle Biographie. Mit einem Nachwort versehen von Adolf Opel* (Vienna: Wiener Frauenverlag, 1996), 301–2.

28. Bernard Michel, *Sacher-Masoch. 1836–1895* (Paris: Laffont, 1989), 287.

In autobiographical narratives the opening sentences are often intended to mirror the precarious beginnings of the narrator's life. Not unlike the first paragraphs of Goethe's *Poetry and Truth,* the first lines of *Confessions* suggest that this autobiography almost remained unwritten. The newborn Goethe almost did not survive the first three days of his life; Wanda von Sacher-Masoch's mother nearly lost her pregnancy. "In 1845 I was born in Graz, Austria to Wilhelm Rümelin, a military clerk," the narrator begins, legitimizes herself with a reference to her patriarchal lineage (4; translation modified). Only the name of the father possesses the power to provide the subject with the necessary legal identity. Without transition the narrative continues: "Several months before my birth my mother suffered an accident" (4; translation modified). Even though the unnamed maternal body cannot endow the autobiographical subject with a legal status, *Confessions* privileges the mother-child relationship as a bond that precedes and outlives patriarchal social structures.

The opening section of *Confessions* ends with the reminiscence of a proposed suicide. "I was three years old when death and despair brushed me for the first time," the narrator states, recalling her father's suggestion of a communal suicide whose motivation remains unexplained (4). The autobiographical subject introduces herself to the reader as a survivor of events that contrast the figure of the weak yet life-affirming mother with a father figure who fails in his traditional function as the provider and protector of the family. Familial turmoil turns into social upheaval, and the following segment shows the narrator in a monastery during the 1848 revolution, where she takes a liking to the "pale-faced nuns, with their renouncing *(entsagenden)* eyes and melancholy smiles" (4; translation modified). As wives and mothers, the narrative implies, women are threatened by potential death; outside the institution of marriage, they carry the signs of renunciation, an appearance that makes them strangely attractive to the narrator's young self.

These introductory scenes set the stage for a narrative that endorses a conventional female gender role while bemoaning its unrealizability in lived reality. Sacher-Masoch concurs with many nineteenth-century thinkers when she focuses on male sexuality as an unpredictable force that even the institution of marriage cannot always successfully contain. Adultery, the violation of the marital contract's mandate of sexual exclusiveness, leads to the breakup of the narrator's family and runs through the autobiography like a leitmotif. The narrator's discovery of her father's illicit relationship with a prostitute ushers in the demise of her family. Mounting financial difficulties and her father's ineptness as a provider destroy the family unit. "I never saw him again" (8), her valediction, not only signifies her father's disappearance from the narrative but foreshadows the ultimate break with Leopold. "I never saw Sacher-Masoch again," the narrator comments when Leopold fails to keep his appointment with her because "there was a woman," as the maid informs her, "with that discreet and so expressive smile with which French servants confide news of this sort" (118).

Confessions attests to the failure of marriage to control male sexuality. As a result, the family cannot guarantee the female role of wife and mother that it creates and sanctions in the first place. Wanda von Sacher-Masoch casts her autobiographical self within the parameters of traditional female gender roles, yet, like many women writers of her time, she uses the language of gender conservatism to tell a story of transgression. Her story of constant struggle against the private and social circumstances that prevented her from sustaining the desired position of wife and mother exposes the unreliability of the boundaries that separate normality from perversion.

Readers perusing the pages of Wanda von Sacher-Masoch's autobiography expect to find the true story of a transgressive sexuality with which they are already familiar: Leopold von Sacher-Masoch's repetitious tales of the male masochistic fantasy with its endless cycle of impending punishment, the execution of punishment, and elaborate anticipation of more refined torture. Let me briefly recapitulate the story of masochism's most famous male fantasy, Leopold von Sacher-Masoch's novella *Venus in Furs.*

A nameless narrator reading Hegel falls asleep and dreams about a talking Venus statue clad in furs. He recounts his dream to his friend Severin von Kuziemski, the main protagonist of *Venus in Furs.* Severin gives him a manuscript titled "Confessions of a Supersensualist," the story of his masochistic relationship with a beautiful young widow named Wanda von Dunajew, whom he persuades to treat him like a slave. She complies, albeit reluctantly, but grows into a role that requires her to whip and humiliate the protagonist. Wanda forces Severin von Kuziemski to sign a contract in which he relinquishes his freedom and submits to whatever cruelty she pleases to inflict. In return, Wanda promises to wear furs as often as possible, especially when she abuses him. A triangular relationship develops with the appearance of "the Greek," who becomes Severin's fortunate rival. In the final scene the Greek whips Severin in front of an amused Wanda. Under the Greek's cruel blows, Severin declares, he cured himself of his fantasy. After his father's death he assumes responsibility for his family's possessions and engages in conventional relationships with women. Severin's despotic treatment of his current lover in the novella's final scene convinces the reader that this man will never again be whipped by a woman. *Venus in Furs* is Leopold von Sacher-Masoch's life-text, the script that shaped his relationship with Wanda von Sacher-Masoch into a continuous "staging of a perversion."[29] In *Confessions,* masochism's foremost female protagonist revised the lines and the role of masochism's cruel woman and presented another version of the master text.

Venus in Furs is the most important but not the first of Sacher-Masoch's masochist fictions. In 1869 he published *Die geschiedene Frau* (The divorced woman), the novel in which he introduced the narrative elements of the masochistic plot. In this work, which is based on real-life experience, he turned his "dramatic" relationship with a woman called Anna von Kottowitz into literature.[30] In *The Divorced Woman,* Frau von Kossow, the female protagonist and Anna von Kottowitz's fictional counterpart, relates the tale of her affair with a young man named Julian von Romaschkan to a figure called Sacher-Masoch. In a plot within a plot, Julian invents the masochistic fantasy of female domination and male submission in an unfinished novella (entitled *Wanda*) that he gives Frau von Kossow to read and that she understands as a series of instructions. "I was incapable of *being Wanda,* but he had disclosed to me through his novella what I had to do to *appear to be Wanda.*"[31] Anna von Kossow turns herself into the masculinized woman who smokes, shoots pistols, and, most importantly, at the next ball appears in a lavish fur coat.[32] Julian's completed novella becomes a literary success. Nonetheless, Frau von Kossow's love affair with Julian ends in a tragic breakup. She is left rich, but socially isolated, her fate encapsulated in Julian's diary, which she reads and rereads. Frau von Kossow's life has been transformed into art. In her living room looms her life-size portrait painted by a local artist. By contrast, Julian continues to be a creative and prolific writer. "He works, he creates, he is useful. *His life will not be wasted,*" are the final words of the novel.[33]

The Divorced Woman is the literary birthplace of the transformation of the female protagonist into "Wanda." The male fantasy becomes the master text for the woman to read at its inception—Julian had not yet finished his novella when he handed it to Frau von Kossow—and to teach her the role of the mannish woman. But in *The Divorced Woman,* the scenes of male masochism, the torturing of the male protagonist by the cruel woman, take place only in Frau von Kossow's imagination, inspired by her perusal of *Wanda.* She confesses her domination fantasies to the

29. Koschorke's subtitle, *Die Inszenierung einer Perversion,* emphasizes the theatricality of Leopold von Sacher-Masoch's life and work.

30. Leopold von Sacher-Masoch in a letter from May 18, 1868; Leopold von Sacher-Masoch, *Die geschiedene Frau: Passionsgeschichte eines Idealisten* (1869; reprinted with an essay by Alexander von Sacher-Masoch and a dossier edited by Michael Farin, Nördlingen: Greno, 1989), 183.

31. Sacher-Masoch, *Die geschiedene Frau,* 71.

32. Ibid., 72.

33. Ibid., 182.

character Sacher-Masoch, and they thus enter into the body of the text but are not (yet) acted out on the body of the male protagonist. A year later, on the pages of *Venus in Furs,* "Wanda von Dunajew" executes the torture Frau von Kossow had fantasized in becoming "Wanda." The written text initiates the staging of the masochistic plot in the interplay between the male protagonist, who transforms his fantasy of the cruel woman into a narrative, and his female counterpart, whose function it is to adopt the prescribed role and to implement the masochistic acts of his invention. The narrative principles of the masochistic plot place the female protagonist at the threshold between the male protagonist's literary imagination and his lived fantasy. The masochist thus creates and delimits the female partner's role, yet his fantasy is such that it allows him to view her as the source of the cruelty he craves.

As if to assure themselves of their identity and subject position, the male heroes of both *The Divorced Woman* and *Venus in Furs* write autobiographical texts. "Passion of an Idealist," Julian von Romaschkan's diary that chronicles Frau von Kossow's life, and "Confessions of a Supersensualist," Severin von Kuziemski's life story, define the male protagonist through his authorship and his ability to write beyond the masochistic plot. Whereas "Wanda," in her various appearances, remains bound by literary invention, Julian and Severin are "useful" as her creator.

In *The Divorced Woman,* Sacher-Masoch portrayed himself as both Julian von Romaschkan, the successful writer of the novella that taught Frau von Kossow to become "Wanda," and the figure of Sacher-Masoch, the author's namesake and first-person narrator who transforms Frau von Kossow's story into a literary text. Thus, Sacher-Masoch maintains an authorial presence both within the narrative itself and as the novelist whose name on the front page asserts his authorship. Anna von Kottowitz, the woman on whom Sacher-Masoch modeled his "Frau von Kossow," did not leave behind a literary work. In *Confessions,* Wanda von Sacher-Masoch liberates the female subject position from the prescript of the male text and writes herself into the authorial function.

Women's complex relationship to self-representation, their implication in the "male gaze" and the "feminist reappropriation of the mirror," motivates many female autobiographies and continues to be of concern to feminist scholars.[34] In *Confessions* Sacher-Masoch traces her desire for self-representation to a short scene of erotic attraction between herself and

---

34. Bella Brodzki and Celeste Schenk, eds., *Life/Lines: Theorizing Women's Autobiography* (Ithaca: Cornell University Press, 1988), 7. The discussion of the "male gaze," which originates from feminist film studies, has become an important issue also in autobiography studies. See Smith, *Poetics of Women's Autobiography;* Gilmore, *Autobiographics;* and Sigrid Weigel, "Double Focus: On the History of Women's Writing," in *Feminist Aesthetics,* ed. Gisela Ecker, trans. Harriet Anderson (London: Women's Press, 1985), 59–80.

Anna von Kottowitz. Walking with her father in a park in Graz as a little girl, the narrator feels strangely drawn to an elegant woman named Frau von K., whose "singular beauty acted on me like a spell—unnerving, ravishing, almost painful" (4). Unbeknownst to the narrator at this early moment in her life, both of them are to fall victim to the same "occult power" (4). This power, however, is not simply Leopold von Sacher-Masoch, who became both women's lover, but the phenomenon of encountering one's self as a work of art. Frau von K. had this experience twice in her life: she had been painted by an artist, who displayed the picture in a Graz art gallery even though it failed to convey her beauty; and a second time through Leopold von Sacher-Masoch, whose *Divorced Woman,* Wanda concedes, does justice to Frau von K.'s beauty but casts her in a "false light" (6).

The scene in the park might well not be "true." Its inclusion in the autobiography, however, suggests that Wanda von Sacher-Masoch viewed the transformation of life into art as a process reflective of the uneven distribution of power between the male artist and his muse. Contrasting her memories of this meeting with the artistic renditions of Frau von K., the narrator assigns a higher truth value to her recollection and rejects the male artistic works as either inadequate or unsympathetic portrayals of Frau von K. Wanda von Sacher-Masoch thus challenges the "false" representation of female life in male art and confronts it with her own version. Whereas Frau von K. remained an object of art, Wanda von Sacher-Masoch reversed the process of objectification and became author and subject of her story. In *Confessions,* the narrator couples her desire for self-representation with her desire for the other woman, "reappropriating the mirror" by juxtaposing male models of sexuality and writing with female homoeroticism and female self-representation.

Wanda von Sacher-Masoch identifies *The Divorced Woman* as the urtext from which the female position in masochism originates, with Anna von Kottowitz as her less fortunate alter ego. *Venus in Furs,* the masochistic master text that Leopold wished to relive, and *Confessions,* Wanda's countertext, thus present two versions of the masochistic plot that offer competing interpretations of the female role. In his famous essay "Coldness and Cruelty," Gilles Deleuze defended Wanda's book against the critics who cast her in the role of the sadist, simply describing it as "excellent."[35] In his efforts to uncouple sadism from masochism and to establish them as two distinct perversions, Deleuze argued that the "woman tor-

---

35. Gilles Deleuze, "Coldness and Cruelty," trans. Jean McNeil, in Gilles Deleuze and Leopold von Sacher-Masoch, *Masochism* (New York: Zone Books, 1991), 9.

turer of masochism [is] . . . a realization of the masochistic fantasy,"[36] and emphasized that the male masochist "definitely has no need of another subject, i.e., the sadistic subject."[37] The masochistic plot depends on the woman's renunciation of her subjectivity; she must, in other words, become "Wanda." Wanda von Sacher-Masoch appropriated the figure of "Wanda" and turned her into the subject for which the heterosexual masochistic plot had no need.

Confessions traces the beginnings of the relationship between its narrator and Leopold von Sacher-Masoch to the mystery of "autobiographical truth" that governs the boundaries between reality and text. The narrator and Frau Frischauer, her Jewish friend, closely observe Leopold walking in the streets of Graz, read his books, and discuss the possible connections between Sacher-Masoch's texts and his life. Are his books "true"? Do his texts represent his desire? Frau Frischauer thinks so. To prove her point, she initiates an exchange of letters with Sacher-Masoch, which she signs "Wanda von Dunajew," the heroine of *Venus in Furs*. After the exposure of her identity prevents Frau Frischauer from continuing the relationship, she dispatches the narrator to retrieve her letters from Sacher-Masoch. Instead of simply collecting the letters, the narrator yields to Sacher-Masoch's pleas to take her friend's place and continues the exchange. With his suggestion that "it would be best if I kept the name of 'Wanda von Dunajew' as an address" Sacher-Masoch conducts an act of baptism by transferring a literary identity from one female interlocutor to another (14; translation modified). The adoption of a literary name initiates Wanda von Sacher-Masoch into a form of "masochistic" authorship. She begins to write "cruel" letters to Leopold, thus bringing his text back to life, while at the same time transforming herself according to the script of his text.

Her success as a writer, Sacher-Masoch acknowledged in *Confessions,* would not have been possible without Leopold's encouragement and his willingness to use his connections to get her short stories and novels published. Some critics have gone so far as to call into question her ability to write altogether, simply attributing her literary output to him. Under his guidance, Wanda von Sacher-Masoch began to publish a series of prose works, using "Wanda von Dunajew" as a pseudonym. In a succession of texts and countertexts she weaves together his and her life stories. Wanda von Sacher-Masoch subtitled her *Roman einer tugendhaften Frau* (Novel

---

36. Ibid., 41.
37. Ibid., 42–43.

of a virtuous woman) "a counterpart to Sacher-Masoch's 'divorced woman'";[38] her 1879 collection *Echter Hermlin* (Genuine ermine)[39] echoes his 1873 volume *Falscher Hermlin* (Fake ermine); and *Die Damen im Pelz* (The ladies in furs), which went into seven editions between 1881 and 1910, reverberates to his *Venus in Furs.*[40] Finally, Sacher-Masoch's autobiography responds to Leopold's *The Divorced Woman* and his *Venus in Furs,* both of which were promoted by their author as autobiographical texts. With its allusion to the Catholic practice of confessional truth-telling and absolution, the title *Confessions* establishes a link to the "Confessions of a Supersensualist," the title of the central narrative within *Venus in Furs,* and to the "Passion of an Idealist," the title of the male protagonist's diary in *The Divorced Woman.* All three works suggest that the act of confession, the telling of one's story, holds the key to redemption. Further, they allude to the high literary tradition of Goethe's "Confessions of a Beautiful Soul." Leopold's male sexual fantasy as text and Wanda's female counternarrative, her autobiography *Confessions,* constitute a sequence of autobiographical acts that negotiate the transformation of sexuality into textual identity. Decades before the controversy between Wanda von Sacher-Masoch and her critics ensued over her "true" life story, Leopold and Wanda engaged in inventing multiple versions of the masochistic tale of the cruel woman and her male slave. In *Confessions* Wanda von Sacher-Masoch tells this story, which yokes together his and her life/writing, one more time; this time she writes beyond the narrative boundaries of his master text.

The cover and title page of *Confessions* feature the words "Wanda von Sacher-Masoch" in the position reserved for the name of the author. After this prominent display of authorship, the narrator abstains from any further self-naming in her text. Nor does "Angelica Aurora Rümelin," which literary encyclopedias insist is her "real" name, enter into the pages of this autobiography. "Wanda" remains the only first name used in *Confessions,* yet, in keeping with Leopold's suggestion, only as an "address" used by other characters in the autobiography. "Wanda von Sacher-Masoch," then, not only signifies the narrator's legal status as a married woman who has adopted her husband's last name, it also blurs the boundaries between literature and life. In coupling "Wanda," the first name of the infamous literary figure of the cruel woman, with "von Sacher-

---

38. Wanda von Sacher-Masoch, *Roman einer tugendhaften Frau: Ein Gegenstück zur "geschiedenen Frau" von Sacher-Masoch* (Prague: Bohemia, 1873).

39. Wanda von Sacher-Masoch, *Echter Hermlin. Geschichten aus der vornehmen Welt* (Bern: Frobeen, 1879).

40. Wanda von Sacher-Masoch, *Die Damen im Pelz. Geschichten* (Leipzig: Morgenstern, 1882).

Masoch," the surname of a literary author from a respected aristocratic Galician family, *Confessions* outlines an identity rooted in both literature and reality, in patriarchy as much as in its subversion.

Wanda von Sacher-Masoch's autobiographical references to her career as a writer remain sparse and are not without self-irony. About the creation of her first novel, *Der Roman einer tugendhaften Frau,* she writes: "I stopped making gloves and started a little novel. Three months later I finished it, and it brought me three hundred florins" (15). At a later point, she comments on her lack of artistic drive and ability. "For a moment I considered taking up writing again to supplement our income, but quickly I discarded the idea. I had a husband, a household, and children. . . . Besides, the ease with which I had given up writing was proof to me that basically I had no great talent" (32). Most importantly, Sacher-Masoch attributes her choice of subject matter to Leopold and his insistence that her literary activities be part of their erotic contract: "My work also had to please my husband—therefore I had to write 'cruel' stories. In order to put myself in an appropriate frame of mind, I had to wear fur and place a huge dog whip on the table before me" (87). The paraphernalia of the cruel woman are essential not only for masochistic role play but also for masochistic literary production. Once she had slipped into "Wanda's" furs, Leopold assumed, she could simply write herself. The autobiographer distances herself from both her sexual and her literary performances, attributing them to her husband's desires and the family's need for economic survival. While Leopold allowed the masochist fantasy to merge his life and writing into an inseparable unit, Wanda von Sacher-Masoch engaged in the opposite strategy and offered *Confessions* as a corrective to her earlier literary creations.

Wanda von Sacher-Masoch's stories of the 1870s and 1880s indeed contain many of the elements in Leopold von Sacher-Masoch's works, including whips, furs, and men begging beautiful women to flog them. Yet in contrast to his texts, in which the female protagonists learn to "become Wanda," she proffers alternative explanations for the cruelty of her women characters. Gilles Deleuze's interpretation of Leopold's cruel women provides a useful analytical model for Wanda's female figures as well. Masochism, Deleuze insists in "Coldness and Cruelty," is a fantasy about the mother. "The masochistic contract excludes the father and displaces onto the mother the task of exercising and applying the paternal law."[41] Deleuze's groundbreaking essay thus challenges Freudian psychoanalysis and the assumption that the woman torturer in the masochist situation represents a stand-in for the father. Male masochism, Deleuze sug-

---

41. Deleuze, "Coldness and Cruelty," 93.

gests, rearranges the symbolic order by expelling the father from his all-powerful position and transferring his attributes to the woman and mother. The all-powerful mother of the masochist fantasy then gives rebirth to an "ideal ego" and thus ultimately confirms the identity of the male masochist subject.[42] In her autobiographical as well as in her fictional responses to the masochist fantasy, Wanda von Sacher-Masoch shifted emphasis from the masochist symbolic to female subject positions in the "reality" of patriarchal society. Her female figures resort to the role of the cruel woman because their realities force them out of their traditional gender identity.

Sacher-Masoch introduced her 1879 volume *Genuine Ermine,* a collection of short stories, with a brief theoretical exploration titled "Das Mysterium der Liebe" (The mystery of love). The enigma of love finds its solution in a reversal of gender roles. Male and female subject positions are located on the extreme ends of a thermal scale: "The colder one partner, the more scorching the other."[43] Female coldness is not an innate female quality but a means to preserve and to stoke male sexual desire. "The gentle, faithful, weak Gretchen will always and everywhere be abandoned for a proud, cold, cruel woman for whom love is but a game; the tenderness of a wife is tiresome, whereas the kicks of a lover give pleasure; her cold, scornful laughter allures and intoxicates."[44] Coldness, cruelty, and the denial of sexual fulfillment protect women against the fate of a "Gretchen," the young woman of Goethe's famous tragedy who gave in to Faust's wooing only to be betrayed by him. Cruel women, by contrast, who keep their male lovers in a permanent state of sexual arousal can expect to be loved with a passion that borders on insanity.

The writer finds the explanation to why gender relationships have strayed so far from traditional notions in the vicissitudes of her time. Romantic love and the devotion of a Gretchen have run their course, forcing women to adopt a new model of female sociosexual conduct. The "pathologically nervous man of modern times," she suggests, has lost his "sense for the simple love of an unpretentious wife."[45] Having diagnosed a crisis of masculine identity and declining virility, Wanda von Sacher-Masoch outlines how women should respond to this pathology of the modern age. "Woman must not love and only as long as she does not love will she maintain the mysterious power with which she renders every man

---

42. Ibid., 127.
43. Wanda von Sacher-Masoch, "Das Mysterium der Liebe," in *Damen mit Pelz und Peitsche,* 8.
44. Ibid.
45. Ibid., 10.

her slave, making him rejoice under her kicks."[46] Wanda von Sacher-Masoch exposes gender relationships as power relationships and tells women how to maintain their "mysterious" omnipotence. Under the cruel blows of the "Greek," Severin, the hero of *Venus in Furs,* resolved to be hammer rather than anvil. In "The Mystery of Love" there is no third element that breaks the heroine's spell over her lover.[47] Advising her female readers how to sustain male heat with their coldness, Wanda von Sacher-Masoch insists that women have a vital interest in keeping male and female subject positions in opposition to one another. If they do not succeed, they will be abandoned. Deleuze, similarly, interprets the woman partner's coldness as a strategy of desexualization that, however, for the male masochist serves as the "precondition of instantaneous resexualization."[48] Wanda von Sacher-Masoch urges her readers to defer this "leap," as Deleuze imaginatively calls it, indefinitely. The jump into resexualization signals the end of the masochist role-play and thus marks the limits of the cruel woman's power. The sex act reintroduces traditional gender roles and reinstates the male partner in his position of superiority. Coldness and cruelty, in other words, are weapons the woman must deploy in the battle of the sexes if she wants to emerge victorious, and Wanda von Sacher-Masoch advises her readers how to use them most effectively.

"The Mystery of Love" also considers class difference. Women of the demimonde, the writer acknowledges, might be capable of play-acting the role of the cruel woman for their upper-class male clients. But in the long run their performances will not sustain the necessary erotic tension. Only the women of the aristocracy, born to rule, are "always noble, always elegant, never *ordinary* and ugly."[49] This distinction between aristocratic cruelty and the base ugliness of the demimonde hints at the precarious position of the cruel woman not only vis-à-vis her male partner but also in terms of her own role. According to Deleuze, there are three distinct yet interrelated types of women in Leopold von Sacher-Masoch's stories. The sensual and independent hetaera is at one extreme, the sadist woman at the other. The masochist's ideal—"cold, maternal, severe; icy, sentimental, cruel"—is positioned between them, constantly controlling her own desires to avoid slipping into one of the extremes.[50] "The character of the

---

46. Ibid., 11.
47. Deleuze remarks that "where the sadistic man happens to triumph, as he does at the end of 'Venus,' all masochistic activity ceases" ("Coldness and Cruelty," 61). Wanda von Sacher-Masoch understood very well that the end of masochistic activity also meant the subjugation of the female partner.
48. Ibid., 118.
49. Sacher-Masoch, "Das Mysterium der Liebe," 10.
50. Deleuze, "Coldness and Cruelty," 51.

woman torturer regards the outer limits with a mixture of fear, revulsion, and attraction, since she never quite knows whether she will be able to maintain her prescribed role, and fears that she might at any moment fall back into primitive hetaerism or forward into the other extreme of sadism."[51] Wanda von Sacher-Masoch interpreted the cruel woman's precarious position between hetaera and sadist as a question of class. Only the aristocratic woman can be secure in her dominant role, a conclusion that might well be based on the writer's observation of social reality.

"The Mystery of Love" reiterates Leopold's fantasy of the dominating woman whose cruelty and near abstinence pushes her lover's passion to insanity. Wanda von Sacher-Masoch, however, locates the demise of the "tender wives" in the pathology of modern men. In the end, the mysterium of love that she claims to have uncovered in her essay is not so much that men long for cruelty, but that women must be cold if they want to play any role at all in the modern version of the ancient battle between the sexes. Both Wanda's and Leopold's novels offer numerous reincarnations of the cruel woman and her treatment of her male slaves. Wanda, however, shifts the emphasis to the female perspective by investigating the cruel woman's stakes in the masochist plot.[52]

Wanda von Sacher-Masoch published her first novel, *The Novel of a Virtuous Woman,* in 1873, the same year that she married Leopold and gave birth to their first child. Subtitled *A Counterpiece to the "Divorced Woman" by Sacher-Masoch,* the 150-page narrative signals its intention to challenge the literary fantasy of the cruel woman while at the same time using the renown of Sacher-Masoch's name and work as a point of reference. *Novel of a Virtuous Woman* tells the story of the young countess Adrienne von Neunkirchen, the beautiful and intelligent daughter of a doting father and a flirtatious, philandering mother, who prefers her studies and serious conversations with her father over the diversions in which high society expects rich young ladies to indulge. Adrienne is indifferent to the advances of young men and rejects her female friends' suggestions to get involved in love affairs. The rational Adrienne refuses to allow her emotions to interfere with her "happiness" and possesses a Nietzschean will to power. Her philosophy of life is best described as social Darwinism, a theory that arouses her curiosity when she reads about "survival of the fittest" in the newspaper. As befits a "cruel story," Adrienne's intellectual interest in Darwinism quickly develops into a power struggle with her

---

51. Ibid., 50.
52. In the closing lines of "Das Mysterium der Liebe," Sacher-Masoch distances herself from her paradigm of gender relationships and identifies herself as the notable exception to the rule outlined in her essay (11).

tutor, Dr. Borchard. Dr. Borchard, who embodies the masochist male in *Virtuous Woman,* interprets "survival of the fittest" as a masochist site of female domination and male submission, offering himself as a subservient "prisoner" to Adrienne's superior strength.[53] While Leopold's Anna von Kossow was willing to "become Wanda," Wanda's "counterpiece" Adrienne von Neunkirchen rejects the masochist contract. A true aristocrat, she possesses the iciness of the "ideal" cruel woman, but she deploys her coldness to stifle her own emotions rather than to stoke a lover's passionate heat. Dr. Borchard threatens and later commits suicide over Adrienne's rejection of his offer of masochist submission, an act that Adrienne condemns as irrational and effeminate. The narrative describes Adrienne as a "true child of modernity" whose "practical reason" not only distinguishes her from her flirtatious mother and her romantic peers but also protects her against entering into a masochist contract.[54] Adrienne's "practical reason" modifies nineteenth-century conventions of femininity without forcing her into the temporary role reversal that underlies the masochist performance. Neither "Gretchen" nor "cruel woman," Adrienne charts a third course.

After the hapless masochist's death, Adrienne falls in love with Prinz Karl Greif-Bernburg. When she learns that Prince Karl, a younger son, will not inherit the family's large fortune, she severs the engagement. "Either I marry rich, or not at all," she informs the distraught prince.[55] Both Karl, as a second son, and Adrienne, as a woman, are subject to the laws of patriarchy. The law of the father prevents Karl's access to Adrienne. Adrienne's renunciation of Karl's love illustrates the economic underpinnings of her coldness, for she knows that she must depend on male providers to maintain her aristocratic lifestyle.

In the second half of the novel, Prince Karl's widowed father, the immensely rich Fürst Greif-Bernburg, courts Adrienne and wins her hand in marriage. Before agreeing to the Fürst's proposal, Adrienne insists on a contract: she demands financial security after her considerably older husband's death; she wants him to know that she does not love him; and she demands equality.[56] Unlike the cruel woman, who must continuously play her role to maintain her superiority, Adrienne's prenuptial requests secure her subject position without masochist performances. Her successful deployment of "coldness" for the sake of economic security liberates her from the necessity of keeping her husband in a state of perpetual erotic torridity.

---

53. Sacher-Masoch, *Roman einer tugendhaften Frau,* 20.
54. Ibid., 60.
55. Ibid., 81.
56. Ibid., 106.

Novel of a Virtuous Woman strips the masochist fantasy of its essential components. Most importantly, fur coats and whips, the indispensable paraphernalia of the cruel woman, are stripped of their masochist significance. Adrienne refuses to wear furs because they are a "symbol of sensuality and dominance."[57] Once, she reports, she wore one of her mother's coats at the request of her father. He was so aroused that she decided to swear off this "Toilettenstück" forever.[58] Sacher-Masoch's cruel woman wears fur to achieve and uphold male sexual arousal. Adrienne rejects the garment for that very reason.

The father's arousal at the sight of his daughter in her mother's fur testifies to the incestuous nature of the father-daughter relationship. Through her marriage to her lover's father, Adrienne transfers her incestuous relationship with her own father to a legitimate object. Like her father, Fürst Greif-Bernburg pleads with Adrienne to wear fur coats. She obliges him by wearing them only in the privacy of her own house. As a married woman, she reasons, she has to obey her husband and, furthermore, thinks it appropriate to appear "intoxicating" in the eyes of her husband.[59] Adrienne thus agrees to furs and the sensuality they signify only in a relationship in which she already has contractually secured power. Similarly, the use of the whip, which in Leopold von Sacher-Masoch's fiction secures the cruel woman's power over her male slave, is here reserved for a situation in which Adrienne is in complete possession of power. In the only whipping scene of the novel, Adrienne punishes a thief among the servants in her father's house with thirty lashes. Class difference, punishment for a concrete offense rather than an imagined one, and the complete absence of erotic tension between the whipping woman and her victim underscore the sexual neutrality of the whipping scene. Dr. Borchard, Adrienne's masochist admirer and witness to this punishment, begs Adrienne to allow him to take the position of the culprit. Predictably, Adrienne refuses to "become Wanda" and declines to fulfill the tutor's masochist fantasies. For Adrienne, furs and whips cannot be the accouterments of the cruel woman because she is not a cruel woman. She allows them only as the rightful insignia of the married upper-class woman, whose power over her subjects is beyond question. Wanda von Sacher-Masoch's "virtuous woman" dons fur and cracks the whip to dissociate herself from her cruel counterpart.

Virtuous Woman shows the female protagonist involved in a network of oedipal constellations. Adrienne and her father are bound to one another by a relationship that is both oedipal and economic. In marrying

---

57. Ibid., 52.
58. Ibid., 109.
59. Ibid., 110.

the immensely rich Fürst, Adrienne aligns her "happiness" with yet another father figure. At the same time, she becomes "mother" to Karl, her former lover and her husband's impecunious son. She thus assumes the position of the "oedipal mother," whom Deleuze describes as the sadistic father's accomplice.[60] The "formula of masochism," Deleuze maintains, "is the humiliated father,"[61] who is "not so much the beater as the beaten."[62] In Wanda von Sacher-Masoch's oedipal drama, the father does not relinquish his power over his son, and the woman aligns herself with his virility and his economic prowess. In a primal scene in the second half of the novel, Karl, looking up to his "mother's" window from the garden below, is about to witness the first sexual encounter between his father and Adrienne. The father and new husband draws the curtain on his son, "as if he had a premonition that his happiness was being spied on."[63] Overwhelmed by his pain, Karl flees the scene of his crime "with the panic of a murderer who fears to be tracked."[64] Importantly, the oedipal rivalry between father and son over the mother's body does not translate into male masochist pleasure. The narrative expresses sympathy with the emasculated son's pain, a victim of the sadistic father and the oedipal mother's compliance with him. In Leopold von Sacher-Masoch's stories the woman torturer's decision to side with the sadistic father puts an end to the masochist fantasy, as did Wanda von Dunajew's alliance with the "Greek" in *Venus in Furs*. Adrienne, by contrast, carefully avoids masochist situations. Masochism's cruel woman retains her power through the deferral of the sexual act. Adrienne consummates it under circumstances that she controls at a contractually guaranteed price.

Having fled the scene of his humiliation, Karl participates in the Prussian-Austrian war of 1866, excels in battle, and thus regains his masculinity. Severely wounded, he returns to his father's house, where Adrienne takes on the arduous task of nursing him back to health with utmost self-sacrifice. As the "mother" of an ill child, she can legitimately give Karl her untiring love and care. At her former lover's sickbed, Adrienne indulges in fantasies of "possessing the man as a son whom she had to renounce as a husband . . . applying hot kisses on his pale mouth."[65]

Adrienne's incestuous desire for "her" son offers a glimpse of the sexual passion oppressed by her "practical reason." In his feverish state Karl alludes to the beautiful fur he had seen Adrienne wear in her wedding

---

60. Deleuze, "Coldness and Cruelty," 55.

61. Ibid., 60.

62. Ibid., 61.

63. Sacher-Masoch, *Roman einer tugendhaften Frau,* 117.

64. Ibid.

65. Ibid., 131.

night, begging her to don it for him. Adrienne grants her ailing son this wish and appears before him in the garment in which she had received his father for their first sexual encounter. Karl, like Adrienne's father before him, is intoxicated by the sexual allure of his "mother." Yet again the fur coat conjures up incestuous wishes rather than masochist fantasies. After Karl recovers from his war injuries, Adrienne returns to her customary coldness toward him and impels him to join an Africa expedition from which he is never to return. He does not leave without a display of violent desire. As he storms into the room in which the scantily clad Adrienne lies on the couch, "The prince's eyes devoured the opulent charms of his mother."[66] Karl flings himself at Adrienne's feet like a "madman," and she in turn threatens him with a pistol.[67] In a reversal of the original voyeuristic incest scene, Karl's father secretly observes the encounter between his wife and his son. Deeply moved by what he interprets as Adrienne's fidelity, he kneels before the "worshiped" woman, kissing her hands in gratitude.

Adrienne explains her behavior to her husband and the reader. Motivation for her conduct was neither love for her husband nor concern for his honor, but her sense of duty and law, her materialistic selfishness and desire for "peace." She rejects Karl as the last battle in her Darwinian struggle for survival in a patriarchal world. Adrienne's "virtue" is in fact her coldness and cruelty against herself and her desires; it gains her a life of material luxury and a large circle of admirers, who shiver in the presence of her "cold majesty." They do not feel the burning passion that the cruel woman incites in her lovers.

Through her protagonist's alliance with the patriarchal male, Wanda von Sacher-Masoch prevents Adrienne from becoming masochism's cruel woman. Karl, moreover, the emasculated son and displaced lover, is no masochist who fantasizes the "good" mother in place of the father. He unsuccessfully demands sexual gratification rather than deferral, and the father's intervention cannot "cure" him. Sentenced to a lonely existence in Africa, he will never take the father's place, nor will he win the "ideal ego" promised by the masochist fantasy. Leopold von Sacher-Masoch's cruel woman "generates the symbolism through which the masochist expresses himself."[68] Adrienne, by contrast, refuses to expel the father and thus prevents masochist expression. Neither she nor Karl can expect to inherit their fathers' position, that is, his money. Adrienne thus uses patriarchal law to her advantage and forms an alliance with the father figure who can provide her with the desired "happiness" at the exclusion of the son.

---

66. Ibid., 149.
67. Ibid.
68. Deleuze, "Coldness and Cruelty," 63.

Both "Mystery of Love" and *Novel of a Virtuous Woman* are "counterpieces" to Leopold von Sacher-Masoch's masochist fantasy. In his work and life, the figure of the cruel woman remained an elusive ideal that he tried to capture and secure. In *Virtuous Woman,* Wanda von Sacher-Masoch introduces a female protagonist who refuses to enter into the masochist contract by siding with patriarchy. "The Mystery of Love," published six years later, explains female cruelty as a strategy of self-defense in a struggle that only the cruel woman can hope to win. Both of these texts subvert the masochist paradigm by shifting attention from the male masochist and his psychosexual needs to the "realities" of the woman partner.

Patriarchal power relationships, in the realm of the symbolic as well as their socioeconomic realities, define both Leopold's and Wanda's approach to the figure of the cruel woman. The masochist fantasy is a temporary reversal of patriarchal power relationships that is played out in the realm of the symbolic. Wanda von Sacher-Masoch, in her fiction as well as in her autobiography, challenges this model by insisting on the "real" implications of this reversal. For her, reality is most aptly expressed as the question of who controls the money. She stresses the primacy of the distribution of socioeconomic power between men and women over the symbolic reversal of male and female subject positions.

A contract governs the relationship between the masochist and the woman torturer, assigning the gendered subject positions *in* the masochistic situation. The stipulations of this contract dictate that the male participant be stripped of his subjecthood, whereas his female partner attains limitless power over her slave. According to Deleuze, the masochist relies on this contract to "exorcise the danger of the father and to ensure that the temporal order of reality and experience will be in conformity with the symbolic order, in which the father has been abolished for all time."[69] The contract dictates the duration of the period during which the masochist relinquishes all rights, although he must imagine that contractual reversal is eternal. The male partner initiates and orchestrates the exchange, thus creating the contract's cruel woman. In *Venus in Furs,* Severin feverishly repeats his declaration of total submission until Wanda von Dunajew draws up the unalterable document whose terms are to expire when Severin dies. Patriarchy is the prerequisite for the masochistic contract, whose attractiveness for the masochistic subject, the man, is grounded in the temporary reversal of existing—"normal"—social power relationships. Wanda von Dunajew loses her contractually guaranteed power in the

---

69. Ibid., 66.

instant Severin declares himself cured and returns to the normalcy of male domination, which he predicts will prevail until women are men's "equal in education and work."[70] The male partner not only creates the cruel woman but also determines the length of her reign. Adrienne von Neunkirchen, by contrast, understood that she had to extend her contractually guaranteed rights beyond her husband's death.

In *Confessions,* Wanda von Sacher-Masoch exposes the materialist foundation of patriarchal family relationships and thus roots the masochist contract in economic reality. The couple draws up its initial contract after a discussion of the family's precarious financial situation and the pecuniary side of Leopold's literary production. The contract, written out by Wanda at Leopold's instigation, transfers control over the family income to the narrator. "It is necessary that you put on a fur to write, so that I may have the sensation of being dominated by you," Leopold insists, heightening the pleasure of the masochistic stimulation he derives from relinquishing his financial power to his wife (32). After the signing of the document he rejoices: "Now you are my mistress, and I your slave." The autobiographer's approach is less dramatic: "I put on the fur and drew up the contract. . . . To inaugurate the new era, I put an end to all extravagances," she notes (32). For Wanda von Sacher-Masoch the contract is not sexual but economic. Both the writer and her literary creation Adrienne draw up contracts to achieve financial security.

A few weeks later, the family is again threatened with economic crisis. French literary critics alleged that Sacher-Masoch's cruel female figures had lost their literary novelty. Responding to the critics' assumption that there were too many cruel women in his life, Leopold insists that writing is a substitute for life. He must write cruel scenes because there is no truly cruel woman in his life as long as Wanda refuses to whip him. Leopold suggests an arrangement in which life will provide him with an adequate substitute for his textual fantasy. "For me it is a sensual pleasure to be mistreated by my wife. Mistreat me and I promise you by everything that is most sacred—I give you my word of honor that starting from today there will be no more cruel women in my books. Do you accept?" (33). The narrator consents to whip her husband for the sake of the family budget. Indeed, in Leopold's subsequent books, she acknowledges, there were "neither furs, nor whips, nor cruel deeds" (33). Wanda von Sacher-Masoch thus distinguishes between the male and the female subject position in the masochist situation. "Reluctantly" she carries out the whippings to give Leopold "sensual pleasure" (33). She desexualizes the female

---

70. Leopold von Sacher-Masoch, *Venus in Furs,* in Deleuze and Sacher-Masoch, *Masochism,* 271.

position in the masochist situation and offers economic need as an alternative explanation for her involvement.

The final stage of the masochist plot is, of course, Wanda's affair with the Greek. In a divergence from the script of *Venus in Furs,* she solicits a written contract from her husband before she submits to the reenactment of the master text's third and ultimate stage. According to nineteenth-century Austrian civil law, a husband whose wife had committed adultery could divorce her against her will and claim custody over the children.[71] To reassure her, Leopold gives Wanda a contract stating that any extramarital affairs take place with the full knowledge and approval of her husband. This "declaration" confirms rather than reverses the power relationships inscribed in a legal system that grants the husband jurisdiction over his wife, and, the terms of the agreement notwithstanding, Wanda von Sacher-Masoch's "infidelity" provided the legal basis for the couple's divorce in 1886—against her will. Leopold's masochist reversal of gender roles did not protect her from the legal realities of turn-of-the-century Austria.

Contracts play different roles in *Confessions, Virtuous Woman,* and in *Venus in Furs.* Both Wanda von Sacher-Masoch and her literary creation Adrienne von Neunkirchen attempt to draw up contracts to redress the economic and legal vulnerabilities of women, both denying any identification with the sexual significance of the contracts. Wanda von Sacher-Masoch insists that she was never truly the cruel woman of *Venus in Furs* but merely acted out the role for her children's sake. Unlike the fictional Adrienne, she did not succeed in protecting her economic position. More gravely, perhaps, she could not separate her identity from the figure of the cruel woman.

Did Wanda von Sacher-Masoch really believe that her *Confessions,* her attempt to dissociate herself from Leopold's textual fantasies and his sexual practices, would clear her name in the public perception? More likely, she was well aware of the transgressive nature of her scandalous story and could not have been entirely surprised that several critics sharply contested her truth. What was important to her, it seems, was to create her autobiographical self through contexts and constellations for which the masochist plot had no model.

Confessions relates several episodes of lesbian desire. Frau X stimulates the narrator's interest, "as for a long time she had seemed mysterious to me" (39). Pretending not to know what she knows, the narrator contin-

---

71. See Viktor Pitter, *Die rechtliche Stellung der Frau in Österreich: Eine Zusammenstellung* (Vienna and Leipzig: Braumüller, 1911), 14.

ues: "Under this [Frau X's] surface, which was always cold and calm, I felt
an ardent vitality—a mystery which those two eyes guarded and also
betrayed" (39). The lesbian's gaze bespeaks her desire for the narrator.
"Finally I realized that she loved me passionately" (40). The relationship
between the two women culminates in an "overheated" dressing room, so
hot that the narrator falls into a semisomnolent state. In this intimate
female space Frau X kisses Wanda's shoulders and arms. "Was that you?"
the narrator asks, feigning ignorance (40). Frau X responds by describing
the narrator's innocent beauty, "so white and delicate," and continues to
kiss her. Wanda, passively accepting Frau X's gaze and touch, is now the
conventional female playing the object of lesbian desire. Frau X restores
to the narrator the traditional female position denied her in the masochistic relationship with her husband.

The next encounter involves the narrator's French teacher, a Parisian
refugee who had fled France after the defeat of the Commune. "She
seemed bathed in mystery" is our introduction to Madame Marie; the
"warmth in her voice" identifies her as a lesbian (57). The narrator controls "relations" with her French teacher by insisting on "certain barriers"
(57). As an object of lesbian desire, the narrator asserts traditional female
privilege to control the degree of intimacy in her relationship with
Madame Marie, which comes to an end only when the French teacher's
jealous female lover threatens suicide. As the passive recipient of lesbian
sexual desire, the narrator breaks away completely from her contractual
role of the cruel woman, with its mandate to dominate her husband and to
yield to the heterosexual requests of the Greek. In her autobiographical
counternarrative to Leopold's masochistic scripts, Wanda von Sacher-
Masoch introduces traditional gender roles within nontraditional constellations. Her role as the object of a gaze that is not male allows her to
become the subject of her own plot.

Kathrin Strebinger, the young Swiss woman who translated Leopold
von Sacher-Masoch's texts into French, is the autobiographer's most
significant challenge to Leopold's fantasy, and Strebinger's biography
becomes part of Wanda von Sacher-Masoch's autobiography. The narrator's close friend and counterpart, Kathrin is the "mannish" woman who
insists on acting out her own plots, declining to play the part prescribed by
the masochistic male. Unlike the narrator, who reluctantly plays the heterosexual cruel woman and reclaims her female passivity in lesbian relationships, Kathrin actively pursues sexual relationships with both men
and women, and, as she relates one evening at the dinner table, she has
given herself to poor men out of pity.[72] Kathrin enters the text of the auto-

---

72. In the English translation this account is characterized as fantasy (67); in the German original the scene is related as reality (*Meine Lebensbeichte,* 70).

biography just after the narrator has accepted the role of the cruel woman and agreed to reenact *Venus in Furs* (34). Kathrin's presence, however, delays Wanda's affair with the Greek, the last act prescribed by the novella, because Kathrin herself enters into relations with the men Leopold thought suitable for the role of the Greek: "*Venus in Furs* was the most important matter in his life, and Kathrin had blithely destroyed, blow by blow, his best-founded hopes" (80, translation modified). Kathrin appropriates the narrator's place in the Greek's bed. Wanda's affair with the Greek occurs only after Kathrin's departure. Kathrin thus not only refuses to enact Leopold's script, she also prevents the narrator from fulfilling her role. After some disparaging remarks about fur coats Kathrin disappears, never to return (80).

Kathrin restores the narrator to the female subject position that Leopold's script denies her. Wanda's attraction to Kathrin is more powerful than her earlier encounters with lesbians: "Kathrin certainly exercised a physical influence on me, but for a long time I was not conscious of it. When she entered my room I felt brighter inside, and darker when she exited" (69, translation modified). After a disastrous river-crossing that the two women had undertaken upon Kathrin's insistence, the narrator finds comfort in Kathrin's strong arms (64), and during a trip "Kathrin slept with me, in the bed meant for my husband" (78, translation modified). Kathrin physically occupies the male space, allowing the narrator to reclaim a female subject position. The same evening Kathrin accidentally steps into a large needle. Instead of removing it, as the narrator urges her to do, she leaves the pointed metal in her toe for an hour, blissfully anticipating the pain of its extraction (79). The scene shows Kathrin as a woman who refuses to do what Deleuze describes as fundamental to the masochistic situation, to renounce "her own subjective masochism."[73] Kathrin does not enter into any kind of a contract, be it a conventional marriage or a masochistic contract.

Wanda's subsequent affair with the Greek begins to undermine Wanda and Leopold's marriage. When she takes Jakob Rosenthal as a lover (with whom, she states, she did not have "physical relations"), Wanda and Leopold separate and subsequently divorce (110). The figure of Kathrin, however, is the most radical departure from Leopold von Sacher-Masoch's text, whose master plot provides no role for the female masochist. If only temporarily, Wanda writes herself into a female subject position outside the heterosexual paradigm and its patriarchal representations.

The appearance of the Greek marks the turning point in both *Venus*

---

73. Deleuze, "Coldness and Cruelty," 42–43.

in Furs and *Confessions.* In *Venus in Furs,* the Greek's introduction into the masochist plot breaks the cruel woman's spell over Severin and transforms him into a sadist; in *Confessions,* the Greek testifies to the autobiographer's forced adultery. In addition to placing classified ads in newspapers, Leopold used his wide range of contacts in the literary world to find an appropriate partner for the reenactment of the final act of *Venus in Furs.* The story of the search, which occupies a substantial part of the narrative, includes a range of delaying moments such as Wanda's attempts to talk Leopold out of his favorite fantasy, the appearance of Kathrin, lack of interest on the part of the prospective Greek, or the compassion shown to Wanda despite her suitor's expectation of sexual gratification. Ultimately, of course, the autobiographer cannot escape the plot that has been scripted for her.

Leopold von Sacher-Masoch's stories about Jewish life in eastern Europe had gained him the respect of Jewish readers and critics. He was a "cosmopolitan" who "appreciated difference," and Wanda shared her husband's unprovincial attitudes.[74] When the Sacher-Masochs spent the summer of 1880 in the Hungarian countryside with a Jewish family named Ries, Wanda immersed herself in Jewish life (85–95). As she writes about the time with their Jewish hosts, "At first we often committed solecisms against Jewish customs; but little by little we became more knowledgeable until sometimes it seemed we had *become* Jewish" (86). For Leopold, however, Jewish country life was just another opportunity to play his "cruel" games with the family's servant girls and friends (86). After the end of this summer, Wanda chooses one of these friends, a young Jew from Budapest named Alexander Gross and her junior by almost ten years, to be her partner in adultery. Gross's youth and dissimilarity to the Greek, she explains, enabled her to retain a degree of control in a dilemma whose consequences she could no longer escape. Leopold's threats to abandon her for another woman unless she complied with his request to stage an act of "infidelity" forced her to fulfill her "duty" (93). Her affair with the Greek not only violates the bourgeois marital contract but also the racial divide that separates Gentiles and Jews in late-nineteenth-century Austria.

Wanda von Sacher-Masoch's positive experience of Jewish life in the antisemitic Habsburg empire, Leopold's pursuit of his erotic fantasies in this setting, and the impending act of adultery link sexual with racial transgression. To many of her critics the fact that her partner in adultery was a Jew was as scandalous as the infidelity itself. For Leopold the day of the adultery was to be the "happiest day of his life" (95). The encounter with

---

74. See Hyams, "Whip and Lamp," 71.

Gross itself remains veiled. "Then I opened the door and I passed into the little room, where another awaited me." And afterward: "I had only one very strong sensation: remorse—piercing remorse—at what I had done" (95). After the adultery, Wanda states in *Confessions,* she no longer had sexual relations with her husband. Her "affair" with the Greek has "cured" the autobiographer of her role in his masochist plot. She remains silent on Leopold's response to her performance of the final act.

With the confession of her prescripted adultery, Wanda von Sacher-Masoch severs her links to masochism and returns to the pre-scribed normalcy of female conduct. Her feelings of guilt and her subsequent suffering are intended to arouse the reader's sympathies for a woman who was forced to fulfill this abnormal marital duty. Her confession of an act of adultery she could not escape and her revelation of a "secret" already known to the reader raises certain questions. What did she hope to achieve with her "confession"? How did she want readers to view her participation in the masochistic plot? The inclusion of a detail immediately preceding the adultery scene gives us a clue. At Leopold's insistence, she puts on the white dress she had worn to the "ball at Leoben," the occasion of her homoerotic experience with Frau X, reminding the reader that Wanda had access to an alternative erotic that Leopold's fantasy did not allow and of whose existence he was unaware. With *Confessions,* Wanda von Sacher-Masoch told the truth about her sexuality. For many of her critics, the act of confession was more transgressive than the sexual act to which it referred.

Immediately after the publication of *Confessions,* Carl Felix von Schlichtegroll (1862–1946), Leopold von Sacher-Masoch's first biographer, wrote a two-hundred-page rebuttal titled *"Wanda" ohne Pelz und Maske* ("Wanda" without fur and mask).[75] Schlichtegroll, author of works with titles such as *Die Bestie im Weibe* (The beast within woman) and *Sacher-Masoch und der Masochismus* (Sacher-Masoch and masochism) undertook to "undress" and "unmask" the autobiographer, suggesting the existence of a truth to be found underneath her masochistic paraphernalia.[76] Schlichtegroll's main sources were Leopold's diaries and letters, from

---

75. Carl Felix von Schlichtegroll, *"Wanda" ohne Pelz und Maske. Eine Antwort auf "Wanda" von Sacher-Masochs "Meine Lebensbeichte" nebst Veröffentlichungen aus Sacher-Masochs Tagebuch* (Leipzig: Leipziger Verlag, 1906).

76. Carl Felix von Schlichtegroll, *Die Bestie im Weibe. Beiträge zur Geschichte menschlicher Verirrung und Grausamkeit* (Leipzig: Leipziger Verlag, 1903), and *Sacher-Masoch und der Masochismus: Litterarhistorische und kunsthistorische Studien* (Dresden: Dohrn, 1901).

which he quotes extensively with the aim of invalidating Wanda's version and the intention to expose her as a notorious liar.[77] The quotation marks around Wanda's name in Schlichtegroll's title, moreover, call into question the authenticity of her identity. Like Theodor Lessing, Schlichtegroll does not deny Leopold's sexual fantasies and practices. Instead, he tells his version of Wanda's sexual conduct; he continues, for instance, where she left off in her description of her infidelity with young Alexander Gross. After the encounter with Gross, Schlichtegroll asserts, followed a passionate sex act with Leopold. Quoting selectively from Leopold's diary, he breaks off at a different juncture than does Wanda: "I: I felt terrible, I thought I could not bear it any longer, I wanted to beg you to do away with me . . . —Wanda . . . . (here follow overly realistic descriptions of the pleasures she enjoyed, from the mouth of Madam herself)."[78] Schlichtegroll thus appeals to the reader's imagination to expose the truth underneath Wanda's mask: her voracious female sexuality.

Wanda von Sacher-Masoch published a second autobiographical narrative in response to Schlichtegroll's book. Titled *Masochismus und Masochisten,* this one-hundred-page rebuttal is both a personal justification and, as its title suggests, an attempt to situate her life story in the larger context of "masochism, " which by the first decade of the twentieth century had evolved into a veritable industry both for literati and sexologists. Hulda Meister, Leopold's second wife and mother of three of his children, is the prime target of Wanda's efforts to clarify her involvement with masochism. Schlichtegroll and others privileged Meister as the woman who cured Leopold of his predisposition, suggesting that Wanda failed where Meister succeeded. Wanda, who accuses Meister of extramarital sex with Leopold as well as greed, insists that Meister's marriage to Leopold, performed on the British island of Heligoland, had no validity in Catholic Austria, where she, Wanda von Sacher-Masoch, was considered Leopold's rightful widow and their son Demetrius his only legitimate child.[79] She cites letters that Leopold addressed to her in 1885, a year before the divorce, indicating that both he and Hulda Meister deceived her about the intimate nature of their relationship. The quarrel over who was the "true" Madame von Sacher-Masoch and who could legitimately claim the late writer's name suggests that only she whose truth prevailed could

---

77. Leopold's letters and diaries were lost in World War II and have not resurfaced. Schlichtegroll's quotations, which he almost certainly edited to suit his needs, remain the only copy of these documents. Hulda von Sacher-Masoch gave Schlichtegroll access to her late husband's diaries and letters and asked him to publish his rebuttal (*Wanda und Leopold von Sacher-Masoch,* 283).

78. Schlichtegroll, *"Wanda" ohne Pelz,* 172.

79. Sacher-Masoch, *Masochismus,* 38.

assert a public identity. Only as Leopold's legitimate widow could Wanda tell the story of her marriage to the man whose name signified the perversion that had also dominated her life. When Schlichtegroll exposed the truth about Wanda's sexuality, he stripped her of her legitimacy as an autobiographer, as a wife, and as a woman. In insisting on her truth about Leopold's sexuality Wanda von Sacher-Masoch authorized the story of her life.

Masochism and Masochists is more than a personal vendetta. The integrity of the autobiographer's self-representation was at stake as much as her desire to be acknowledged as a central figure in masochism. Wanda von Sacher-Masoch was familiar with Krafft-Ebing's writings on the subject in *Psychopathia Sexualis* and objected to his and others' popularization of masochism as a "fashionable disease" *(Modekrankheit)* without admitting the harm it caused to the masochist's family.[80] She reports having written to Krafft-Ebing to eliminate her from his list of masochist writers since she wrote stories such as the ones collected in *The Ladies in Furs* under duress rather than out of inclination.[81] Despite her efforts to distance herself from masochism, however, masochist men persisted in identifying her with her female characters and corresponded with her hoping to find in her their ideal cruel woman. In the name of science she made available to Krafft-Ebing a sequence of letters written by a masochist admirer from Prague. In his appreciative reply the famous sexologist spelled out what she had long known: that her husband's "pathological disposition" *(krankhafte Organisation)* alone was responsible for the literature he produced.[82] *Masochism and Masochists* ends with an appeal to the judges of this world to allow women to divorce their husbands on account of masochism. Women, she pleads, are masochism's real victims.

Wanda von Sacher-Masoch's autobiographical writings serve a number of purposes. She attempted to justify her role in Leopold von Sacher-Masoch's well-known masochistic plot by telling her version of the story; she certainly sought to draw attention to herself a decade after his death; and, without doubt, she strove to hurt those she perceived to be her enemies, in particular Leopold's second wife, Hulda Meister. Petty perhaps, her personal objectives recall the social and financial disadvantages that divorced women faced in the late nineteenth century. In recounting how she "became Wanda" the autobiographer shows that as woman and a member of the lower class she had to inscribe her self into a male text to claim a voice. She then proceeds to subvert this text and make it her own. Her counternarratives, in their autobiographical as well as their literary

---

80. Ibid., 56.
81. Ibid., 77.
82. Ibid., 78.

versions, challenge the authority of the master text by suggesting alternative models of female representation. Wanda von Sacher-Masoch understood that male masochism has no use for female subjects. She introduced into her plot the lesbian, the masochist woman, and the oedipal mother to represent female subjectivity outside of masochism. Leopold strove to realize his ideal by continuously devising new versions of his masochist master plot. Wanda tried to approximate her interpretation of this plot through her autobiography. In the end, the "real" Wanda remains elusive.

André Salmon's spirited recollection of the scene at the Mercure de France lets us witness the aging Wanda von Sacher-Masoch as she enacted the part of Venus one more time. The multiple versions of Wanda and Leopold's masochist performance incited the fears as well as the fantasies of late-nineteenth-century society. The interest in "perversion" reflects the profound impact of sexual deviancy on traditional gender relationships. That Leopold's defenders should have blamed Wanda for his sexual "tragedy" does not come as a surprise, but the viciousness of the reactions shows just how deep the fears of changing gender relations ran. Wanda von Sacher-Masoch understood that shifting gender roles were a key element of modernity. She, too, appealed to the sanctity of tradition, but she used the sexual crisis to push against the limitations of female self-representation with her story of sexual, racial, and class transgression. For her, the question of femininity and its function in modern society did not have the urgency it had for Lazarus, von Eckenbrecher, and Popp. Instead, she manipulated the crisis of masculinity to claim agency as a woman and as a writer.

autobiography — only within larger mvn.
autobiographical context —
much plot stuff (not re autobiography)

Witnessing Change: The Crisis of Modernity and the Limits of Autobiography

Autobiography reflects the self-understanding of turn-of-the-century culture in a dual way. The anxieties caused by the shift from a traditional to a modern mass society are felt in the autobiographies themselves as well as in their reception and the debates surrounding the genre. For many, the upsurge in autobiographical production was a symptom of the modern age, and commentators interpreted the autobiography boom as an outgrowth of contemporary culture.

Autobiography, like any other modern literary genre, straddles both sides of the "great divide" between mass culture and high culture. The advocates of the autobiographical boom existed in a tension with the critics of mass culture, who regarded the flood of autobiography as a serious threat to literary standards. However, both advocates and detractors assumed that autobiographical literature was truer to social realities than other forms of literature. They agreed, the one applauding and the other despairing, that more lax literary standards and the closer relationship to social realities explained the appeal of autobiography to large audiences.

The demographics of the reading and writing public boosted the publishing industry's economic stakes in autobiography. Various sociopolitical groups seized on autobiography for their political agendas. Some critics promoted autobiography as readily accessible historical sources for a biography of the German nation, while others enlisted them in the battle against social ills such as poverty and prostitution. While the high modernists, whose works are typically thought to reflect the crisis of identity, saw themselves as elite commentators on their epoch, the majority of autobiographers defined themselves as ordinary people whose life stories bore witness to the changing times. Autobiography's presumed proximity to reality, its status as a historical document, and its general accessibility to readers and writers privileged it as a form of expression through which contemporaries tried to understand themselves and their time.

The democratization of literary culture inherent in memoir writing challenged cultural commentators to link autobiography to three interrelated projects: the defense of high culture, the avowal of German national identity, and the confirmation of gender difference. Yet the proliferation of autobiography was not easily contained or sworn to a particular purpose. "In our fast-moving and profusely scribbling time," a reviewer for the *Prussian Yearbooks* wrote as early as 1899, autobiographies are becoming "distressingly fashionable."[1] Modernity manifested itself through cultural overproduction, which for this writer culminated in the gendered link between autobiography and the fashion of his time. For many, the upsurge in autobiography confirmed the feminization of turn-of-the-century culture. In his 1906 article "The Meaning of Autobiography" literary critic Hermann Eßwein put forth a similar argument when he summarized Friedrich Schlegel's condemnation of autobiography as a "nervous disease, narcissism in every form including the effeminate predilection to coquet with posteriority, pedantry, the need to give public testimony."[2] The association of the autobiographical genre with femininity, and, conversely, the equation of all women's writing with autobiography, was a favorite theme among literary critics. An 1896 article in *New German Review* traced the difference between male- and female-authored texts to the uniquely autobiographical elements of women's writing: "Indeed, in just about all of women's literature the aesthetic or the objective psychological interest is insignificant compared to the delightful way in which the author consciously reveals or unconsciously betrays herself."[3] In assuming that all women's literature was autobiographical in essence, the reviewer feminized autobiography as a genre of lesser aesthetic value.[4] The association of autobiography with femininity and modern mass culture reflects the fear of feminization that pervaded turn-of-the-century culture. On the other hand, autobiography was thought to provide privileged insights into the lives of women, workers, or other groups who pushed to the fore as a result of social change. Contemporaries viewed the memoir

---

1. Arthur Brausewetter, "W. Beyschlags Autobiographie," review of *Aus meinem Leben,* by Willibald Beyschlag, *Preußische Jahrbücher* 96 (1899): 417.

2. Hermann Eßwein, "Der Sinn der Autobiographie," *Das Literarische Echo* 8 (1905–6): 1696.

3. Hans Paul, "Frauen-Litteratur," *Neue Deutsche Rundschau* 7 (1896): 276.

4. This idea has not lost its appeal. Michaela Holdenried critiques the autobiographical approach to all literature by women and argues that it results in a continuing neglect of women's autobiographies (introduction to *Geschriebenes Leben,* 9).

boom as a modern phenomenon. In struggling to explain the fascination with autobiography, cultural critics interpreted the meanings of modernization. The contradictions inherent in these debates reflect the conflicted responses to the changes they witnessed.

For female autobiographers the memoir boom meant first of all an opportunity to write and publish their life stories. The general interest in women encouraged them to become autobiographers, but the prevailing assumptions about femininity prescribed what kind of stories could be committed into writing. In a society preoccupied with gender difference, female autobiographers could not afford to ignore gender. The autobiographers assembled in this book attribute considerable importance to the impact of gender on their lives. They take pride in their exceptional achievements, while at the same time insisting that they are "ordinary" women who do not violate the boundaries of acceptable female conduct. All of them explain their extraordinary lives as their desire to overcome the circumstances that prevented them from being "normal" women. Nahida Lazarus's conversion to Judaism, for instance, required persistence as well as courage to withstand the socioeconomic pressures on unmarried or widowed women in nineteenth-century society. In her autobiography she maintains that only as a Jew could she lead the life of an ordinary woman. Adelheid Popp identifies the sexual victimization she experienced as a child and adolescent as a catalyst for her remarkable career as a working-class activist and member of the Social Democratic Party. Her narrative ends with her marriage and the respectability that it afforded her as a woman. Wanda von Sacher-Masoch contrasts her life of sexual deviancy with her desire to be an ordinary wife, justifying her compliance with her husband's requests for masochistic role-play by the need to provide for her children. Colonizer Margarethe von Eckenbrecher, who lived her exotic life geographically remote from ordinary German women, proclaimed that she wanted nothing more than to lead a normal housewife's life in Africa. The writers resolved the tension between ordinary womanhood and their extraordinary female lives by assuring the reader (and perhaps themselves) that the conventional life was the goal to which they aspired.

The appeal to tradition reflects social expectations as much as the undeniable conflicts these autobiographers faced in representing their gender to the reading public. Individual differences aside, they all experienced modernization most acutely through women's changing roles in society. Contained in the tensions between normalcy and extraordinariness that run through their narratives are their responses to the promises of modernity and the allure of tradition. Their "modern" achievements as writers, public speakers, and autobiographers notwithstanding, the family and women's traditional role within it was the bellwether that signaled to them the condition of the society in which they lived. They assessed the modern age by measuring their own experience of family life against the bourgeois family ideal.

Class had a profound impact on the autobiographers' experience of family and gender relationships. For the middle-class subjects Nahida Lazarus and Margarethe von Eckenbrecher the discrepancies between lived reality and ideal translated into a profoundly felt *Modernisierungs-schmerz* (pain of modernization) for which they tried to compensate outside of German majority culture.[5] For them, modernization manifested itself in the loss of women's revered status in bourgeois society; more objectively, they and their families suffered a decline in class status that forced women to adopt new roles. The lower-class writers Popp and von Sacher-Masoch also bemoan the absence of traditional family structures, but neither of them searched for premodern alternatives. Popp advocated socialism as a solution to the problems of the working-class family; von Sacher-Masoch placed herself outside of the conventional paradigm altogether. Popp and von Sacher-Masoch were less threatened by change than their middle-class counterparts. Even though they, too, relied on the traditional family ideal for self-definition, they conceived of themselves as women in a society of the future rather than an imagined past.

The topic of sexuality inspired an immense amount of medical, juridical, social, and aesthetic commentary in turn-of-the-century German society. Professional observers, among them doctors, lawyers, and writers, focused their attention largely on deviant sexualities. As Michel Foucault has noted, the "legitimate couple, with its regular sexuality, had a right to more discretion."[6] The autobiographers discussed in this study all married; only von Eckenbrecher and Lazarus, however, were married at the time of writing. Popp was widowed when she wrote her autobiography; von Sacher-Masoch was divorced. Apart from the twice-married Nahida Lazarus, they all became mothers. With the notable exception of Wanda von Sacher-Masoch, sexuality within marriage is not a topic for these autobiographers. Experiences of sexuality in premarital or extramarital contexts, by contrast, play a role in all narratives. In these situations, the writers perceive themselves as victims or observers of deviant practices. Lazarus and Popp, who narrate their lives in the form of the conversion autobiography, experience sexuality at a young age as assault and victimization. Von Eckenbrecher's descriptions of the omnipresent hypersexuality of the Africans around her echo Popp's criticism of the working-class women's sexualized conduct in the factories. The interest in deviant sexu-

5. Wolfgang Mantl, "Modernisierung und Dekadenz," in Nautz and Vahrenkamp, *Die Wiener Jahrhundertwende,* 91.

6. Foucault, *The History of Sexuality,* 38.

ality allowed them to write about sexuality at a time when presumably "regular sexuality" could not yet be put into words in a female autobiography. For Lazarus, Popp, and von Eckenbrecher marriage serves as shorthand for sociosexual respectability; neither felt compelled to devote much space to the relationships with their husbands. Wanda von Sacher-Masoch, by contrast, dedicated almost the entire autobiography to her courtship, marriage, and divorce. With her story of deviant male sexuality she forfeited her claim to ordinary womanhood.

Gender does not appear as an isolated category in these autobiographies. Lazarus and von Eckenbrecher, in different ways, linked gender to their identity as Germans. In the colonial setting von Eckenbrecher's understanding of Germanness shifted from a cultural to a racial definition, her whiteness offsetting the disadvantages she suffered as a woman in Wilhelmine Germany. Lazarus, by contrast, continued to draw on the older model of Germanness as a cultural category when she appealed to German high culture as the umbrella that united educated Jews and Germans. Her model, which reconciled religious difference and sameness based on German high culture, enabled her to identify with Jewish culture and its gender arrangements while retaining her Germanness despite the growing pressures of racial antisemitism. For the Austrians Popp and Sacher-Masoch knowledge of German high culture served to overcome the disadvantages they associated with their lower-class birth and their gender rather than as a claim to national identity. Neither of them reflects on her status as a citizen of Austria. Von Sacher-Masoch's journey through deviant sexuality, however, could not have taken place outside of the multinational Habsburg empire. Popp's Czech-Bohemian background, on the other hand, is of no interest to her as she identifies with the cultural politics of German Social Democracy.

The narratives of the female convert, the colonizer, and the worker confirmed their readers' religious, racial, and class values. The writers could assume that they would find a positive reception among the groups that they primarily addressed. Confessional memoirs such as Wanda von Sacher-Masoch's, by contrast, were read as illustrations of the modern age and its vicissitudes. Because these narratives pushed against the sexual, racial, and class boundaries fin de siècle society tried to enforce, they testify to the crisis of modernity perhaps better than any other literary form. Confessing books were marketed as a forum to present the truth about aberrant sexuality in the authentic voices of those who participated in it, voluntarily or as victims, often justifying their publication with the need to return to conventional gender roles and relations. Neither the case studies of the sexologists whose voluminousness and Latin quotations appealed only to specialists nor the products of high art had the popular appeal, the accessibility, or the immediacy of the confessional memoir. Confessional memoirs were so successful that fictitious confessions appeared side by side with the "true relations" of prostitutes and unfaithful wives. Some, such as Felix Salten's anonymously published *Josefine Mutzenbacher: Die Lebensgeschichte einer wienerischen Dirne, von ihr selbst erzählt* (1906; Josefine Mutzenbacher: the story of a Viennese strumpet told by herself), were authored by men. Salten imitated the confessional form for the purpose of telling a pornographic story. In addition to the many revelatory narratives about female sexuality, women began to offer their opinions on male sexuality. Literary magazines printed exchanges between women with titles such as "Aus den Bekenntnissen einer Frau" (From the confessions of a woman) and "Intimes aus dem Seelenleben einer anderen Frau" (Intimacies from the soul of another woman), in which the writers ascertained their conflicting positions on the topic of male marital infidelity.[7] The one-hundred-page narrative *Eine für Viele: Aus dem Tagebuche eines Mädchens* (One for many: From the diary of a girl), the story of a young woman who commits suicide after she finds out that her fiancé had premarital relations, caused a literary sensation in turn-of-the-century Vienna.[8] In his review of this book, the Viennese critic Oskar Friedländer described *One for Many* as an outgrowth of the latest fashion. *Mode* and *modern,* he argued, were not only etymologically related but defined by their shared lack of cultural substance.[9] He had to concede, however, that "fashion" and the "modern" characterized the consciousness of the majority of his contemporaries and went on to condemn those critics who tried to assess the "mood of the time" in the name of culture.[10] For Friedländer, "modern" signified a loss of culture. Moreover, *One for Many* to him was a prime example of women's literature. "In the relatively short period of concentrated literary activity women have proven their aptitude in at least one respect; in the area of sexuality they are also *theoretically* at least as versed as the stronger sex."[11] Friedländer intended his review not as the "evaluation of a book but the explication of a symptom."[12] *Mode,* the modern, and *Frauenlitteratur* form a continuum of cultural decline.

The confessional memoir, then, for many readers signified what was wrong with contemporary culture. While not all critics shared Friedlän-

---

7. Anna Bernau, "Aus den Bekenntnissen einer Frau," *Die Gesellschaft* 15, no. 4 (1899): 115–17; and Maxi Sontoneff, "Intimes aus dem Seelenleben einer anderen Frau. Erwiderung auf die 'Bekenntnisse einer Frau,'" *Die Gesellschaft* 16, no. 1 (1900): 108–11.

8. Vera [Betty Kris], *Eine für Viele: Aus dem Tagebuche eines Mädchens* (Leipzig: Hermann Seemann Nachfolger, 1902).

9. Oskar Friedländer, "'Eine für Viele,'" *Die Gesellschaft* 18, no. 3 (1902): 159.

10. Ibid., 158.

11. Ibid., 161.

12. Ibid., 160.

der's pessimism, they agreed that the confessional memoir was a modern phenomenon. More than any other form of autobiography, the confessional memoir, in which the prevalent issues of sexuality, writing, and gender converged, was regarded as a measuring device for the status of culture itself. In her *Confessions,* Wanda von Sacher-Masoch probed the limits of female self-representation, not so much because she violated gendered codes of conduct but because, as a woman, she dared to write about it. The short-lived scandal that accompanied her book and her own subsequent descent into oblivion illustrate the anxieties raised by female autobiography and the possible sanctions their authors faced. In dismissing it as untruthful and aesthetically inferior, critics discredited her version of a well-known story of sexual deviancy with arguments that have been traditionally used to keep at bay women and their writing.

The majority of women's autobiographies from the turn of the century were only quietly subversive of reigning gender paradigms. Even though many women told stories of extraordinary lives and achievements, most of them insisted on being ordinary women. Critics for the most part welcomed autobiographies by women as roads into the interior of the female psyche. These narratives, however, were often less affirmative of traditional femininity than the contemporary reception wanted to believe.[13] The growing number of female autobiographers and the expanding range of topics they addressed pushed against the constraints on the lives women could live and write. Adelheid Popp's use of autobiography to make acceptable women's presence in politics is just one example. In that sense, autobiography indeed shaped historical reality.

The autobiography wave around the turn of the century was fueled by an interest in the past and the desire to better understand the present. In the twentieth century personal narratives evolved into highly varied forms. In the 1970s, women wrote autobiography to explore the meanings of femininity and female sexuality. These confessional narratives no longer caused the scandal stirred up by their turn-of-the-century counterparts, but they, too, aimed to hold a critical mirror up to patriarchal society. In the 1990s Germany witnessed another memoir boom as autobiographers contributed their personal histories to the historiography of the twentieth century.[14] Fifty years after the Holocaust the autobiographies of survivors

---

13. On subversion and masquerade see Michaela Holdenried, "'Ich, die schlechteste von allen.' Zum Zusammenhang von Rechtfertigung, Schuldbekenntnis und Subversion in autobiographischen Werken von Frauen," in *Geschriebenes Leben,* 402–20.

14. See Andreas Huyssen's analysis of the "obsession with memory in contemporary culture," in *Twilight Memories: Marking Time in a Culture of Amnesia* (New York: Routledge, 1995), 3. Huyssen's study goes beyond autobiography and includes museum and media culture.

found a growing audience;[15] childhood and youth during fascism became the material of autobiographical reflections;[16] and, most recently, East Germans published personal documents and documentations of their lives under Communism.[17] The optimism expressed in many autobiographies from the previous turn of the century has vanished. The question is no longer whether modernity is a threat to tradition or liberation from convention but how to interpret one's life in the context of the twentieth century's traumas. What remains is the belief that autobiography tells us something about who we are and the times in which we live.

[handwritten marginal notes:]

repetition of what was already said —
autobiography above all as historical document (176)
" German" unmarked category - i.e. little (if any) comparative work
not much historical contextualization -
i.e. what pre-turn-of-century attitudes re women + autobiog. were
also not in least but interdisciplinary - since it is not much about primarily a historical approach - form

---

15. Ruth Klüger, *Weiter leben: Eine Jugend* (Göttingen: Wallstein, 1992); and Victor Klemperer, *Ich will Zeugnis ablegen bis zum letzten. Tagebücher, 1933–1945,* ed. Walter Nowojski (Berlin: Aufbau, 1995). Benjamin Wilkomirski's *Bruchstücke: Aus einer Kindheit, 1939–1948* (Frankfurt am Main; Suhrkamp, 1995) earned critical acclaim. It created another sensation when the Swiss novelist Daniel Ganzfried, himself the author of a novel on the Holocaust, exposed Wilkomirski's autobiography as a forgery.

16. A recent example is Martin Walser's autobiographical novel *Ein springender Brunnen* (Frankfurt am Main: Suhrkamp, 1998); Jost Hermand, *Als Pimpf in Polen: Erweiterte Kinderlandverschickung, 1940–1945* (Frankfurt am Main: Fischer, 1993).

17. Daniela Dahn, *Westwärts und nicht vergessen: Vom Unbehagen in der Einheit* (Berlin: Rowohlt, 1996). A number of autobiographies chronicle a youth under fascism and adulthood in the GDR; among these are Günter de Bruyn, *Zwischenbilanz: Eine Jugend in Berlin* (Frankfurt am Main: Fischer, 1992), and *Vierzig Jahre: Ein Lebensbericht* (Frankfurt am Main: Fischer, 1996); and Heiner Müller, *Krieg ohne Schlacht: Leben unter zwei Dikaturen* (Cologne: Kiepenheuer und Witsch, 1992).

Bibliography

Aas, Norbert, and Werena Rosenke, eds. *Kolonialgeschichte im Familienalbum: Frühe Fotos aus der Kolonie Deutsch-Ostafrika.* Münster: Unrast, 1992.

Adelmann, Helene. *Aus meiner Kinderzeit.* Berlin: Appelius, 1892.

Als unsre großen Dichterinnen noch kleine Mädchen waren. Leipzig: Moeser, 1912.

Anderson, Benedict. *Imagined Communities: Reflections on the Origin and Spread of Nationalism.* Rev. ed. London: Verso, 1991.

Anderson, Harriet. *Utopian Feminism: Women's Movements in Fin-de-Siècle Vienna.* New Haven: Yale University Press, 1992.

Apter, Emily. *Feminizing the Fetish: Psychoanalysis and Narrative Obsession in Turn-of-the-Century France.* Ithaca: Cornell University Press, 1991.

Arnim, Bettina von. *Ein Lesebuch.* Edited by Christa Bürger and Birgitt Diefenbach. Stuttgart: Reclam, 1987.

Ashley, Kathleen, Leigh Gilmore, and Gerald Peters, eds. *Autobiography and Postmodernism.* Amherst: University of Massachusetts Press, 1994.

Bammé, Arno, ed. *Margarete Böhme: Die Erfolgsschriftstellerin aus Husum.* Munich: Profil, 1994.

Banéth, Noëmi. *Soziale Hilfsarbeit der modernen Jüdin.* Berlin: Louis Lamm, 1907.

Bebel, August. *My Life.* London: Unwin, 1912.

———. *Woman under Socialism.* Translated by Daniel de Leon. New York: Schocken, 1971.

Belgum, Kirsten. *Popularizing the Nation: Audience, Representation, and the Production of Identity in "Die Gartenlaube," 1853–1900.* Lincoln: Nebraska University Press, 1998.

Belke, Ingrid, ed. *Moritz Lazarus und Heymann Steinthal. Die Begründer der Völkerpsychologie in ihren Briefen.* Tübingen: Mohr, 1971.

Benstock, Shari, ed. *The Private Self: Theory and Practice of Women's Autobiographical Writings.* Chapel Hill: University of North Carolina Press, 1988.

Berger, Renate. *Malerinnen auf dem Weg ins 20. Jahrhundert.* Cologne: DuMont, 1982.

Bering, Dietz. *The Stigma of Names: Antisemitism in German Daily Life, 1812–1933.* Translated by Neville Plaice. Ann Arbor: University of Michigan Press, 1992.

Berman, Nina. *Orientalismus, Kolonialismus und Moderne: Zum Bild des Orients in der deutschen Kultur um 1900.* Stuttgart: Metzler, 1997.

Berman, Russell A. *Enlightenment or Empire: Colonial Discourse and German Culture.* Lincoln: University of Nebraska Press, 1998.

Bernau, Anna. "Aus den Bekenntnissen einer Frau." *Die Gesellschaft* 15, no. 4 (1899): 115–17.

Bernold, Monika. "Representations of the Beginning: Shaping Gender Identity in Written Life Stories of Women and Men." In *Austrian Women in the Nineteenth and Twentieth Centuries: Cross-Disciplinary Perspectives,* edited by David F. Good, Margarete Gardner, and Mary Jo Maynes, 197–212. Providence: Berghahn, 1996.

Bieberfeld, Eduard. "Das jüdische Weib." Review of *Das jüdische Weib,* by Nahida Remy. *Israelitische Monatsschrift* 10 (1891): 37–38.

Blackwell, Jeanine. "Herzensgespräche mit Gott. Bekenntnisse deutscher Pietistinnen im 17. und 18. Jahrhundert." In *Deutsche Literatur von Frauen,* edited by Gisela Brinker-Gabler, 1:265–89. Munich: Beck, 1988.

Bley, Helmut. *South-West Africa under German Rule, 1894–1914.* London: Heinemann, 1971.

Böhme, Margarete. *Tagebuch einer Verlorenen: Von einer Toten.* Edited by Hanne Kulessa. Frankfurt am Main: Suhrkamp, 1989.

Boyer, John W. *Culture and Political Crisis in Vienna: Christian Socialism in Power, 1897–1918.* Chicago: University of Chicago Press, 1995.

Brackel, Ferdinande Freiin von. *Mein Leben.* Cologne: Bachem, 1905.

Brantlinger, Patrick. "Victorians and Africans: The Genealogy of the Myth of the Dark Continent." In *"Race," Writing, and Difference,* edited by Henry Louis Gates, 185–222. Chicago: University of Chicago Press, 1985.

Brausewetter, Arthur. "W. Beyschlags Autobiographie." Review of *Aus meinem Leben,* by Willibald Beyschlag. *Preußische Jahrbücher* 96 (1899): 417–31.

Brée, Germaine. Foreword to *Life/Lines: Theorizing Women's Autobiography,* edited by Bella Brodzki and Celeste Schenck, ix–xii. Ithaca: Cornell University Press, 1988.

Brereton, Virginia Lieson. *From Sin to Salvation: Stories of Women's Conversions, 1800 to the Present.* Bloomington: Indiana University Press, 1991.

Breuer, Raphael. *Aus dem Tagebuch einer jüdischen Studentin.* Frankfurt am Main: Knauer, 1907.

Brinker-Gabler, Gisela, and Sidonie Smith, eds. *Writing New Identities: Gender, Nation, and Immigration in Contemporary Europe.* Minneapolis: University of Minnesota Press, 1997.

Brockmann, Clara. *Briefe eines deutschen Mädchens aus Südwest.* Berlin: Mittler, 1910.

Brodzki, Bella, and Celeste Schenck, eds. *Life/Lines: Theorizing Women's Autobiography.* Ithaca: Cornell University Press, 1988.

Bromme, Moritz Th. W. *Lebensgeschichte eines modernen Fabrikarbeiters.* 1905; reprint, with an afterword by Bernd Neumann, Frankfurt am Main: Athenäum, 1971.

Bronner, Stephen Eric, and F. Peter Wagner, eds. *Vienna: The World of Yesterday, 1889–1914*. Atlantic Highlands, N.J.: Humanities Press, 1997.

Brümmer, Franz. *Lexikon der deutschen Dichter und Prosaisten des neunzehnten Jahrhunderts*. 5th ed. 3 vols. Leipzig: Reclam, 1901.

Burgtheater, 1776–1976. Aufführungen und Besetzungen von zweihundert Jahren. Edited by Österreichischer Bundestheaterverband. 2 vols. Vienna: Ueber-reuter, 1979.

Coetzee, J. M. *White Writing: On the Culture of Letters in South Africa*. New Haven: Yale University Press, 1988.

Conway, Jill Ker. *When Memory Speaks: Reflections on Autobiography*. New York: Knopf, 1998.

Crew, David. "The Ambiguities of Modernity: Welfare and the German State from Wilhelm to Hitler." In *Society, Culture, and the State in Germany, 1870–1930*, edited by Geoff Eley, 319–44. Ann Arbor: University of Michigan Press, 1997.

Cvetkovich, Ann. *Mixed Feelings: Feminism, Mass Culture, and Victorian Sensationalism*. New Brunswick: Rutgers University Press, 1992.

Dahn, Daniela. *Westwärts und nicht vergessen: Vom Unbehagen in der Einheit*. Berlin: Rowohlt, 1996.

Daly, Brenda O., and Maureen T. Reddy, eds. *Narrating Mothers: Theorizing Maternal Subjectivities*. Knoxville: University of Tennessee Press, 1991.

Davidson, Cathy, and E. Broner. *The Lost Tradition: Mothers and Daughters in Literature*. New York: Frederick Ungar, 1980.

de Bruyn, Günter. *Vierzig Jahre: Ein Lebensbericht*. Frankfurt am Main: Fischer, 1996.

———. *Zwischenbilanz: Eine Jugend in Berlin*. Frankfurt am Main: Fischer, 1992.

Deleuze, Gilles. "Coldness and Cruelty," trans. Jean McNeil. In Gilles Deleuze and Leopold von Sacher-Masoch, *Masochism*, 9–138. New York: Zone Books, 1991.

de Man, Paul. "Autobiography as Defacement." *MLN* 94 (1979): 919–30.

Dijkstra, Bram. *Idols of Perversity: Fantasies of Feminine Evil in Fin-de-Siècle Culture*. New York: Oxford University Press, 1986.

Drechsler, Horst. *"Let Us Die Fighting:" The Struggle of the Herero and Nama against German Imperialism 1884–1915*. London: Zed Press, 1980.

Ebner-Eschenbach, Marie von. *Meine Kinderjahre*. Berlin: Paetel, 1906.

Eckenbrecher, Margarethe von. *Im dichten Pori. Reise- und Jagdbilder aus Deutsch-Ostafrika*. Berlin: Mittler, 1912.

———. "Padleben in Südwest-Afrika." In *Deutsch-Südwestafrika. Kriegs- und Friedensbilder. Selbsterlebnisse geschildert von Frau Margarethe von Eckenbrecher, Frau Helene von Falkenhausen, Stabsarzt Dr. Kuhn, Oberleutnant Stuhlmann*, 1–20. Leipzig: Weicher, 1907.

———. *Was Afrika mir gab und nahm. Erlebnisse einer deutschen Ansiedlerfrau in Südwestafrika*. Berlin: Mittler, 1907.

———. *Was Afrika mir gab und nahm. Erlebnisse einer deutschen Frau in Südwestafrika, 1902–1936*. 7th. ed. Berlin: Mittler, 1937.

Eigler, Friederike. "Engendering German Nationalism: Gender and Race in Frieda von Bülow's Colonial Writings." In *The Imperialist Imagination: German Colonialism and Its Legacy,* edited by Sara Friedrichsmeyer, Sara Lennox, and Susanne Zantop, 69–85. Ann Arbor: University of Michigan Press, 1998.

Emmerich, Wolfgang, ed. *Proletarische Lebensläufe: Autobiographische Dokumente zur Entstehung der Zweiten Kultur in Deutschland.* 2 vols. Reinbek bei Hamburg: Rowohlt, 1974.

Eßwein, Hermann. "Der Sinn der Autobiographie." *Das Literarische Echo* 8 (1905–6): 1696–98.

Esterhuyse, J. H. *South West Africa, 1880–1894: The Establishment of German Authority in South West Africa.* Cape Town: Struik, 1968.

Falkenhausen, Helene von. *Ansiedlerschicksale: Elf Jahre in Deutsch-Südwestafrika, 1893–1904.* Berlin: Reimer, 1905.

Farin, Michael, ed. *Leopold von Sacher-Masoch: Materialien zu Leben und Werk.* Bonn: Bouvier, 1987.

Feilchenfeld, Alfred, ed. *Denkwürdigkeiten der Glückel von Hameln.* Berlin: Jüdischer Verlag, 1913.

Felski, Rita. *Beyond Feminist Aesthetics: Feminist Literature and Social Change.* Cambridge: Harvard University Press, 1989.

———. *The Gender of Modernity.* Cambridge: Harvard University Press, 1995.

Finney, Gail. *Women in Modern Drama: Freud, Feminism, and European Theater of the Turn of the Century.* Ithaca: Cornell University Press, 1989.

Fischer, Karl. *Denkwürdigkeiten und Erinnerungen eines Arbeiters.* Leipzig: Diederich, 1903.

Folkenflik, Robert. "Introduction: The Institution of Autobiography." In *The Culture of Autobiography: Constructions of Self-Representation,* edited by Robert Folkenflik, 1–20. Stanford, Calif.: Stanford University Press, 1993.

Foucault, Michel. *The History of Sexuality.* Vol. 1, *An Introduction.* Translated by Robert Hurley. New York: Vintage Books, 1980.

Frederiksen, Elke, ed. *Die Frauenfrage in Deutschland, 1865–1915.* Stuttgart: Reclam, 1981.

Frenssen, Gustav. *Peter Moors Fahrt nach Südwest: Ein Feldzugsbericht.* Berlin: Grote, 1906.

Friedländer, Oskar. "Eine für Viele." Review of *Eine für Viele,* by Vera. *Die Gesellschaft* 18, no. 3 (1902): 157–84.

Friedman, Susan Stanford. "Women's Autobiographical Selves: Theory and Practice." In *The Private Self: Theory and Practice of Women's Autobiographical Writings,* edited by Shari Benstock, 34–62. Chapel Hill: University of North Carolina Press, 1988.

Friedrich, Cäcilia, ed. *Aus dem Schaffen früher sozialistischer Schriftstellerinnen.* Berlin: Akademie-Verlag, 1966.

Friedrichs, Elisabeth. *Die deutschsprachigen Schriftstellerinnen des 18. und 19. Jahrhunderts. Ein Lexikon.* Stuttgart: Metzler, 1981.

Friedrichsmeyer, Sara, Sara Lennox, and Susanne Zantop, eds. *The Imperialist*

Imagination: German Colonialism and its Legacy. Ann Arbor: University of Michigan Press, 1998.

Frobenius, Else. *Zehn Jahre Frauenbund der Deutschen Kolonialgesellschaft.* Berlin: Kolonie und Heimat, 1918.

Gagnier, Regenia. "Social Atoms: Working-Class Autobiography, Subjectivity, and Gender." *Victorian Studies* 30 (1987): 335–63.

———. *Subjectivities: The Pragmatics of Self-Representation.* New York: Oxford University Press, 1991.

Geary, Christraud M. *Images from Bamum: German Colonial Photography at the Court of King Njoya, Cameroon, West Africa, 1902–1915.* Washington, D.C.: Smithsonian Institution Press, 1988.

Gehrecke, Siegfried. *Themistokles von Eckenbrecher, 1842–1921.* Goslar: Museumsverein Goslar, 1985.

Gerhard, Ute. *Unerhört: Die Geschichte der deutschen Frauenbewegung.* Reinbek bei Hamburg: Rowohlt, 1990.

Gerstenberger, Katharina. "January 31, 1850: Conversion to Judaism Is Protected under the Constitution of the North German Confederation." In *Yale Companion to Jewish Writing and Thought in German Culture, 1096–1996,* edited by Sander Gilman and Jack Zipes, 186–92. New Haven: Yale University Press, 1997.

———. "Nahida Ruth Lazarus's 'Ich suchte dich!': A Female Autobiography from the Turn of the Century." *Monatshefte* 86 (1994): 525–42.

Gilman, Sander L. *Disease and Representation: Images of Illness from Madness to AIDS.* Ithaca: Cornell University Press, 1988.

———. *Freud, Race, and Gender.* Princeton: Princeton University Press, 1993.

———. *The Jew's Body.* New York: Routledge, 1991.

———. *Jewish Self-Hatred: Anti-Semitism and the Hidden Language of the Jew.* Baltimore: Johns Hopkins University Press, 1986.

Gilmore, Leigh. *Autobiographics: A Feminist Theory of Women's Self-Representation.* Ithaca: Cornell University Press, 1994.

Goldman, Karla. "The Ambivalence of Reform Judaism: Kaufmann Kohler and the Ideal Jewish Woman." *American Jewish History* 79 (1990): 477–99.

Goodman, Katherine. *Dis/Closures: Women's Autobiography in Germany between 1790 and 1914.* New York: Peter Lang, 1986.

Green, Barbara. *Spectacular Confessions: Autobiography, Performative Activism, and the Sites of Suffrage 1905–1938.* New York: St. Martin's Press, 1997.

Grunwald, Max. *Die moderne Frauenbewegung und das Judentum: Vortrag gehalten im Verein "Oesterreichisch-Israelitische Union."* Vienna: Beck, 1903.

Gürtler, Christa. "Damen mit Pelz und Peitsche. Zu Texten von Wanda von Sacher-Masoch." In *Schwierige Verhältnisse: Liebe und Sexualität in der Frauenliteratur um 1900,* edited by Theresia Klugsberger, 71–82. Stuttgarter Arbeiten zur Germanistik, 262. Stuttgart: Heinz Verlag, 1992.

Hahn, Barbara. "Die Jüdin Pallas Athene. Ortsbestimmungen im 19. und 20. Jahrhundert." In *Von einer Welt in die andere: Jüdinnen im 19. und 20 Jahrhundert,* edited by Jutta Dick and Barbara Hahn, 9–28. Vienna: Brandstätter, 1993.

————. "Lazarus, Nahida Ruth." In *Jüdische Frauen im 19. und 20. Jahrhundert: Lexikon zu Leben und Werk,* edited by Jutta Dick and Marina Sassenberg, 238–39. Reinbek bei Hamburg: Rowohlt, 1993.

————. *Unter falschem Namen: Von der schwierigen Autorschaft der Frauen.* Frankfurt am Main: Suhrkamp, 1991.

Hegeler, Wilhelm. "Erinnerungen eines Arbeiters." Review of *Denkwürdigkeiten und Erinnerungen eines Arbeiters,* by Karl Fischer. *Das litterarische Echo* 6 (1903–4): 30–35.

Henderson, W. O. *The German Colonial Empire, 1884–1919.* London: Frank Cass, 1993.

Herkner, Heinrich. "Seelenleben und Lebenslauf in der Arbeiterklasse." *Preußische Jahrbücher* 140 (1910): 393–412.

Hermand, Jost. *Als Pimpf in Polen: Erweiterte Kinderlandverschickung, 1940–1945.* Frankfurt am Main: Fischer, 1993.

Herre, Franz. *Jahrhundertwende 1900: Untergangsstimmung und Fortschrittsglauben.* Stuttgart: dva, 1998.

Herrmann, Hans Peter, Hans-Martin Blitz, and Susanna Moßmann, eds. *Machtphantasie Deutschland: Nationalismus, Männlichkeit und Fremdenhaß im Vaterlandsdiskurs deutscher Schriftsteller des 18. Jahrhunderts.* Frankfurt am Main: Suhrkamp, 1996.

Herwig, Franz. "Neue Romane." Review of *Memoiren einer Sozialistin,* by Lily Braun. *Hochland* 7, no. 2 (1910): 95–98.

Heuser, Magdalene, ed. *Autobiographien von Frauen: Beiträge zu ihrer Geschichte.* Tübingen: Niemeyer, 1996.

Hinrichsen, Adolf. *Das literarische Deutschland.* 2d ed. Berlin: Verlag des "literarischen Deutschlands," 1891.

Hirsch, Marianne. *The Mother/Daughter Plot: Narrative, Psychoanalysis, Feminism.* Bloomington: Indiana University Press, 1989.

Holdenried, Michaela, ed. *Geschriebenes Leben: Autobiographik von Frauen.* Berlin: Schmidt, 1995.

————. "'Ich, die schlechteste von allen.' Zum Zusammenhang von Rechtfertigung, Schuldbekenntnis und Subversion in autobiographischen Werken von Frauen." In *Geschriebenes Leben: Autobiographik von Frauen,* 402–20. Edited by Michaela Holdenried. Berlin: Schmidt, 1995.

Horton, Susan R. *Difficult Women, Artful Lives: Olive Schreiner and Isak Dinesen, in and out of Africa.* Baltimore: Johns Hopkins University Press, 1995.

Hroch, Miroslav. "From National Movement to the Fully-Formed Nation: The Nation-Building Process in Europe." In *Becoming National: A Reader,* edited by Geoff Eley and Ronald Grigor Suny, 60–77. Oxford: Oxford University Press, 1996.

Hull, Isabel. "The Bourgeoisie and Its Discontent." *Journal of Contemporary History* 17 (1982): 247–68.

Huyssen, Andreas. *After the Great Divide: Modernism, Mass Culture, Postmodernism.* Bloomington: Indiana University Press, 1986.

————. *Twilight Memories: Marking Time in a Culture of Amnesia.* New York: Routledge, 1995.

Hyams, Barbara. "The Whip and the Lamp: Leopold von Sacher-Masoch, the Woman Question, and the Jewish Question." *Women in German Yearbook* 13 (1997): 67–79.

Ihringer, Bernhard, ed. *Frauenbriefe aller Zeiten.* Stuttgart: Krabbe, 1910.

Jacobi, Hosea. *Über die Stellung des Weibes im Judenthum: Mit besonderer Berücksichtigung der Eheschliessung, wie sie uns in den Schriften des Alten-Testaments vorliegt.* Berlin: Julius Sittenfeld, 1865.

Jacobi-Dittrich, Juliane. "The Struggle for an Identity: Working-Class Autobiographies by Women in Nineteenth-Century Germany." In *German Women in the Eighteenth and Nineteenth Centuries: A Social and Literary History,* edited by Ruth-Ellen Joeres and Mary Jo Maynes, 321–45. Bloomington: Indiana University Press, 1986.

Jacobowski, Ludwig. "Nahida Ruth Lazarus." Review of *Ich suchte Dich!* by Nahida Ruth Lazarus. *Die Gesellschaft* 15, no. 1 (1899): 235.

Janik, Allan, and Stephen Toulmin. *Wittgenstein's Vienna.* New York: Simon and Schuster, 1973.

Jelinek, Estelle. *Women's Autobiography: Essays in Criticism.* Bloomington: Indiana University Press, 1980.

Juchacz, Marie. *Sie lebten für eine bessere Welt: Lebensbilder führender Frauen des 19. und 20. Jahrhunderts.* Berlin: Dietz, 1955.

Jusek, Karin J. *Auf der Suche nach der Verlorenen: Die Prostitutionsdebatten im Wien der Jahrhundertwende.* Vienna: Löcker, 1994.

Kaplan, E. Ann. *Motherhood and Representation: The Mother in Popular Culture and Melodrama.* London: Routledge, 1992.

Kaplan, Marion. *The Making of the Jewish Middle Class: Women, Family, and Identity in Imperial Germany.* New York: Oxford University Press, 1991.

Karpeles, Gustav. "Ein autobiographisches Glaubensbekenntnis." Review of *Ich suchte Dich!* by Nahida Lazarus. *Allgemeine Zeitung des Judenthums,* October 15, 1897, 499–501.

———. *Die Frauen der jüdischen Literatur: Ein Vortrag, gehalten zum Besten des Sefath-Emeth-Vereins in Berlin.* Berlin: Poppelauer, 1871.

Kaufmann, David. *Wie heben wir den religiösen Sinn unserer Mädchen und Frauen?* Trier: Sigmund Mayer, 1893.

Kautsky, Karl. "Der Werdegang einer kämpfenden Proletarierin." Review of *Die Jugendgeschichte einer Arbeiterin,* by Adelheid Popp. *Die neue Zeit* 27, no. 2 (1909): 313–16.

Kayserling, Meyer. *Die jüdischen Frauen in der Geschichte, Literatur und Kunst.* Leipzig: Brockhaus, 1879.

Keller, Helen. *Die Geschichte meines Lebens.* Stuttgart: Lutz, 1905.

Kelly, Alfred, ed. *The German Worker: Working-Class Autobiographies from the Age of Industrialization.* Berkeley and Los Angeles: University of California Press, 1987.

Kingsley, Mary H. *Travels in West Africa: Congo Français, Corisco, and Cameroons.* London: Macmillan, 1897.

Klemm, Gustav Friedrich. *Allgemeine Culturgeschichte der Menschheit.* 10 vols. Leipzig: Teubner, 1843–52.

Klemperer, Victor. *Ich will Zeugnis ablegen bis zum letzten. Tagebücher, 1933–1945.* Edited by Walter Nowojski. 2 vols. Berlin: Aufbau, 1995.

Klotz, Marcia. "Memoirs from a German Colony: What Do White Women Want?" In *Eroticism and Containment: Notes from the Flood Plain,* edited by Carol Siegel and Ann Kibbey, 154–87. New York: New York University Press, 1994.

Klucsarits, Richard, and Friedrich G. Kürbisch, eds. *Arbeiterinnen kämpfen um ihr Recht: Autobiographische Texte rechtloser und entrechteter "Frauenspersonen" in Deutschland, Österreich und der Schweiz des 19. und 20. Jahrhunderts.* Wuppertal: Hammer, 1975.

Klüger, Ruth. *Weiter leben: Eine Jugend.* Göttingen: Wallstein, 1992.

Knapp, Vincent J. *Austrian Social Democracy, 1889–1914.* Washington, D.C.: University Press of America, 1980.

Knoll, Arthur J., and Lewis H. Gann, eds. *Germans in the Tropics: Essays in German Colonial History.* New York: Greenwood, 1987.

Kord, Susanne. *Ein Blick hinter die Kulissen. Deutschsprachige Dramatikerinnen im 18. und 19. Jahrhundert.* Stuttgart: Metzler, 1992.

Kosch, Wilhelm. *Deutsches Literatur-Lexikon. Biographisches und bibliographisches Handbuch.* 2d ed. Vol. 3. Bern: Francke, 1956.

Koschorke, Albrecht. *Leopold von Sacher-Masoch: Die Inszenierung einer Perversion.* Munich: Piper, 1988.

Kosta, Barbara. *Recasting Autobiography: Women's Counterfictions in Contemporary German Literature and Film.* Ithaca: Cornell University Press, 1994.

Krafft-Ebing, Richard von. *Psychopathia Sexualis with Especial Reference to the Antipathic Sexual Instinct: A Medico-Forensic Study.* Translated by F. J. Rebman. New York: Physicians and Surgeons Book Company, 1929.

Kratz-Ritter, Bettina. "Konversion als Antwort auf den Berliner Antisemitismusstreit? Nahida Ruth Lazarus und ihr Weg zum Judentum." *Zeitschrift für Religions- und Geistesgeschichte* 46 (1994): 14–30.

Kristeva, Julia. *Powers of Horror: An Essay on Abjection.* Translated by Leon S. Roudiez. New York: Columbia University Press, 1982.

Krull, Edith. *Women in Art.* London: Studio Vista, 1989.

Kuntze, Lisa. *"Was hält Euch denn hier fest?"* Windhoek: Wissenschaftliche Gesellschaft, 1982.

Kurrein, Adolf. *Die Frau im jüdischen Volke: Vortrag gehalten zu Gunsten des israelitischen Frauenvereins in Bielitz.* Frankfurt am Main: Kauffmann, 1885.

Lange, Helene, and Gertrud Bäumer, eds. *Handbuch der Frauenbewegung.* Berlin: Moeser, 1906.

Lazarus, Moritz. *Aus meiner Jugend.* Edited by Nahida Lazarus. Frankfurt am Main: J. Kauffmann, 1913.

———. *Ein deutscher Professor in der Schweiz.* Edited by Nahida Lazarus. Berlin: Dümmler, 1910.

———. *Moritz Lazarus's Lebenserinnerungen.* Edited by Nahida Lazarus and Alfred Leicht. Berlin: Georg Reimer, 1906.

———. *Sprüche von Moritz Lazarus.* Edited by Nahida Ruth Lazarus. Leipzig: E. H. Mayer, 1899.

————. *Was heisst national?* 2d ed. Berlin: Dümmler, 1880.

Lazarus, Nahida. *Bikashtikha.* Translation by Israel Schapira of *Ich suchte Dich!* into Hebrew. Tel-Aviv: Mitspah, 1932.

————. "Frühlingsfabel." *Allgemeine Zeitung des Judenthums,* March 24, 1899, 144.

————. *Ich suchte Dich!* Berlin: Siegfried Cronbach, 1898.

————. *Das jüdische Haus.* 2d ed. Culturstudien über das Judentum. Berlin: Carl Duncker, 1898.

————. "Eine Spazierfahrt." *Allgemeine Zeitung des Judenthums,* November 2, 1894, 527–28, November 16, 1894, 550–52.

"Wie Steinthal und Lazarus Brüder wurden." *Jahrbuch für jüdische Geschichte und Literatur* (1900): 149–66.

————. "Zweiter Lazarusabend. Vortrag der Frau Nahida Ruth Lazarus." *Oesterreichische Wochenschrift* 17 (1897): 361–63.

Le Rider, Jacques. *Modernity and Crises of Identity: Culture and Society in Fin-de-Siècle Vienna.* Translated by Rosemary Morris. New York: Continuum, 1993.

Leimbach, Karl A., ed. *Die deutschen Dichter der Neuzeit und Gegenwart. Biographien, Charakteristiken und Auswahl ihrer Dichtungen.* Leipzig: Kesselringsche Hofbuchhandlung, 1899.

Lejeune, Philippe. *On Autobiography.* Edited by Paul John Eakin. Translated by Katherine Leary. Minneapolis: University of Minnesota Press, 1989.

Lessing, Theodor. "*Meine Lebensbeichte:* Eine Ehrenrettung." Review of *Meine Lebensbeichte,* by Wanda von Sacher-Masoch. *Die Gegenwart* 35, no. 32 (1906): 85–88; 35, no. 33 (1906): 104–7. Reprinted in *Leopold von Sacher-Masoch: Materialien zu Leben und Werk,* edited by Michael Farin, 205–20. Bonn: Bouvier, 1987.

Leutwein, Theodor. *Elf Jahre Gouverneur in Deutsch-Südwestafrika.* Berlin: Ernst Mittler, 1907.

Levenson, Alan T. "An Adventure in Otherness: Nahida Remy-Ruth Lazarus (1849–1928)." In *Gender and Judaism: The Transformation of Tradition,* edited by T. M. Rudavsky, 99–111. New York: New York University Press, 1995.

Liebknecht, Wilhelm. *Wissen ist Macht—Macht ist Wissen, und andere bildungspolitisch-pädagogische Äußerungen.* Edited by Hans Brumme. Berlin: Volk und Wissen, 1968.

Loreck, Jochen. *Wie man früher Sozialdemokrat wurde: Das Kommunikationsverhalten in der deutschen Arbeiterbewegung und die Konzeption der sozialistischen Parteipublizistik durch August Bebel.* Bonn: Verlag Neue Gesellschaft, 1977.

Lorenz, Max. "Memoiren einer Idealistin von Malwida von Meysenbug." Review of *Memoiren einer Idealistin,* by Malwida von Meysenbug. *Preußische Jahrbücher* 98 (1899): 559–61.

Lublinski, S. "Eine Bekehrte." Review of *Ich suchte Dich!* by Nahida Lazarus. *Die Zeit,* July 16, 1898, 38–39.

Mamozai, Martha. *Schwarze Frau, weiße Herrin: Frauenleben in den deutschen Kolonien.* Reinbek bei Hamburg: Rowohlt, 1982.

Mantl, Wolfgang. "Modernisierung und Dekadenz." In *Die Wiener Jahrhundert-*

wende: Einflüsse, Umwelt, Wirkungen, edited by Jürgen Nautz and Richard Vahrenkamp, 80–100. Vienna: Böhlau, 1993.

Manz, Gustav. "Memoirenwerke." *Das Litterarische Echo* 4 (1901–2): 309–14.

Martin, Biddy. "Lesbian Identity and Autobiographical Difference[s]." In *Life/Lines: Theorizing Women's Autobiography,* edited by Bella Brodzki and Celeste Schenck, 77–103. Ithaca: Cornell University Press, 1988.

———. *Woman and Modernity: The Life Styles of Lou Andreas-Salomé.* Ithaca: Cornell University Press, 1991.

Mason, Mary G., and Carol Hurd Green, eds. *Journeys: Autobiographical Writings by Women.* Boston: G.K. Hall, 1979.

Maynes, Mary Jo. "Childhood Memories, Political Visions, and Working-Class Formation in Imperial Germany: Some Comparative Observations." In *Society, Culture, and the State in Germany 1870–1930,* edited by Geoff Eley, 143–62. Ann Arbor: University of Michigan Press, 1997.

———. "Gender and Class in Working-Class Women's Autobiographies." In *German Women in the Eighteenth and Nineteenth Centuries: A Social and Literary History,* edited by Ruth-Ellen Joeres and Mary Jo Maynes, 230–46. Bloomington: Indiana University Press, 1986.

———. "Gender and Narrative Form in French and German Working-Class Autobiographies." In *Interpreting Women's Lives: Feminist Theory and Personal Narratives,* edited by Personal Narratives Group, 103–17. Bloomington: Indiana University Press, 1989.

———. *Taking the Hard Road: Life Course in French and German Worker's Autobiographies in the Era of Industrialization.* Chapel Hill: University of North Carolina Press, 1995.

McClintock, Anne. *Imperial Leather: Race, Gender, and Sexuality in the Colonial Contest.* New York: Routledge, 1995.

Mehring, Franz. "Lebensgang eines deutsch-tschechischen Handarbeiters." Review of *Lebensgang eines deutsch-tschechischen Handarbeiters,* by Wenzel Holek. *Die neue Zeit* 27, no 2 (1909): 762–64.

Meisel-Hess, Grete. *The Sexual Crisis: A Critique of Our Sex Life.* Translated by Eden and Cedar Paul. New York: Critic and Guide, 1917.

———. *Die sexuelle Krise: Eine sozial-psychologische Untersuchung.* Jena: Biederich, 1909.

Mensi, Alfred von. "Die Memoiren Bertha von Suttners." Review of *Memoiren,* by Bertha von Suttner. *Hochland* 6, no. 2 (1909): 219–22.

Meyer, Michael A. *Response to Modernity: A History of the Reform Movement in Judaism.* New York: Oxford University Press, 1988.

Michel, Bernard. *Sacher-Masoch. 1836–1895.* Paris: Laffont, 1989.

Misch, Georg. *A History of Autobiography in Antiquity.* Translated by E. W. Dickes. Cambridge: Harvard University Press, 1951.

Morrison, Toni. *Playing in the Dark: Whiteness and the Literary Imagination.* Cambridge: Harvard University Press, 1992.

Mosse, George L. *Nationalism and Sexuality: Middle-Class Morality and Sexual Norms in Modern Europe.* Madison: University of Wisconsin Press, 1985.

Mudimbe, V. Y. *The Invention of Africa: Gnosis, Philosophy, and the Order of Knowledge.* Bloomington: Indiana University Press, 1988.

Müller, Heiner. *Krieg ohne Schlacht: Leben unter zwei Diktaturen.* Cologne: Kiepenheuer & Witsch, 1992.

Münchow, Ursula. *Frühe deutsche Arbeiterautobiographie.* Berlin: Akademie Verlag, 1973.

Nautz, Jürgen, and Richard Vahrenkamp, eds. *Die Wiener Jahrhundertwende: Einflüsse, Umwelt, Wirkungen.* Vienna: Böhlau, 1993.

Nekrolog zu Kürschners Literatur-Kalender. Edited by Gerhard Lüdtke. 1901–35. Berlin: de Gruyter, 1936.

Neumann, Bernd. Afterword to *Lebensgeschichte eines modernen Fabrikarbeiters,* by Moritz Th. W. Bromme, 369–82. 1905; reprint, Frankfurt am Main: Athenäum, 1971.

Niggl, Gunter. *Geschichte der deutschen Autobiographie im 18. Jahrhundert: Theoretische Grundlegung und literarische Entfaltung.* Stuttgart: Metzler, 1977.

Nipperdey, Thomas. *Deutsche Geschichte, 1866–1918.* Vol. 1, *Arbeitswelt und Bürgergeist.* Munich: Beck, 1994.

Noyes, John. *Colonial Space: Spatiality in the Discourse of German South West Africa, 1884–1915.* Chur: Harwood, 1992.

———. "National Identity, Nomadism, and Narration in Gustav Frenssen's 'Peter Moor's Journey to Southwest Africa.'" In *The Imperialist Imagination: German Colonialism and Its Legacy,* edited by Sara Friedrichsmeyer, Sara Lennox, and Susanne Zantop, 87–105. Ann Arbor: University of Michigan Press, 1998.

Nussbaum, Felicity A. *The Autobiographical Subject: Gender and Ideology in Eighteenth-Century England.* Baltimore: Johns Hopkins University Press, 1989.

Nusser, Peter. *Trivialliteratur.* Stuttgart: Metzler, 1991.

Oncken, Hermann. "Aus der neueren Memoirenliteratur." *Deutsche Monatsschrift* 7 (1905): 616–24.

O'Pecko, Michael T. "Comedy and Didactic in Leopold von Sacher-Masoch's *Venus im Pelz.*" *Modern Austrian Literature* 25, no. 2 (1992): 1–13.

Osterhammel, Jürgen. *Kolonialismus: Geschichte, Formen, Folgen.* Munich: Beck, 1995.

Otto-Peters, Louise. "Das Recht der Frauen auf Erwerb." In *Die Frauenfrage in Deutschland, 1865–1915: Texte und Dokumente,* edited by Elke Frederiksen, 297–304. Stuttgart: Reclam, 1981.

Pataky, Sophie. *Lexikon deutscher Frauen der Feder: Eine Zusammenstellung der seit dem Jahre 1840 erschienenen Werke weiblicher Autoren, nebst Biographieen der lebenden und einem Verzeichnis der Pseudonyme.* 2 vols. Berlin: Schuster und Loeffler, 1898.

Paul, Hans. "Frauen-Litteratur." *Neue Deutsche Rundschau* 7 (1896): 276–81.

Paxton, Nancy L. "Disembodied Subjects: English Women's Autobiography under the Raj." In *De/Colonizing the Subject: The Politics of Gender in Women's Autobiography,* edited by Sidonie Smith and Julia Watson, 387–409. Minneapolis: University of Minnesota Press, 1992.

Peterson, Linda H. "Institutionalizing Women's Autobiography: Nineteenth-Century Editors and the Shaping of an Autobiographical Tradition." In *The Culture of Autobiography: Constructions of Self-Representation,* edited by Robert Folkenflik, 80–103. Stanford, Calif.: Stanford University Press, 1993.

Pfabigan, Alfred. *Ornament und Askese: Im Zeitgeist des Wien der Jahrhundertwende.* Vienna: Brandstätter, 1985.

Pietz, William. "The Problem of the Fetish, I." *Res* 9 (spring 1985): 5–17.

Pitter, Viktor. *Die rechtliche Stellung der Frau in Österreich: Eine Zusammenstellung.* Vienna: Braumüller, 1911.

Planert, Ute. *Antifeminismus im Kaiserreich: Diskurs, soziale Formation und politische Mentalität.* Göttingen: Vandenhoeck & Ruprecht, 1998.

Popp, Adelheid. *Die Arbeiterin im Kampf ums Dasein.* Vienna: Verlag der Wiener Volksbuchhandlung Ignaz Brand, 1911.

———. *The Autobiography of a Working Woman.* Translated by E. C. Harvey. 1913; reprint, Westport, Conn.: Hyperion Press, 1983.

———. *Erinnerungen. Aus meinen Kindheits- und Mädchenjahren. Aus der Agitation und anderes.* Stuttgart: Dietz, 1915.

———. *Frauenarbeit in der kapitalistischen Gesellschaft.* Vienna: Verlag des Frauenzentralkomitees, 1922.

———. *Jugend einer Arbeiterin.* Berlin: Dietz Nachfahren, 1983.

———. *Die Jugendgeschichte einer Arbeiterin von ihr selbst erzählt.* Munich: Ernst Reinhardt, 1909.

———. *Der Weg zur Höhe: Die sozialdemokratische Frauenbewegung Österreichs. Ihr Aufbau, ihre Entwicklung und ihr Aufstieg.* Vienna: Frauenzentralkomitee der Sozialdemokratischen Arbeiterpartei Deutschösterreichs, 1929.

———, ed. *Gedenkbuch. 20 Jahre österreichische Arbeiterinnenbewegung.* Vienna: Kommissionsverlag der Wiener Volksbuchhandlung, 1912.

Poppenberg, Felix. "Frauen-Bekenntnisse." *Die Gegenwart* 49 (1896): 165–67.

Pratt, Mary Louise. *Imperial Eyes: Travel Writing and Transculturation.* New York: Routledge, 1992.

Pultz, John. *The Body and the Lens: Photography, 1839 to the Present.* New York: Abrams, 1995.

Quataert, Jean H. *Reluctant Feminists in German Social Democracy, 1885–1917.* Princeton: Princeton University Press, 1979.

Radkau, Joachim. *Das Zeitalter der Nervosität: Deutschland zwischen Bismarck und Hitler.* Munich: Hanser, 1998.

Radway, Janice A. *A Feeling for Books: The Book-of-the-Month Club, Literary Taste, and Middle-Class Desire.* Chapel Hill: University of North Carolina Press, 1997.

Ragussis, Michael. *Figures of Conversion: "The Jewish Question" and English National Identity.* Durham: Duke University Press, 1995.

Raisin, Jacob. S. *Gentile Reactions to Jewish Ideals: With Special Reference to Proselytes.* Edited by Herman Hailperin. New York: Philosophical Library, 1953.

Rambo, Lewis R. *Understanding Religious Conversion.* New Haven: Yale University Press, 1993.

Remy, Nahida. "Auch eine Geistergeschichte!" *Allgemeine Zeitung des Judenthums,* June 30, 1893, 311–12.

———. *Culturstudien über das Judentum.* Berlin: Carl Duncker, 1893.

———. *Domeniko.* Schauspiel, 1884.

———. *Das Gebet in Bibel und Talmud.* Berlin: E. Apolant, 1892.

———. *Geheime Gewalten.* Dresden: Pierson, 1890.

———. *Die Grafen Eckhardstein.* Schauspiel, 1880.

———. *Das jüdische Weib.* Foreword by Prof. Dr. M. Lazarus. Leipzig: Malende, 1891.

———. *Konstanze.* Berlin, 1879.

———. *Liebeszauber.* Berlin, 1887.

———. *Nationale Gegensätze.* Berlin, 1884. Jewish National and University Library, Jerusalem, Arc. Ms. Var. 124a.

———. *Rechnung ohne Wirth.* 1871. Jewish National and University Library, Jerusalem, Arc. Ms. Var. 298/138.

———. *Schicksalswege.* Schauspiel. 1880. Jewish National and University Library, Jerusalem, Arc. Ms. Var. 298/124a.

———. *Sizilianische Novellen.* Berlin: Verlag Richard Eckstein Nachfahren Carl Hammer, 1886.

Richter. "Die Südwesterin im Kriegssturm." Review of *Was Afrika mir gab und nahm,* by Margarethe von Eckenbrecher. *Deutsche Kolonialzeitung* 19 (1907): 189–91.

Romero, Patricia W., ed. *Women's Voices on Africa: A Century of Travel Writing.* Princeton, N.J.: Markus Wiener, 1992.

Rose, Jacqueline. *States of Fantasy.* New York: Oxford University Press, 1996.

Rosenbaum, Heidi. *Formen der Familie: Untersuchungen zum Zusammenhang von Familienverhältnissen, Sozialstrukturen und sozialem Wandel in der deutschen Gesellschaft des 19. Jahrhunderts.* Frankfurt am Main: Suhrkamp, 1982.

Rosin, David. "Zerline Meyer." *Allgemeine Zeitung des Judenthums,* June 15, 1894, 278–80.

Roth, Günther. "Die kulturellen Bestrebungen der Sozialdemokratie." In *Moderne deutsche Sozialgeschichte,* edited by Hans-Ulrich Wehler, 342–65. Düsseldorf: Droste, 1981.

Rubin, Joan Shelley. *The Making of Middle Brow Culture.* Chapel Hill: University of North Carolina Press, 1992.

Rudloff, Holger. *Pelzdamen: Weiblichkeitsbilder bei Thomas Mann und Leopold von Sacher-Masoch.* Frankfurt am Main: Fischer, 1994.

Sacher-Masoch, Leopold von. *Die geschiedene Frau: Passionsgeschichte eines Idealisten.* 1869; reprint, with an essay by Alexander von Sacher-Masoch and a dossier edited by Michael Farin, Nördlingen: Greno, 1989.

———. *Venus in Furs.* In Gilles Deleuze and Leopold von Sacher-Masoch, *Masochism,* 143–271. New York: Zone Books, 1991.

Sacher-Masoch, Wanda von. *Die Beichte der Dame im Pelz.* Edited by Michael Farin. Munich: Moewig, 1986.

———. *Confession de ma vie.* Paris: Mercure de France, 1907.

———. *Confession de ma vie.* Paris: Claude Tchou, 1967.

———. *The Confessions of Wanda von Sacher-Masoch.* Translated by Marian Phillips, Caroline Hébert, and V. Vale. San Francisco: Re/Search, 1990.

———. *Die Damen im Pelz. Geschichten.* Leipzig: Morgenstern, 1882.

———. *Damen mit Pelz und Peitsche.* Edited by Christa Gürtler. Frankfurt am Main: Ullstein, 1995.

———. *Echter Hermlin. Geschichten aus der vornehmen Welt.* Bern: Frobeen, 1879.

———. *Masochismus und Masochisten. Nachtrag zur Lebensbeichte.* Berlin: Schuster & Loeffler, [1908].

———. *Meine Lebensbeichte. Memoiren.* Berlin: Schuster & Loeffler, 1906.

———. "Das Mysterium der Liebe." In *Damen mit Pelz und Peitsche,* edited by Christa Gürtler, 7–12. Frankfurt am Main: Ullstein, 1995.

———. *Der Roman einer tugendhaften Frau. Ein Gegenstück zur 'geschiedenen Frau' von Sacher-Masoch.* Prague: Bohemia, 1873.

Sadji, Amadou Booker. *Das Bild des Negro-Afrikaners in der deutschen Kolonialliteratur, 1884–1945. Ein Beitrag zur literarischen Imagologie Schwarzafrikas.* Berlin: Reimer, 1985.

Sagarra, Eda. "Dienstbotenautobiographien der Jahrhundertwende." In *Autobiographien von Frauen: Beiträge zu ihrer Geschichte,* edited by Magdalene Heuser, 318–29. Tübingen: Niemeyer, 1996.

———. "Quellenbibliographie autobiographischer Schriften von Frauen im deutschen Kulturraum, 1730–1918." *Internationales Archiv für Sozialgeschichte* 11 (1986): 175–231.

Salmon, André. *Souvenirs sans fin: Premiere Epoque, 1903–1908.* Paris: Gallimard, 1955.

Salten, Felix. *Josefine Mutzenbacher: Die Lebensgeschichte einer wienerischen Dirne, von ihr selbst erzählt.* Munich: Rogner & Bernard, 1996.

Sansgêne, Marie. *Jugenderinnerungen eines armen Dienstmädchens.* Berlin: Fontane, 1905.

Schackmann, Isolde. "Das Bild der 'Emanzipierten': Herrin und/oder Gefährtin. Zu zwei Novellen von Wanda von Sacher-Masoch und Irma Troll-Borostyáni." In *Schwierige Verhältnisse: Liebe und Sexualität in der Frauenliteratur um 1900,* edited by Theresia Klugsberger, 83–102. Stuttgarter Arbeiten zur Germanistik, 262. Stuttgart: Heinz Verlag, 1992.

Scherr, Johannes. *Deutsche Kultur- und Sittengeschichte.* 5th ed. Leipzig: Wiegand, 1873.

Schleiden, Mathias Jacob. *Die Bedeutung der Juden für Erhaltung und Wiederbelebung der Wissenschaften im Mittelalter.* Leipzig: Commissionsverlag von Baumgaertner's Buchhandlung, 1877.

Schlichtegroll, Carl Felix von. *Die Bestie im Weibe. Beiträge zur Geschichte menschlicher Verirrung und Grausamkeit.* Leipzig: Leipziger Verlag, 1903.

———. *Sacher-Masoch und der Masochismus: Litterarhistorische und kunsthistorische Studien.* Dresden: Dohrn, 1901.

———. *"Wanda" ohne Pelz und Maske. Eine Antwort auf "Wanda" von Sacher-Masochs "Meine Lebensbeichte" nebst Veröffentlichungen aus Sacher-Masochs Tagebuch.* Leipzig: Leipziger Verlag, 1906.

Schmid-Bortenschlager, Sigrid. "Frauenliteratur im 19. Jahrhundert—Ideologie,

Fiktion, Realität. Dargestellt am Beispiel der Thematik "Versorgungsehe." In *Begegnung mit dem "Fremden": Grenzen-Traditionen-Vergleiche,* edited by Eijiro Iwasaki, 246–50. Akten des 8. Internationalen Germanisten-Kongresses, Tokyo 1990. Munich: Iudicium, 1991.

Schmid-Bortenschlager, Sigrid, and Hanna Schnedl-Bubeniček. *Österreichische Schriftstellerinnen, 1880–1938: Eine Bio-Bibliographie.* Stuttgart: Heinz, 1982.

Schmiedt, Helmut. *Ringo in Weimar: Begegnungen zwischen Hochkultur und Popularkultur.* Würzburg: Köngishausen & Neumann, 1996.

Schmokel, Wolfe W. "The Myth of the White Farmer: Commercial Agriculture in Namibia, 1900–1983." *International Journal of African Historical Studies* 18 (1985): 93–108.

Schneider, Manfred. *Die erkaltete Herzensschrift: Der autobiographische Text im 20. Jahrhundert.* Munich: Hanser, 1986.

Schorske, Carl E. *Fin-de-Siècle Vienna: Politics and Culture.* New York: Vintage, 1981.

Schütz, Hans J. Introduction to *Jugend einer Arbeiterin,* by Adelheid Popp. Berlin: Dietz, 1983.

Schwabe, Kurd. *Der Krieg in Deutsch-Südwestafrika, 1904–1906.* Berlin: Weller, 1907.

Schwerin, Sophie. *Ein Lebensbild aus ihren eigenen hinterlassenen Papieren zusammengestellt von ihrer jüngeren Schwester Amalie von Romberg.* Edited by Paul Schreckenbach. Leipzig: Eckart, 1911.

Scott, Joan W. "Experience." In *Feminists Theorize the Political,* edited by Judith Butler and Joan W. Scott, 22–40. New York: Routledge, 1992.

Sekula, Allan. "On the Invention of Photographic Meaning." In *Photography against the Grain: Essays and Photo Works, 1973–1983,* 3–22. Halifax: Press of the Nova Scotia College of Art and Design, 1984.

Sharpe, Jenny. *Allegories of Empire: The Figure of Woman in the Colonial Text.* Minneapolis: University of Minnesota Press, 1993.

Showalter, Elaine. *The Female Malady: Women, Madness, and English Culture, 1830–1980.* New York: Penguin, 1985.

———. *Sexual Anarchy: Gender and Culture at the Fin de Siècle.* New York: Viking, 1990.

Simmel, Georg. "The Relative and the Absolute in the Problem of the Sexes" In *On Women, Sexuality, and Love,* translated by Guy Oakes, 102–32. New Haven: Yale University Press, 1984.

Sitzungsberichte der Königlich Preussischen Akademie der Wissenschaften zu Berlin. Berlin: Verlag der Königlichen Akademie der Wissenschaften, 1900.

Smith, Helmut Walser. "The Talk of Genocide, the Rhetoric of Miscegenation: Notes on the Debates in the German Reichstag concerning Southwest Africa, 1904–14." In *The Imperialist Imagination: German Colonialism and Its Legacy,* edited by Sara Friedrichsmeyer, Sara Lennox, and Susanne Zantop, 107–23. Ann Arbor: University of Michigan Press, 1998.

Smith, Sidonie. "Construing Truths in Lying Mouths." *Studies in the Literary Imagination* 23 (1990): 145–63.

———. "The Other Woman and the Racial Politics of Gender: Isak Dinesen and

Beryl Markham in Kenya." In *De/Colonizing the Subject: The Politics of Gender in Women's Autobiography,* edited by Sidonie Smith and Julia Watson, 410–35. Minneapolis: University of Minnesota Press, 1992.

———. *A Poetics of Women's Autobiography: Marginality and the Fictions of Self-Representation.* Bloomington: Indiana University Press, 1987.

———. *Subjectivity, Identity, and the Body: Women's Autobiographical Practices in the Twentieth Century.* Bloomington: Indiana University Press, 1993.

Smith, Sidonie, and Julia Watson, eds. *De/Colonizing the Subject: The Politics of Gender in Women's Autobiography.* Minneapolis: University of Minnesota Press, 1992.

———. *Getting a Life: The Everyday Uses of Autobiography.* Minneapolis: University of Minnesota Press, 1996.

Smith, Woodrow. *The German Colonial Empire.* Chapel Hill: University of North Carolina Press, 1978.

Sonnenberg, Else. *Wie es am Waterberg zuging: Ein Beitrag zur Geschichte des Hereoaufstandes.* Braunschweig: Wollermann, 1906.

Sontoneff, Maxi. "Intimes aus dem Seelenleben einer anderen Frau. Erwiderung auf die 'Bekenntnisse einer Frau.'" *Die Gesellschaft* 16, no. 1 (1900): 108–11.

Spiel, Hilde. *Vienna's Golden Autumn.* New York: Weidenfeld and Nicolson, 1987.

Stanton, Domna C. "Autogynography: Is the Subject Different?" In *The Female Autograph: Theory and Practice of Autobiography from the Tenth to the Twentieth Century,* edited by Domna C. Stanton, 3–20. Chicago: University of Chicago Press, 1984.

Stauff, Philipp. *Semi-Kürschner oder Literarisches Lexikon der Schriftsteller, Dichter, Bankiers, Geldleute, Ärzte, Schauspieler, Künstler, Musiker, Offiziere, Rechtsanwälte, Revolutionäre, Frauenrechtlerinnen, Sozialdemokraten usw., jüdischer Rasse und Versippung, die von 1813–1913 in Deutschland tätig und bekannt waren.* Berlin: Selbstverlag Philipp Stauff, 1913.

Steedman, Carolyn. *Landscape for a Good Woman: The Story of Two Lives.* New Brunswick, N.J.: Rutgers University Press, 1986.

Steinthal, Heymann. "Giebt es noch Jüdinnen?" Review of *Das jüdische Weib,* by Nahida Remy. *Allgemeine Zeitung des Judentums,* October 16, 1891, 494–95. Reprinted in *Juden und Judentum,* edited by Gustav Karpeles, 31–36. Berlin: M. Poppelauer, 1906.

Stoecker, Helmuth, and Peter Sebald. "Enemies of the Colonial Idea." In *Germans in the Tropics: Essays in German Colonial History,* edited by Arthur J. Knoll and Lewis H. Gann, 59–72. New York: Greenwood, 1987.

Strauß und Torney, Lulu von. "Memoirenwerke." *Das Literarische Echo* 14 (1911–12): 1272–77.

Strobel, Margaret. "Gender and Race in the Nineteenth- and Twentieth-Century British Empire." In *Becoming Visible: Women in European History,* edited by Renate Bridenthal, Claudia Koonz, and Susan Stuart, 375–95. Boston: Houghton Mifflin, 1987.

Sturmhoefel, Nahida. *Neulatein als Weltsprache.* Berlin: Apolant, 1884.

Sturrock, John. "Theory versus Autobiography." In *The Culture of Autobiogra-*

phy: Constructions of Self-Representation, edited by Robert Folkenflik, 21–37. Stanford, Calif.: Stanford University Press, 1993.

Tambling, Jeremy. *Confession: Sexuality, Sin, the Subject.* Manchester: Manchester University Press, 1990.

Tebben, Karin. *Literarische Intimität: Subjektkonstitution und Erzählstruktur in autobiographischen Romanen von Frauen.* Tübingen: Francke, 1997.

Theweleit, Klaus. *Male Fantasies.* Translated by Erica Carter and Chris Turner. 2 vols. Minneapolis: University of Minnesota Press, 1989.

Timm, Uwe. *Deutsche Kolonien.* Cologne: Kiepenheuer & Witsch, 1986.

Treut, Monika. *Die grausame Frau: Zum Frauenbild bei de Sade und Sacher-Masoch.* Basel: Stroemfeld/Roter Stern, 1984.

Trotter, David. "Colonial Subjects." *Critical Quarterly* 32 (1990): 3–20.

Twellmann, Margrit. *Die deutsche Frauenbewegung: Ihre Anfänge und erste Entwicklung 1843–1889.* Meisenheim: Hain, 1972.

Vaughan, Megan. *Curing Their Ills: Colonial Power and African Illness.* Stanford, Calif.: Stanford University Press, 1991.

Vera [Betty Kris]. *Eine für Viele: Aus dem Tagebuche eines Mädchens.* Leipzig: Hermann Seemann Nachfolger, 1902.

Vogtmeier, Michael. *Die proletarische Autobiographie, 1903–1914: Studien zur Gattungs-und Funktionsgeschichte der Arbeiterautobiographie.* Frankfurt am Main: Peter Lang, 1984.

Wagner, Nike. *Geist und Geschlecht: Karl Kraus und die Erotik der Wiener Moderne.* Frankfurt am Main: Suhrkamp, 1982.

Walser, Martin. *Ein springender Brunnen.* Frankfurt am Main: Suhrkamp, 1998.

Wanda und Leopold von Sacher-Masoch: Szenen einer Ehe. Eine kontroversielle Biographie. With an afterword by Adolf Opel. Vienna: Wiener Frauenverlag, 1996.

Warmbold, Joachim. *"Ein Stückchen neudeutsche Erd' . . .": Deutsche Kolonial-Literatur. Aspekte ihrer Geschichte, Eigenart und Wirkung, dargestellt am Beispiel Afrikas.* Frankfurt am Main: Haag + Herchen, 1982. Translated as *Germania in Africa: Germany's Colonial Literature* (New York: Peter Lang, 1989).

Warneken, Bernd Jürgen. *Populare Autobiographik: Empirische Studien zu einer Quellengattung der Alltagsgeschichtsforschung.* Tübingen: Tübinger Vereinigung für Volkskunde, 1985.

Weigel, Sigrid. "Double Focus: On the History of Women's Writing." In *Feminist Aesthetics,* edited by Gisela Ecker, translated by Harriet Anderson, 59–80. London: Women's Press, 1985.

Wettstein-Adelt, Minna. *3½ Monate Fabrik-Arbeiterin.* Berlin: Leiser, 1893.

Wildenthal, Lora Joyce. "Colonizers and Citizens: Bourgeois Women and the Woman Question in the German Colonial Movement, 1886–1914." Ph.D. diss., University of Michigan, 1994.

———. "'She Is the Victor': Bourgeois Women, Nationalist Identities, and the Ideal of the Independent Woman Farmer in German Southwest Africa." *Social Analysis* 33 (1993): 68–88. Reprinted in *Society, Culture, and the State in Germany, 1870–1930,* edited by Geoff Eley, 371–96. Ann Arbor: University of Michigan Press, 1997.

Wilke, Fritz. *Das Frauenideal und die Schätzung des Weibes im Alten Testament: Eine Studie zur israelitischen Kultur- und Religionsgeschichte.* Leipzig: Dieterich'sche Verlagsbuchhandung, 1907.

Wilkomirski, Benjamin. *Bruchstücke: Aus einer Kindheit, 1939–1948.* Frankfurt am Main: Suhrkamp, 1995.

Wininger, Salomon. *Große jüdische National-Biographie, mit mehr als 8000 Lebensbeschreibungen namhafter jüdischer Männer und Frauen aller Zeiten und Länder. Ein Nachschlagewerk für das jüdische Volk und dessen Freunde.* Cernauti: Druck "Orient," 1925–36.

Winkler, Paula. "Betrachtungen einer Philozionistin." *Die Welt* 36 (1901): 4–6.

Wohlfeld, S. K. "Sacher-Masochs Ehegeschichte." Review of *"Wanda" ohne Maske und Pelz,* by Carl Felix von Schlichtegroll. *Die Wage* 9, no. 40 (1906): 972–74. Reprinted in *Leopold von Sacher-Masoch: Materialien zu Leben und Werk,* edited by Michael Farin, 223–25. Bonn: Bouvier, 1987.

Wolzogen, Ernst von. "Marie Ebners Kinderjahre." Review of *Meine Kinderjahre,* by Marie von Ebner-Eschenbach. *Das Literarische Echo* 9 (1906): 1440–42.

Worbs, Michael. *Nervenkunst: Literatur und Psychoanalyse im Wien der Jahrhundertwende.* Frankfurt am Main: Europäische Verlagsanstalt, 1983.

Wuthenow, Ralph-Rainer. *Das erinnerte Ich: Europäische Literatur und Selbstdarstellung im 18. Jahrhundert.* Munich: Beck, 1974.

Young, Robert J. C. *Colonial Desire: Hybridity in Theory, Culture, and Race.* London: Routledge, 1995.

Zagori, Emmeline. *Aus dem Leben eines Weihnachtskindes.* Leipzig: Ungleich, 1908.

Zantop, Susanne. *Colonial Fantasies: Conquest, Family, and Nation in Precolonial Germany, 1770–1870.* Durham: Duke University Press, 1997.

Zobeltitz, Hanns von. *Frauenleben.* Bielefeld: Velhagen und Klasing, 1903.

Index